SUPERMANAGING

SUPERMANAGING

How to Harness
Change for
Personal and
Organizational
Success

Arnold Brown

Edith Weiner

McGraw-Hill Book Company

New York   St. Louis   San Francisco   Auckland
Bogotá   Hamburg   Johannesburg   London
Madrid   Mexico   Montreal   New Delhi
Panama   Paris   São Paulo   Singapore
Sydney   Tokyo   Toronto

Library of Congress Cataloging in Publication Data

Brown, Arnold, date
  Supermanaging: how to harness change for personal
and organizational success.
  Includes index.
  1. Organizational change.   2. Technological
innovations.   3. Social change.   4. Management.
5. Success.   I. Weiner, Edith.   II. Title.
HD58.8.B76   1984   658.4   83-20002
ISBN 0-07-008201-4

  234567890   DOC/DOC   8987654

ISBN 0-07-008201-4

The editors for this book were William A. Sabin and
Galen H. Fleck, the designer was Dennis Sharkey,
and the production supervisor was Sally Fliess.
It was set in Baskerville by Achorn Graphic Services, Inc.

Printed and bound by R. R. Donnelley & Sons Company

For
Jared
and
Pam, Kathy, and Cindy
and
Derek

CONTENTS

PART 4: Where Today Clashes with Tomorrow: Exploding Old Myths 124

A broadside view of change, and the difference between
transient and fundamental shifts. The importance to you of
accepting the idea of transition.

How you acquire organizational vision, understanding,
communication skills, power, and managerial excellence.

Making the most of the options available to you in choosing
one or more careers, moving through your life cycle, making
investment decisions, and achieving personal satisfaction.

PREFACE

Since Alvin Toffler's *Future Shock* captured the public fancy in the early 1970s, there has been a swarm of books on the future. This book is also about what is to come, but more importantly it is about how to deal with change. Specifically, how to master it. And in doing so, how to become a *supermanager*.

The first step in mastering change is having a good and objective description of the current environment, out of which will come the future. We describe much of that environment. But it is also necessary to have an awareness of what priorities to assign and how best to respond to the elements that make up that environment. Knowing how to respond is critical. Knowing how to respond *positively* is perhaps even more critical, because a key factor in mastering change is capitalizing on it. René Dubós once said that trend is not destiny; you do not have to be a spectator or an ostrich. You can achieve a control over change by determining how to benefit from it—for yourself and your organization.

For more than fifteen years, we have been helping managers and organizations see, understand, and respond effectively to change. Our clients range from Fortune 500 corporations to government agencies, from think tanks to academic institutions. But as we see change coming ever more rapidly and institutions becoming even larger and slower, we see a need becoming greater—the need to help the contemporary manager make the leap from yesterday to tomorrow without getting stuck in the immediate present. Our society is mired in socioeconomic malaise; our institutions are trapped in a sticky web of ritual practices that render them incapable of flexibility; our managers themselves are confused, burdened with reconciling their dual roles of organizational protector and individual satisfaction seeker.

There is no magic in how we help managers view emerging issues and opportunities. We have been, for many years, monitoring a core of over fifty carefully selected periodicals (plus numerous conferences, research reports, conversations with experts, books, and entertainment media) in search of developments that will affect our future.

We look for:

■ Items completely new to us that represent events, ideas, or developments we have never before encountered.

■ Items that, when linked with others, begin to form patterns that become larger and more important than the sum of their parts. These patterns are the major tidal forces of change, and it is necessary to know them in order to understand the external environment. Thus we would connect a new office technology, a political platform plank espousing retraining for displaced workers, and a move to unionize managers to give a more comprehensive idea of potential developments in the workplace than we get from seeing just the discrete elements.

■ Items from surprising sources. There is more to be gleaned about future trends when a traditionally conservative point of view appears in a liberal periodical or when a respected member of a profession rather than an outsider attacks the practices of that profession, or when a nonscientist offers insights into a new technology.

■ Items that contradict previous assumptions about a trend or our own beliefs about what seems to be happening. It is by this fourth effort that we ensure objectivity. This may be the most important point. We cannot be the objective observers we must be without the willingness to look at things that shake our faith.

The publications we read cover the social, political, economic, and technological worlds, and they range from the far right to the far left in ideology. From them we have selected a great deal of pertinent information about how our world is changing; we have over 15,000 items that we have culled, analyzed, and connected to the real world that managers have to operate in.

Our focus has never been solely on providing information about change. One of the first discoveries we made when we began doing this work was that the easiest part of the job for the client was getting the information. Getting it to be used is the critical issue—and the most difficult part of the job.

So our work has been focused on translating information about change into a useful tool, on breaking down institutional impediments to dealing with change, on liberating managers from their reluctance to depart from standard bureaucratic thinking. And that is what this book is all about. We have tried to condense some of our experience and our long-range thinking about change into a usable conceptual framework. This is intended to be a practical book.

To some, this book may seem a bit overwhelming. To some, it will be enlightening. Some will find it threatening. For some, it will be mildly interesting reading. Some will regard this book as an action agenda. Those are the individuals who can capitalize on what they learn. Those are the people who waste little time arguing over words and use their energy to catapult themselves forward toward self-satisfaction and managerial excellence. Those are the people to whom we have dedicated our work. Those, in the main, are the *supermanagers*.

ACKNOWLEDGMENTS

We have been told so many times by so many people—friends, clients, readers of our articles, and listeners to our speeches—that we should write a book. At some point we began to believe it. But our belief was, at best, half-hearted. Early each year, the idea would pop up like the groundhog and quickly go down again in the face of our distractions. There were too many speeches to be written, too many clients to help, too much to read, and so on and so on.

One day a couple of years ago, however, we made the mistake of revealing our latent ambition to Lew Young, editor in chief of *Business Week*. Lew, a true supermanager, had us connected to McGraw-Hill before we knew what was happening, and we shortly found ourselves saddled with a contract *to write a book*!

That's how it began, and this is how it ends. Now that we have endured the agony of rewrite, it is time to thank Lew and the many other people who contributed so much to us and to our book.

First, we would like to express our appreciation to the people who helped us open our eyes and minds, thus enabling us to see and understand better. Often they were people whose points of view we found to be diametrically opposed to each other's and to our own. F. M. Esfandiary, for example, and Hazel Henderson. Yet as we forced ourselves to listen, to resist automatic denial, we found that our minds were being stretched, and we were beginning to understand a little more than we had before. Willis Harman also did that for us, and the late Ray Bauer. Daniel Yankelovich, too, and Daniel Bell and Peter Drucker. We are also indebted to visionary business leaders like Fletcher Byrom and Robert Anderson for giving innovative ideas credibility in the no-nonsense and highly competitive corporate world. A special thanks, too, to Colin Hampton for opening up to us the world of the boardroom and the insides of a truly progressive company. We owe much to our friends and clients, like Marty Edelston and Paul Kolton, and to many others too numerous to mention (they know who they are). They gave us the kind of support and encouragement that we needed to see this project through.

And, of course, we have to thank the important people who helped with the important tasks, such as research and typing: Rose Valenstein, Geoffrey King, and Bob Driscoll.

Finally, we offer heartfelt thanks to our editor, Bill Sabin. He taught us much more than we thought we needed to know, and this would have been much less a book without him and his belief in us. He also put up with an awful lot from us, and he did it with grace and humor.

SUPERMANAGING

PART 1

Understanding and Responding to Change

There is a tide in the affairs of men,
Which, taken at the flood, leads on to fortune;
Omitted, all the voyage of life
Is bound in shallows and in miseries.

Shakespeare
Julius Caesar

Prior to World War II, an American general observing British army maneuvers noted that mobile artillery pieces were served by seven soldiers, one of whom did nothing but stand at attention while the other six readied and fired the gun. Upon inquiring, he discovered that no one could tell him what the seventh man was for. Intrigued, he pursued the matter until he found out that in the old days, before trucks, the seventh man held the horses. The horses went, but the structure, now useless and wasteful, remained.

CHAPTER 1

Mastering Change

Picture, if you will, a racetrack lined with spectators, all betting on different outcomes. This is the great arena in which changes are taking place, changes that affect us, our organizations and our society. How we as individuals respond to these changes determines our roles at the track. The many spectators are passive, powerless to affect the outcome. The horses are the change makers, the engines of change, the powerful forces of life. The reins are the means of control, the change agents. And the riders are in control of the forces for change; they determine the outcome; they are the *supermanagers*.

Sometimes a force for change cannot be mastered; the jockey may be thrown. But the horse goes on, riderless, and that uncontrolled force may greatly affect all the others in the race. To overcome this also calls for skill at mastering the unexpected.

We may not always know how or why things are changing, but none of us can escape the sensation of being at this cosmic racetrack. Perhaps the single most important question each of us asks at post time is: "How can I be a supermanager?"

The Scope of Change

Adlai Stevenson once said of Eleanor Roosevelt, "She would rather light a candle than curse the darkness." For many people today, the sum total of all the books written for the purpose of enlightenment only increases the perception of darkness. Thousands of statistics confuse; hundreds of theories conflict; change causes concern; and the time available to deal with change seems to contract.

Demographics keep changing and keep surprising us with their massive impacts. We can't halt a majority of the shifts, but we can understand potential consequences and thereby diminish the surprises.

Technology moves us ever onward into a future that most science fiction writers envision as scientifically advanced but socially inadequate and politically inept. We don't have to accept that scenario. Emerson's despairing cry that "things are in the saddle and ride mankind" does not have to be the truth. Technology need not be the uncontrolled engine for change that leaves us behind to eat the dust. Indeed, fear that it is, if not resisted, can impair our ability to master the wonders of high technology in a humane, practical, and profitable manner.

Our political institutions, concerned as they are with their own survival, often manifest the inadequacies of such shortsightedness. But out of their inadequacies grow opportunities for those who would serve popular needs through innovative, entrepreneurial, community-based, and/or participatory programs.

Becoming Comfortable with Change

Mastering change requires knowing, and accepting, that some changes cannot be ridden. So many people dissipate their strength by hurling it against gigantic and uncontrollable forces, and as a consequence the smaller forces escape their control as well. But, before we can settle on priorities, we must have the total picture, as much as we are ever able to achieve a panoramic view.

To see not only the changes that are upon us but also those gradually emerging from the shadows of life and commerce as they are constantly evolving, we need a kind of radar to systematically scan the world and signal the new, the unexpected, the major, and the minor. Nowadays, many institutions have such a radar; it is called environmental or strategic scanning. Many more need such a system. Individuals need one too.

Impediments to Mastering Change

Animals in the wild never become insensitive to their environments; to do so can be fatal. But institutional walls have a lulling effect and foster a false sense of security. Walls work two ways: they keep danger out, but they also limit vision. They encourage a form of thinking that deals with the world by refusing to see it. Unfortunately, reality doesn't go away if we refuse to see it.

We all tend to see our institutions as permanent, as lasting forever and as being unchanged from the way we know them now. Indeed, a view of the world from inside an institution is fatally flawed by confidence in the institution's invulnerability. The seabed of human history is cluttered with Atlantises. The tides of history can be vastly more powerful than any human institution, difficult though that may be for us to accept.

It is, unfortunately, so human to see the world through the distorting lenses of our prejudices and preconceptions. We see what we want to see. But today, whether you are managing an organization or trying to manage your own life, your ability to cope successfully, to succeed— even survive—depends upon *objectivity*.

The Japanese word *sunao* translates roughly as "the untrapped mind." It describes the ability to see the world as it is, not as one wishes it to be. Konosuke Matsushita, the pioneering Japanese industrialist, says that the *sunao* spirit is essential for success at managing today. "Without it," he writes, "one can enjoy neither genuine success in management nor genuine happiness in life."

There is a phenomenon known as the Titanic effect: the greater the magnitude of the potential disaster, the greater the tendency to ignore it. But to master change, you must be willing to look real and imagined disasters in the eye.

The leaders of our institutions also tend to try to minimize error. Few make the connection between the punishing of error and the dampening of risk. To remain vibrant and competitive in any era and even more so today, an enterprise *must* become what organizational psychologist Donald Michael has called "error embracing." Yet to not only tolerate but encourage error is anathema to most organizations, as reflected by compensation and promotion schemes that do little to enhance risk taking and much to penalize wrong decisions. For your part, you need to examine just how much personal tolerance you have for errors made by yourself, your peers, your supervisor, your staff. Have you been part of the problem?

The human failing of using the language and concepts of the past to define the developments of today—which we call the horseless carriage phenomenon—is another of the obstacles you must overcome in order to see clearly what is actually happening. The automobile, when it first came along, was defined in terms of existing forms of personal transportation. But it was vastly and fundamentally different, and it took a while before we had a new vocabulary to help us understand just what about it was different. That vocabulary includes such terms as "highways," "infrastructures," "assembly lines," "parking lots," and "commuting."

The problem is magnified by the tendency of most people to rely solely on the media to identify and define events and changes. But people in the media are as much victims of an outdated and inadequate vocabulary as the rest of us, perhaps even more so. Of themselves, facts are not understanding. For example, the political upheavals and realignments in Washington in the late 1970s were almost unanimously attributed by the media to the simplistic and traditional context of liberal versus conservative. In reality, as we describe later, powerful social, economic, and political forces such as populism, ecology, economic nationalism, and limits to growth had already made the traditional political terminology obsolete.

Another obstacle to actually seeing the world is our natural desire for certainty. Scientists have known since the early years of this century that, according to the Heisenberg principle, the best that can be hoped for in complex systems is possibility. Our world system has become almost unbearably complex; and as it has done so, the likelihood of certainty has drastically decreased. To master change, you have to learn to be comfortable with uncertainty.

Perhaps the single most bothersome impediment to mastering change, the hardest thing for any of us to do, is to admit to ignorance.

(Our own, that is. It is not at all difficult to acknowledge someone else's.) We must be prepared to admit that we don't know, so that we can begin to learn.

Unwillingness to appear ignorant leads people into the most appalling follies, for which the tale of the emperor's new clothes is the perfect metaphor. People will cling to myths and fallacies rather than risk the tides. Within institutions, there is a great fear of appearing ignorant or naive, so the questions that are essential to the process of discovery are left unasked.

Overcoming the Obstacles

There are those who do not retreat from the challenges of the times. There are people who are not intimidated or threatened but instead are invigorated by the pace, nature, magnitude, and promise of change. These are the supermanagers, the individuals who achieve not just despite the changes in the world, but because of them. To be a supermanager, you have to share their firm belief that trend is not destiny. You have to share their capacity to understand that for every trend there is a countertrend, that the future is not black *or* white, nor is it gray. In all likelihood, it is black *and* white—and a variety of other colors as well. Thus, there is room for any number of differences of opinion, potential opportunities, lurking challenges, and personal and professional courses of action.

You must take a set of reins with the conviction that, at the very least, you will not be left out of the race. Neither the contradictions of our time nor the uncertainty of the future should deter you. Understand that freedom is the difference between riding a roller coaster and riding a horse. Failure is a disappointment but not a defeat. Your perspective must be not of the trees, but of the forest. Only then can you find the paths that are interesting enough, important enough, and rewarding enough for you to master.

As we recast our perceptions about bigness, about success, about our links to the global community, about justice, about human resources, about systems of work and play, and about the nature of change, we look to those who have been successful at mastering change. Not all are heads of institutions or leaders of people. Indeed, it can be argued that many of those considered to be functionally illiterate are, in their acquisition of "street smarts," survivors by instinct and training. They are masters of change, some within and some without the law, for good or for bad.

And not all who make it to the top of their professions are supermanagers. Some see their personal lives crumbling and feel virtually helpless in the face of legal, social, interpersonal, or economic problems. Indeed, we wonder whether it is a reasonable goal to have complete mastery over all aspects of one's work and life.

To be a supermanager, then, you may need to be less vulnerable to defeat than others, to be not just a survivor but a winner.

The mastery of change implies leadership, and that in turn implies an ability to articulate as well as understand what is happening. The ability to give substance and meaning to barely perceived and even less understood happenings seems more and more to be a hallmark of leadership in today's confusing times.

Finally, and perhaps most importantly, mastering change requires that you make the link to action. The true supermanager can translate the perception and understanding of change to a useful and attainable response. Throughout this book, we will focus on how to help you make such translations.

CHAPTER 2

Impermanence

It is a cliché that the more things change, the more they stay the same. And today many who are over 50 years of age tend to look back across the history of their lives and times and, via anecdotes and philosophy, argue that all things move like a pendulum. Trends come and go; they are given new life decades apart only to swing back again from whence they came. Economic cycles, they say, are just that—cycles—and there is really very little new in the course of human events. In *A Distant Mirror*, historian Barbara Tuchman shows how the tumultuous times and the decline of institutions of religion, government, commerce, and community in fourteenth-century Europe parallel much of what we are seeing today. Descriptions of changes are often greeted with, "Isn't this the same as what happened in the 1920s?" or "Didn't we see this in the 1950s?"

Perhaps the most difficult aspect of analyzing change and detecting emerging issues is that different lenses are needed. When we speak of the future as the next 3 years, our perceptions are different than when we are speaking of 5 to 10 years, and neither, of course, is the same as envisioning the year 2000 and beyond.

History, someone once said, does not repeat itself; people do. People create institutions, and the institutions, in interaction with other elements in the system, develop sore spots that are covered with Band-Aids rather than cured. Eventually the entire system succumbs to the cumulative infection, and something radically new seems more attractive. Some modern thinkers say that this is the second law of thermodynamics in a sociopolitical setting, nothing more than normal entropy. Things tend to break down over time until the energy needed to maintain them exceeds the initial energy needed to build them. This law, they say, applies to all systems, ideas, and processes. And it can be used to explain why things change.

Another possible explanation for the process of change is the so-called Hawthorne effect first noticed many years ago at a factory in Illinois: Any nonthreatening change can improve morale and productivity because it provides a stimulus that is absent in a long-established status quo. Thus, change can be a necessary means of remotivating and revitalizing any system or subsystem.

The hierarchy of needs made famous by psychologist Abraham Maslow tells us that, with few exceptions, the basic human drives for survival and economic well-being generally dominate drives for social affiliation and self-fulfillment; indeed, the latter are pursued only after the first two are satisfied. Within this context also, it is not surprising that many of our existing institutions are undergoing massive change, that many people are clamoring for new approaches (even though some of those approaches are not really new and have been shown to be unworkable in the long term), and that economic and safety issues begin to dominate the concerns of the populace when people feel that their livelihoods and identities are threatened.

But long-term cycles in the course of history seem more pertinent to the historian and philosopher than they do to the managers of modern institutions and to young adults. Perhaps that is a tragedy of contemporary mainstream thinking. In concerning themselves with the next quarter, or the next year, people lose sight of the bigger picture.

No institution has ever achieved permanence; many believe none should. Why, then, the reluctance to accept impermanence along with the fact that some conditions do remain constant? In the midst of vibrant, exciting, threatening, challenging shifts in all of our institutions and expectations for the future, many people respond in one of two ways: some believe everything is completely new or changing, and others think there is nothing new under the sun. Of course, neither position is correct. Those who will master their organizational and personal destinies will understand that some things do change and some things do not.

The Pendulum
versus the Spiral

There are perceptual tools that help illustrate the dichotomy. One requires discarding the analogy of the pendulum. Nothing ever swings back along the same path. You can never cross the same river twice, because the water is different. Circumstances change, and therefore identical events lose their sameness. A more accurate representation of apparently cyclical change is a spiral rather than a pendulum, as shown in Figure 2-1. When things seem to revert to some former stage

A pendulum travels back and forth along the same path.

A spiral turns in on itself, but always in a new plane.

Figure 2-1 The pendulum versus the spiral.

of belief or development, they do so in a new context, and therefore they are never exactly the same.

When, for example, some observers say that there is a turning back to marriage and family, they may be correct about the increased willingness of young people to marry and have children, but they are perhaps missing the more important point of the modern context in which this is occurring. In the past, marriage was considered permanent. Today the notion of permanence does not have so strong a hold on the human mind, and divorce seems likely to rival marriage as an expected life event. Few young people marry today with the vision their grandparents had of one day celebrating golden anniversaries. And many more people are having children out of wedlock than ever before.

When people say there has been a backlash against equal-opportunity programs, that the "pendulum has swung back, away from reverse discrimination," they are not taking into account the bodies of law, the role models, the successes, and the new organizational psychology that would, at the very least, prevent the outright discrimination against qualified candidates that was commonplace decades ago.

The fact that certain aspects of the consumerist movement seem to have moved from the front burner does not mean that caveat emptor is again the rule. It will, in all likelihood, never again be, at least not in the foreseeable future.

Past Shock

This leads us to the second conceptual tool: that the notion of future shock be supplemented by a notion applicable to the 1980s and beyond. Call it *past shock*. After going through several decades of rapid technological change, massive social movements, political ups and downs, and major international crises, as well as personal uncertainties, most managers today are fairly well conditioned to change. If Ms. Executive, a well-schooled senior manager, were to wake up one morning and suddenly find herself, like Rip Van Winkle, 20 years hence, she would probably find it less shocking than if she were to wake up 20 years back. Placed in the past, she would be appalled by the outright discrimination she would face at work, by the very limited expectations her husband and family would have of her, by the primitive technology she would have available to calculate and type, by the refusal of the manufacturers of goods she purchased to accept returns of faulty or malperforming products, by the smokestacks in the city belching out black soot, by the lack of readily available means to detect or cure breast cancer, by the limited media available to her to view and read, by the comments she would get from neighbors if her floors were not spic and span all of the time, by the widespread belief that we could not reach the moon.

Those who are best able to control and advance their own lives and the institutions they manage will find no real comfort in retreating into the past. The real challenge is to accept, adopt, and adapt the positive aspects of the past as part of some newer model of life in the present and future.

Option Shock

This leads to a third conceptual tool for understanding ourselves and others in a time of recognized impermanence: *option shock*. To have all of history, all of contemporary thinking, and all of the envisioned future possibilities from which to choose ideas and actions frightens some people. Others, however, are much stimulated by the challenge. The real leaders to emerge are those who are not traumatized by the choices and who, at the same time, can simplify and rationalize the choices that others need to make.

For a good illustration, look at the computer software business. Managers who see the wide range of opportunities for new products and who effectively appeal to the new markets will succeed and profit if they also make it easy for the consumer to choose and to feel comfortable with the choice. The same is true of the financial services sector. To the extent that a manager is turned on by the challenge of option shock but does not grasp that the consumer could be paralyzed by it, a potential success story could end in failure. The reverse, as it happens, also is true. When consumers like the availability of options, even though unable to take advantage of all of them, a manager who suffers option shock and retreats from offering the options will be left with a declining market share. This might not necessarily be bad, but it might not be what was originally intended as a long-range goal of the organization.

Individuals, no matter how intelligent or advanced in status and authority, face this kind of schizophrenia in their personal lives. We all like to have the many options opened up to us in a time of change, but we also find comfort in locating the adviser, the guru, the sage, or the information service that somehow helps us in making the ultimate choices.

The New Manager

A fourth conceptual tool for a time of impermanence is to envision what Stephen Temlock, a human resources consultant, calls the "bionic

Table 2-1
Concepts of Management Development

Traditional: Short-Term Return on Investment	Forward-Looking: Long-Term Return on Investment
Training	
Of secondary importance	Of primary importance
Candidates come from management ranks and are successful in their current endeavors	Starts with demands of the position and seeks to train several potential candidates to help them get there
Reliance on intensive one-time university management training and seminar courses	Continuing and varied education; lifetime learning mode
Experiential learning and some limited job rotation in closely aligned areas of specialty	Experiential learning outside one's direct area of expertise; rotation of work experience in unexpected and unaligned areas
Identification of Future Senior Managers	
Reliance upon strengths in what they now know and have proved they can already do	Reliance upon already proven competencies *plus* analysis of the kinds of decisions these people make regarding the new skills they wish to develop, new areas they want to explore for the company, and ways in which they are expanding their own base of knowledge
Capabilities	
Ability to motivate others	Ability to create an environment in which workers motivate themselves
Exhibits "rugged" individualism across decision centers	Displays individualism but in an intellectual rather than operational sense
Operates well in a hierarchical decision-making mode	Ability to operate well in both horizontal and vertical decision-making modes

manager," an individual whose "parts" (in the sense of skills, activities, goals, and positions) can be changed like parts of a machine. Most management development programs now are targeted for immediate payoff in terms of success at the next stage of responsibility rather than ultimate longer-term, all-around success as a senior manager. Table 2-1 shows how the current traditional training approach compares with a more forward-looking program that takes into account ultimate organizational and individual needs.

Planning for Change

Accepting impermanence—the idea of change—is a critical step to be taken by those who would achieve success in work or in their personal lives. Although it is true that there are longer-term cycles that may be permanent fixtures of the human landscape, the idea of substantive year-to-year changes must be integrated into life and work. Whether we speak of wildly fluctuating interest rates, devastating climatic changes, high rates of divorce, questionable availability of resources, genetic engineering, one-term presidencies, inflation, the birth and death of major industries, the mobility of society, the unemployment levels of the middle class, or the rapid outdating of scientific knowledge, we are speaking of an overriding notion of impermanence.

Planning for change, not just for the sake of change but for organizational survival, is more than a new discipline; it is a whole new philosophy. In organizations, it requires a new perspective from the top. It requires a new look at how strategies were once devised and carried out. And in these times of new competition, new technologies, new consumer knowledge and expectations, and new work force factors, it requires asking whether traditional institutional structures and procedures are still valid.

We often find it difficult to understand fully how much has really changed since the 1960s because we have lived through those changes. We are like parents who don't notice the changes in their children whom they see every day. Only when they look at old photos or when infrequent visitors stop by are they made aware of how the kids have grown or how their personalities have evolved.

Despite the observations that nothing is really new, the fact is that nothing stays the same. Some periods are tranquil and deliver up their changes slowly. Some are turbulent and play havoc with our perceptions of certainty, predictability, tradition, and continuity. By all observations, we are now living in one of the more turbulent times.

PART 2

The Driving Forces for Change

In Part 2 we sketch in broad strokes the key social, economic, political and technological forces that are shaping today's environment and that of tomorrow. They are known as driving forces, because they provide the impetus of change. Understanding what they are, how they are altering your environment, and what the alterations mean to you and your organization can be your key first step in supermanaging.

CHAPTER 3

Demographics— The Changing American

By the year 2000, world population may reach 7 billion people, a number which, according to some authorities, will strain the carrying capacity of the earth. Although the population growth rate of the United States is well below that of the entire planet, there is concern over what many see as a nonexpanding pie of wealth to be divided. Others, however, think the pie—economic growth—is potentially limitless. The subject is critical, and upon it hangs the fate of both large and small organizations, public and private. In the main, the significant demographic facts of life for the United States are as follows:

■   The vast leading edge of the baby boom begun after World War II has pushed into the thirties age bracket.

■   An echo of that baby boom is now appearing; it is ushering in a new growth in births (if not in birthrate).

■   The older population has increasing longevity, numbers, and clout.

■   A wave of legal and illegal immigration has severely shaken our economic and political system.

■   Mobility has profoundly altered the map of the United States.

■   In spite of all our efforts, there is still a gap in income distribution that leads some observers to predict class warfare.

The Postwar Baby Boom

In the introduction to his book, *Great Expectations: America and the Baby Boom Generation,*[1]* demographer Landon Jones writes:

> The change began after World War II, when the first boom baby was born, and will continue until sometime after the middle of the next century, when the last survivor of the baby boom will die. No single generation has more impact on us than the baby boom, and no single person has been untouched. . . .

> It is, above all, the biggest, richest and best-educated generation America has ever produced. The boom babies were born to be the best and the brightest. They were the first raised in the new suburbs, the first with new television, the first in the new high schools. They were twice as likely as their parents to go to college and three times as likely as their grandparents. They forced the economy to regear

*Superscript numbers indicate references listed at the end of the book.

itself to feed, clothe, educate, and house them. Their collective purchasing power made fads overnight and built entire industries. . . . They are a generational tyranny.

Most projections, based on a baby boom that was nurtured in affluence, are for continued higher levels of consumption throughout the 1980s, despite inflation, high interest rates, and recession. As these people move into the prime income and buying ages from 25 to 44—and form households (in many cases with multiple incomes), analysts expect them to spend, spend, spend. Understanding how they will spend and on what and for what reasons they will spend is the key to success in, for example, marketing and new product development. That will become more apparent as we get into the values of this group later in the book.

However, there are modifying circumstances. Perhaps chief among them is the swelling of middle-management ranks, now one of the nation's prime concerns. Organizations are coming off the expansion highs of the 1960s and 1970s with substantially eroded productivity and profit growth. The days of fast promotion and an exploding managerial force are over. In the eyes of the baby boom elite, it was all supposed to be easy; if you got good grades and went to good schools, you got good jobs. But thousands are realizing that is no longer so, and they are adjusting their expectations downward. Some of the large corporations that employ career-minded graduates not only are employing fewer than in the past but are holding new employees in entry-level positions longer. Promotions are coming much slower and after greater competitive struggle. And many baby-boomers who had been promoted into the managerial ranks are being laid off. No wonder, then, that managers sensitive to change have in recent years looked to alternatives to traditional career patterns in large organizations.

But other sectors are not capable of absorbing the overload. Universities continue to turn out almost five times more doctorates than there are available teaching posts. The professions are getting squeezed. MBAs are in less demand; in 1982, job offers were down 67 percent from the previous year at the University of Pennsylvania's Wharton School.

Dorothy Wickendon, managing editor of *The New Republic,* observed in early 1982 that young men and women in Washington, D.C., no longer think of themselves as young. While the middle-aged cling to the fantasy that youth is a time of freedom and high spirits, much of the younger generation is deeply into presenescence. The faces of young professionals are pasty from 12-hour days at the office; their bones crack when they rise from their desks; they tap their feet impatiently when the bus is late. While oldsters are often maligned for their tedious recounting of bodily ills, young white-collar workers, with a morbid fascination, discuss their job-related nervous afflictions: facial tics, heartburn, insomnia, and unconscious teeth grinding. One friend of Mrs. Wickendon was warned that if he didn't wear a brux bar at night, he'd be toothless by the time he was 40.

When the baby-boomers do enjoy the amenities of easy living, as do those in two-wage-earner households if both workers have managed to hold onto good jobs and high incomes, time has become a commodity second in value perhaps only to money. Time, that is, in terms of convenience and getting rewarding or satisfying experiences. They are likely to be less driven by wanting to *have* than by the desire to *do*, not only because they may already own much of what they want or need but also because of a developing *minimalist culture* that deemphasizes material possessions. The latter could put unexpected limits on the market for hard goods and durables and correspondingly increase the markets for services, particularly those that allow buyers to enjoy such experiences as travel and home entertainment.

One of the key factors you must appreciate today, aside from the work force issues that will be treated in detail in subsequent chapters, is that the postwar baby boom generation is no longer the large uniform audience that American business once addressed. There is no longer uniformity in music, dress, recreation, style, or political belief. Even in the nonconformity of the baby-boomers' earlier days there was a sense of uniformity. That is gone. Many are married; many are single; many are divorced. Many are straight; many are gay. Many are politically liberal; many are politically conservative; many have abandoned political distinctions altogether. Many inhabit luxury high-rise apartments and cooperatives in the cities; many have fled to rural America. Many wish to keep up with the Joneses; many put the Joneses down.

There are, however, certain projections we can make about issues that could unite the baby-boomers as a group. They live in a time of financial uncertainty; they face a decade in which financial institutions and social service programs will be in a state of flux. For those reasons, plus the important fact that by and large they will continue to be affluent, financial institutions can anticipate major markets for new investments, savings, and insurance services. Fear that the Social Security system will not come through will foster many long-term financial concerns, as will their growing inability to afford traditional housing or to plan for financing their children's education.

Pressures for reform of the tax system will come in large part from this age group. The greatest growth in entrepreneurialism, as indicated above, also will come from this group as an alternative to increasingly shaky career possibilities in shrinking major employing institutions. More pressure will be placed on the educational system to perform, and there will be entrepreneurial opportunities for the revamping of the educational service industries as the baby-boomers raise families of their own.

In the Wake of the Baby Boom Generation

According to most demographic projections, our economy can anticipate a shrinking labor force of under-25 workers. The postwar baby boom ended in the early 1960s. In 1965, births dropped below 4 million for the first time in 12 years. Fertility over the following 15 years dropped to the lowest levels in American history. The number of Americans aged 16 to 19 has been falling since 1977, and the proportion of the population 16 to 24 is expected to continue to decline.

Experts have predicted that school and military enrollments will be hardest hit in the decade ahead. In the case of the military, however, high unemployment rates among the young would offset the diminishing pool. Many companies are considering the use of more people over 55 as lower-level employees such as bank tellers and workers in fast-food stores. Faster introduction of robots to eliminate low-skilled jobs is seen as another solution. And, as stated above, employers will also fill their needs by keeping the baby boom generation in lower-level jobs and promoting them more slowly. Furthermore, and perhaps most importantly, if efforts to dam the tide of illegal immigration do not succeed, all of the above forecasts are suspect. The addition of a million or more primarily young people to the labor pool each year would change the picture substantially.

The pressure of living in the wake of the baby boom generation—the fast-paced growth spurred by the baby-boomers and the bursting of the bubble—has not been easy for the under-25s. Punk rock, disliked intensely by the generation that hailed the Beatles, is a bitter response to a world of frustration, fear, and unfulfilled promises. One way to escape that world is the Sony Walkman, the success of which is based on the isolationist tendencies that have sprung from this group and have spread across much of the rest of the population. Those same isolationist tendencies are both the product of and a spur to the further growth of the computerized and video games. Beyond Pac-Man are the fantasy games, which can take up as many as 7 or 8 hours per sitting while projecting players into unique and alien worlds. Gamers claim they reject mass culture. This same attitude characterizes the popular

punk rock group DEVO (for devolution), whose music expresses scorn
for technological advancement and the society and institutions based
on it.

Of course, the *ultimate* escape is death. Over the 1970s the suicide
rate of American teenagers nearly doubled. Suicides are now the third
leading cause of death—with accidents first and homicide second—for
persons from 15 to 24 years old. Some demographers and suicidologists
say the baby boom led to a glut of people vying for limited jobs and that
in turn led to a climate that fosters suicide. Novelist Scott Spencer
(*Endless Summer*) believes society has lost its commitment to children. He says, "Children must compete with the narcissistic lifestyle of
adults. . . . Children sense they can no longer be afforded and, in a final
act of disobedience, oblige their parents by killing themselves."

Certainly, narcissism is reflected in the escalated divorce rate of the
population generally but especially that of the baby-boomers, and this
has had an impact on the children growing up behind them. A 1980
survey by the National Association of Elementary School Principals
reported that children of divorced parents are far more likely to run
into academic and disciplinary trouble than are their classmates who
live with two parents. Some one million more kids each year live with
just one parent, and they represent about 19 percent of all Americans
under age 18. Over half are black. About 45 percent of children born in
the United States today are expected to spend at least one year living
with a single parent. That group represents our future into the early
1990s.

A very basic fact of the coming years is that today's teenagers feel
themselves to be in a pressure cooker. The fact that there are fewer of
them means they stand a better chance of being needed in the work
force but, they fear, mostly in dead-end jobs. They are products of
revolutionary technologies and unstable family backgrounds. They are
to inherit a future fraught with uncertainty. They may be a lost generation, and they may, as a result of the pressures, become a profoundly
disturbing influence on the rest of society, a breeding ground for turmoil, violence, and radicalism—all of which can be seen in the lyrics
and videos of current rock music. Whether as a manager or a parent or
a marketer, you will find that such people will require more individual
attention (but not necessarily direction) than their predecessors.

The Baby Boom Echo

In recent years, American women have been having an average of
fewer than two children each. The total number of births, however, is

now quite high because of the massive number of women of childbearing age. In 1981, when the fertility rate was 1.8 births per woman, more children were born than during the baby boom year 1950 when the fertility rate was 3. A new baby boom, or boomlet, is underway. The Census Bureau reports that by 1990 the under-5 population could rise 19 percent and reach almost 20 million.

Today's women are very different from the generation that bore the baby-boomers. Many are better educated, and such women usually have fewer children. They are much more likely to be in the labor force, and they tend to return to work quickly rather than build large families.

Demographers, school officials, and corporate marketers of products for the young are disagreeing over just how large the echo will be, but one observation is not in dispute. The echo of the 1980s will be a low-order birth boom, which has special economic and social significance. Low-order births have the largest effect on family spending. First births command the lion's share of all the necessary major nursery purchases, and second births often force a family to move to larger quarters and thereby incur new household expenses.

Having and being an only child is becoming more acceptable to Americans for several reasons, including later marriage and women postponing childbearing for the sake of a career. Another factor, not unimportant, is a change in what we know about the only child. It had long been believed that only-children were spoiled, lonely, dependent, and selfish. However, study after study shows that is not true. Maya Pines, in a 1981 issue of *Psychology Today,* says research shows that only-children fare better than children in general when it comes to intelligence, achievement, relations with adults, and educational goals. Only-children are most similar to first-born children, another group that produces a high share of leaders and achievers. Both groups, it appears, benefit from having the undivided attention and devotion of their parents during the early years.

One study showed that many couples neither insist on having an only-child of specific gender nor try to clone themselves by having one child of each sex. This implies that the child is freed of stereotyping by the parents. It has been found that kindergarten children who have siblings are much more rigid about what is appropriate for boys and girls than are only-children, who seem to have a more androgynous perspective.

The baby boom echo, the children now being born to women in their late twenties and thirties, offers hope to marketers of many child-related household products. It may also be a very positive indication of the long-range future in the shape of a work force that will have a high proportion of self-reliant and achievement-oriented workers.

A less positive side to the echo is the epidemic of teenage pregnancies—babies having babies. Almost all unmarried teenage mothers are now deciding to keep their babies, and in Washington, D.C., and New York City, births to unwed teenagers rival in number births to married and older women. When asked why they are having, and keeping, their babies, many of the answers by the young mothers center on the need to be loved unquestioningly and on the need for a permanent bond. Might these be leading indicators of the long-range impact of divorce, serial marriage, and single parenthood on the future childbearing attitudes of today's young?

For you as a manager today, the real message is that the baby boom echo is not only a product of more affluent, upscale couples, as many market research studies would have you believe, but also a product of poorer, less-educated, unstable, bitter, and disenfranchised youth. Thus, if you are a marketer, you may be gleeful about the baby product potential in the boomlet. But as a manager of either a private or a public institution, you must also consider the pressure on housing (already a major problem), work schedules, and limited social and public funds, not to mention the potential for class conflict over private versus public education and health care delivery as the result of this other and sizable segment of new mothers.

Immigration

Emigration has long been seen as a way out of poverty and oppression for individuals, and immigration has long been seen as a source of new strength and vitality for nations. During the growth decades following World War II, there was a constant vast flow of immigrants. But the rise of refugees (now more than 15 million) and declining economies have prompted a change.

Throughout Europe, resentment is building over the immigrant work force at a time of severe competition for jobs and record rates of unemployment. There are, for example, almost 5 million foreigners in West Germany. Over a fifth of them are Turks, most of whom came at West Germany's invitation during a time of labor shortages. But the "guest workers" have remained, even after the need for them tapered off in the 1970s, and West Germany now faces serious housing, school, unemployment, public assistance, and crime rate problems as a result of the foreign situation. The United States is, of course, the globe's Mecca for immigrants. About 1.5 million people may have emigrated each year to this country in recent times; the figures are inexact because of the huge number of illegal entrants. This is more than the number recorded in either of the peak immigration years of 1907 and 1914. Legal and illegal immigration is currently the cause of nearly half of U.S. population growth, and not since the decade 1911–1920 has immigration played so significant a role in U.S. population shifts.

The issue of immigration is charged with emotion, conflicting values, and the harsh realities of economics and resource allocation. In late 1981, the liberal magazine *The Humanist* dedicated an entire issue to the dilemma posed by the pressing immigration problem. The publication began by addressing the following ethical issues. The United States has traditionally been considered the land of opportunity, and there is an obligation to maintain that standard. However, our immigration policy, or lack of one, is creating a situation that is on the verge of being out of control. The government appears to have forgotten its duty to protect its citizens, and the United States is already overpopulated. We also have a duty to help citizens of other nations, and those nations as political and cultural entities, to help themselves.

The publication went on to raise these other issues:

■ The threat to U.S. security from the Catholic church, whose natalist policies encourage immigration to less-populated areas.

■ The push for foolproof identification cards for everyone in the population in order to win the battle against illegal immigration.

■ The mixed feelings of American workers who sympathize with the plight of the immigrants but who have the most to lose from uncontrolled immigration.

Because the United States consumes so much energy, food, and other basic world resources on a per capita basis, any substantial change in our immigration policy would have a corresponding effect on the pattern of such resource use. It could also affect U.S. exports. A continued increase in U.S. population, through continued high immigration rates, combined with potential water shortages, high fuel costs, and the loss of agricultural lands, could result in the domestic consumption of all food produced in the United States, with little or none left for export.

However, although negative consequences of immigration are commanding the major share of media attention, there are some benefits that should not be overlooked. Historically, immigrants have provided the backbone of change, innovation, and revitalization in the United States. One need only look at how immigrants from South Korea have revitalized the retail produce business in New York City to see how well the process continues to work.

More than 300,000 foreigners came to study in the United States in 1981. That figure could double by 1990, when foreigners may account for 10 percent of all college students. Some schools look to them to compensate for a projected decline in American enrollment, and many of the foreigners spend a lot of money here in the states. The percentage of European and Canadian students here has shrunk. Today's largest single group is from Iran. South and east Asia have the biggest regional representation. Foreigners tend to concentrate in high-demand fields like engineering, business administration, and, increasingly, mathematics and computer science. About 1200, or one-half, of the engineering doctorates awarded in 1979 went to non-Americans. Often these students are made attractive offers by U.S. companies and stay on in this country. The influx is critical for the companies seeking scarce technical workers.

But there are powerful pressures to close the golden door, or at least to narrow the opening. These are generated by economic fears and are often manifested in xenophobia. In introducing his immigration reform bill in 1982, Republican Senator Allan Simpson of Wyoming said: "Uncontrolled immigration is one of the greatest threats to the future of this nation, to American values, traditions, institutions, to our public culture and to our way of life." The bill passed the Senate by a vote of 81 to 18 (although House passage now seems unlikely).

Hispanics

The Hispanics comprise the single largest immigration group in the United States. In future generations the Hispanic minorities will command proportionately more attention. In the 18-to-24 group, for example, the proportion of Spanish-speaking people will grow from 6.5 percent in 1980 to 21.7 percent by 1990. Landon Jones points out that the baby boom may be remembered someday as the last American generation to grow up without a sizable and influential Spanish minority. Already over 15 million Hispanics are living here. In Minneapolis–St. Paul, Mexican Americans have replaced blacks as the largest minority. In Los Angeles, over one-third of the students are of Hispanic descent, and the figure is almost half for kindergarten pupils. In Seattle, the Hispanic population is growing almost twice as fast as the white one. The United States is already the fourth-largest Spanish-speaking nation in this hemisphere and is projected to become the third-largest by 1990, according to Roberto Anson in *The Futurist*.

Until recently, it was widely but erroneously believed that the Hispanic community carried little weight in influencing the mainstream

Table 3-1
Hispanic population in the United States

Origin	%	U.S. Residence	%
Mexico	59	California	29
Cuba	6	New York	15
Puerto Rico	15	Texas	20
Central and South America and other	20	Arizona, Colorado, and New Mexico	9
		Other	27

in the United States. The median age of the Hispanic population was lower than the nation's median age, and almost half of the Hispanics were under voting age. Their geographic and cultural composition was nonuniform, as the Bureau of the Census estimates given in Table 3-1 show.

Hispanics are united by a common language and the majority also by strong ties to the Roman Catholic church. However, much of their commonality ends there. Young, urban Mexican Americans call themselves "Chicanos," a term disliked by older Mexican Americans. In Hartford the preferred term is "Hispanics." In Washington, D.C., where there are many Central Americans, the favored term is "Latinos." In New Orleans it is "Latins." Hispanic political clout has been perceived to be relatively minor because of low voter registration, language barriers, the illegal status of some Hispanic people, and a general cultural estrangement from each other and the U.S. mainstream.

But the impact of the Hispanic population will be felt more strongly in the future. Often overlooked culturally is the role the Hispanics have already played in recent fads and trends related to food, clothing, restaurants, religion, dance, and music. Politically, they are patiently focusing on achieving power locally and arriving at regional or national power incrementally. Although observers generally agree that it will take several years before they gain substantial national clout, the Hispanics are making progress. California, Texas, New York, Florida, Illinois, New Jersey, and New Mexico will probably be prime areas of increased political activity.

Hispanics have not yet matched the progress of blacks in income and level of education, but by their growing size they represent enormous potential for overall purchasing power. There has been relatively little study of Hispanics in the marketplace, and the need for better market research is obvious. Robert Staples and Alfredo Mirande of the University of California found that the little research done on the Chicano family in the 1950s and 1960s reflected the stereotype of the macho father who rejects authority and is lord and master of the household.

Their own Mexican American study found, to the contrary, that there is fairly widespread egalitarianism between husband and wife and that parent-child relations are warm and nurturing. They also found that Chicanos are as likely to marry as other groups but are less likely to divorce.

With respect to Hispanics, the two most emotionally charged issues you will face over the next decade are bilingualism (how far will this be pressed in schools, workplace, materials, and consumer products?) and the competition for jobs. Also to be considered are the consequences of Hispanics achieving political clout, the need to conduct lifestyle and life values studies (to support demographic projections and market research), the potential for new service and new product developments geared to the Hispanic market, and the human resources factor to be considered in assimilating vast numbers of Hispanic workers.

Blacks

Recent surveys show increasing alienation among blacks, who represent about 12 percent of the U.S. population. Now competing for scarce jobs with women and Hispanics, they see the opportunities drying up. Michael King, a black reporter for *The Wall Street Journal,* observed in 1981 that black Tuskegee students preparing for professional careers were astonishingly alienated; they felt despised by whites and spurned by black professionals. Many young black MBAs are realizing that the MBA is not the golden passport that they had expected it to be.

In the late 1960s publishers were eager for the works of blacks. Mel Watkins, an editor of *The New York Times Book Review,* recently observed that some publishers now feel the "mere inclusion of the word 'black' in a book's title hurts its chances." More black women than black men are currently being published, perhaps because women are more marketable now. Black movies don't make money, so they are not being made, and many black men and women are convinced that they are not making the kind of gains in white-collar jobs that white women are making.

Race relations on campuses are deteriorating. Joel Achenbach, editorial chairman of the *Daily Princetonian,* observed in 1982 that race relations barely exist at Princeton, and that "the university remains remarkably segregated in academics and extracurricular activities as well as in students' social lives and housing choices." Black students feel unwelcome; they say that white racism has forced them to find support in their own community, in third world unity—which whites interpret as separatism. The tension is visible in the dining halls, in public and private. And there are similar reports from other Ivy League schools such as Harvard and Dartmouth. The situation seems no different throughout higher education. The University of Cincinnati, for example, ordered a 2-year suspension of a fraternity that celebrated the birthday of Dr. Martin Luther King, Jr., in 1982 with a racially demeaning party. These are not isolated observations or events.

The Census Bureau has been reporting a steady climb in black male earnings as a percentage of white male earnings, but the data excluded the unemployed. Indeed, there is reason to believe that a growing black male underclass is masked by the data. This is part of a widening split in the black community. Some are doing far better; many are doing worse. Frustration among the black poor is now compounded by the fact that many blacks have achieved some degree of success in the ranks of white-collar and skilled blue-collar workers. Economist William Wilson believes that we are witnessing a fundamental social stratification among blacks and that there is a disturbing tendency toward intergenerational continuity of economic distress for poor blacks as welfare, unemployment, and low skill levels become institutionalized as family traditions.

One manifestation is the increase in proportion of female-headed black households since the early 1960s: from 23 to almost 40 percent, compared with 15 percent for all American families. Female-headed households are characterized by lower income and higher unemployment. Fifty-two percent of American blacks over the age of 18 are single, compared with one-third of white adults. Robert L. Staples, a sociologist at UC–San Francisco, says the difference is due not to choice but to the acceptance by some blacks of a white-middle-class value system which may conflict with the values of some if not many potential or former mates. Compounding that difficulty is the fact that almost twice as many black women are in college as black men, and the women do not want mates with less education than they have. In addition, about 150,000 black men are in prison, many died in the Vietnamese war, and about 90,000 have married women outside their race. The outlook for a decline in the proportion of black female-headed households is extremely bleak; one set of Census Bureau statistics indicates there may be as many as forty-four middle-class black women for each eligible middle-class black male.

Observers believe the health of most black Americans is getting worse. The death rate from cancer among blacks today is 30 percent higher than among whites, and blacks are more susceptible to virtually every major degenerative disease. Poor diet, lower income, and less education are blamed for much of the difference.

The jobless rate of young blacks is a very elusive figure. Some estimates are that well over a third of 16- to 19-year-olds are looking for and unable to find work. Other estimates are as low as 8 percent. The black teenage labor force has been shrinking: over two-thirds of those 16 to 19 years old say their primary activity is school or college. Many are joining the military. More than one-fifth of all enlisted persons and 5 percent of all officers are black. For black women, the figures are a bit higher.

Although many believe that blacks will not move as rapidly in an age of competition with other population groups for scarce economic opportunities and shrinking social programs, there are signs that some new tactics are propelling this segment further on the track toward participation in the power centers, both political and economic.

The Reverend Jesse Jackson's operation PUSH instituted a "selective buying campaign" against Coca-Cola; the result was an agreement that will channel more than $30 million to black businesses. This signaled a new interest in boycotts—now called selective buying for legal purposes—as a civil rights tactic. There is broad support throughout the black community for the concept that black economic growth is linked to black buying power, which should be used to achieve black business success. PUSH had plans to examine the records of large consumer products companies, such as Procter & Gamble, General Foods, Philip Morris, and McDonald's, to determine the economic relation of the companies with the black community.

Black women are a rising new force for political clout. The Black Women's Forum in California is a potent new political factor in the United States. Of the six blacks elected to the California state legislature from Los Angeles in 1981, four were women; and half of all black officials elected statewide that year were women.

Even if there is, as some observers claim, a backing away from pressures for employment quotas, black power in the marketplace and the political arena, especially at the grass roots level, is a growing reality. It should not be overlooked by managers who may have temporarily lost sight of the economic and strategic importance of blacks, and it certainly remains an area to be much capitalized on by the astute marketer, social professional, academic institution, publisher, and politician.

The Graying of America

It may come as no surprise to learn that 20.8 percent of the U.S. population is over 55. The key fact is that today's older people are quite unlike their predecessor generations. Indeed, today 55 is considered middle-aged.

Older people are better educated and healthier than ever before, but economic uncertainties are taking their toll on expectations. The combination of pension, Social Security, assets, and savings is no longer the protection that many people once believed it would be. Their worth eroded by inflation, their holdings complicated by rising taxes, and their Social Security in jeopardy, many who would once have looked forward to retirement are having second thoughts. As the 1980s began, there was a decline in the number of people claiming Social Security retirement benefits. Early retirement, once encouraged by some employers and eagerly opted for by many in recent prosperous times, is expected to become less and less attractive. Many Americans feel it necessary to work full-time until they reach 70 and at least part time after that. Furthermore, although most older people want to enjoy at least partial retirement, few want to be forcibly, totally sidelined. A Harris poll at the beginning of this decade reported that 46 percent of today's retired people would prefer to work at least some of the time.

The United States is experiencing what some have called a revolution in corporate attitudes and policies toward the older worker. According to Representative Claude Pepper (D-Fla.), chairman of the House Committee on Aging, corporations are turning to the older worker to solve productivity and labor shortage problems. During hearings on new business perspectives for older employees, one witness testified that ACS American Inc., a computer software development company, uses members of the retirement community to write its computer programs. Another said that Grumman Corporation rehires a number of its own retirees on a part- or full-time basis. It is estimated that people over 55 make up about one-fifth of the part-time work force.

Retirees often work for less than permanent employees and can be brought aboard without the usual fringe benefits. Many share what would otherwise be full-time jobs, and others are called in on special projects or as vacation fill-ins. The majority are white-collar workers, because union rules often bar blue-collar workers from resuming their old jobs.

The return of older workers to the labor force is not without attendant controversy. Unions were first to oppose the trend because of the tight job markets. More recently, complaints are being heard from members of the baby boom generation, who now find their careers blocked by their elders. One Detroit attorney has predicted a rise in lawsuits as a result; other observers predict intergenerational conflict as a result not just of jobs, but of government spending allocations.

Barbara Boyle Torrey, a White House budgeter, recently said that unless spending for the elderly slowed, the United States could face a major choice of priorities. By 1986, pension outlays for veterans could almost double as large numbers of World War II veterans reach 65.

Medicare could be the largest single item in the federal budget by 2000. Indeed, outlays for the elderly, currently about 25 percent of the federal budget, could easily reach 30 percent by 1986. Torrey recommends that private sources begin to work now with government to decide how those costs can be split and what the priorities should be.

There is a growing research focus on the problems and concerns of older people—diet, exercise, environment, vitamins, drugs, genetics, artificial organs, and suspended animation. Scientists are concluding that many of us have a real choice of living well beyond the limits of our inherited life span. There is real hope for helping people with cancer, diabetes, and other diseases and symptoms that generally occur with aging.

Thus, as a market and a human resource pool, the older population will be increasingly significant. The split between well-off and poor older people will add to the existing stresses on the social services and tax systems. And the fact that older people vote in greater proportions than other age groups gives them a political clout that makes politicians tremble. Witness the difficulty in making relatively simple reforms in the Social Security system.

Geographic Shifts

During the last half of the 1970s, over 80 million Americans changed their residence within the United States at least once and about one-fifth of them moved to different states. By the end of the 1980s, the nation's population is expected to increase by over 20 million. Almost half of that growth is expected to occur in the southern states, which currently hold less than a third of all Americans and about a third of the increase is projected to take place in the western regions, which now hold less than a fifth of all U.S. inhabitants. The older, northern regions, where half of all Americans now live, may see an increase of less than 5 million. Demographer Fabian Linden of the Conference Board has projected the following for the 1980s:

New England   Outmigration will continue, and so will the decline of relative per capita income.

Middle Atlantic   Little or no population growth and slow economic growth.

East north central   The population and economy will continue to expand. Because of heavy concentration of large industries here, wages may still exceed the national level.

West north central   Slow growth in both population and economy.

South Atlantic Rapid growth. The number of persons is expected to rise by 13 percent, and personal income will expand a good deal more than in most other places. The Florida boom will continue, practically undiminished, through the 1980s.

East south central Good expectations for economic and population growth.

West south central Continued strong growth particularly in Texas, which will grow by more than 17 percent by 1990. A strong growth rate is also anticipated for Louisiana.

Mountain states Population will grow about 20 percent, a rate more than twice that of the total country.

Pacific By decade's end, the population is expected to grow by 14 percent, substantially faster than the national average. California will dominate; it will account for about 75 percent of the total. But the region's economic growth will only marginally exceed the national average. Since population will be growing rapidly, the growth in per capita income of this area will slacken.

Many of the geographic shifts are linked to changed economic conditions. The armies of the semiskilled who populated the older industries (such as steel and auto) and therefore the older industrial centers of the north, have to move on as those industries and areas decline. And in moving on they find themselves competing for jobs with people who will work for less and are not inclined to join unions. Municipal services are also of a lower order generally, partly to keep taxes down so as to attract industry and partly because wage scales in government are somewhat lower.

What is often missed in standard projections is that the salaries and benefits of municipal workers in the sun belt have begun to catch up with those of the northern counterparts. Unions are making inroads and wages are generally going up, so a leveling seems to be taking place. The south and southwest still win on climate, but housing has become a critical problem in the faster-growing regions. Prices are even higher, thus negating some of the living cost advantages.

There are also interesting developments in population shifts among urban, suburban, and rural areas. The dominant movement is still toward the suburbs, but it is less dominant than before. During the 1970s, rural areas grew faster than metropolitan areas for the first time since the early 1800s. Conversely, a *gentrification movement* began, with the middle and upper classes moving into blighted central-city areas. Cost of energy, commuting time, disillusionment with the suburbs, two-income households, poor public transportation, housing shortages, and high prices are the contributors to this new inmigration. But gentrification only adds to the plight of the poor, who are forced to leave as property values soar in once-ignored ghettos.

San Francisco and Toronto have become the first major cities to require office developers to build housing as a condition for getting permits to build offices. To assure that a portion of the work force lives within city borders, San Francisco city officials have designated large portions of a warehouse area within a few blocks of the office district as underutilized and suitable for housing. But that housing will be offered at market rates that will be affordable only to highly paid workers. Clerical staff will still find it necessary to live farther out, and many clerical operations and computer banks are being moved out to the suburbs.

And there are still other considerations not fully explored in often-used demographic projections. *The Wall Street Journal,* in a 1982 editorial, joined with many other publications and observers in predicting that water might be our most undervalued, limited, and critical resource in the coming years. Certainly, little thought has been given by demographers to the impact of future water availability in many U.S. regions currently experiencing fast growth. If you have to consider site planning, investments, products or services that are water-dependent, and costs of doing business, you cannot afford to be blind to the potential impact of water shortages. No one in the business sector should remain indifferent to warnings of the sort we are hearing with regard to water. Energy has already taught us one painful lesson about arrogance and naiveté. Pollution, topsoil destruction, poor planning, weather changes, and waste also are taking their toll. Now is the time, for the sake of your organization and community, to get involved—to participate in the movement for better water management and planning.

A report from the Joint Center of Urban Studies at MIT and Harvard University faults another oversight of traditional demographic projections: failure to recognize that migration patterns have replaced births and deaths as the major determinant of population growth. The report's authors contend that, against the conventional wisdom cited earlier, some sun belt regions will experience slower growth and some frost belt regions will experience new growth. They found that on many past occasions when the Census Bureau predicted slower growth or faster growth, the opposite happened.

Overview

In the 1980s the United States will be made up of a diversity of people. That is not news. Perhaps it would not even be news to say that there will be three major age bulges: the elderly (or older), the baby-boomers, and the baby boom echo (the size of which demographers dispute). But when we look at the population in another way, we see serious rifts developing in what is no longer a mainstream America with a solid middle class.

The older population contains many who are very well off and live comfortably and many who are in abject poverty. A good many of the baby-boomers have made it, and they feel the need to purchase second and third homes to use as tax shelters because of their income levels. But there is also a large number whose expectations have been affected by hard economic realities. Many have slipped down, or off, the ladder. The baby boom echo will also be a group divided. Many will be born to higher-income, better-educated parents, but perhaps an equal number will be born to juveniles and unwed mothers with lower education or income levels and an environment of deprivation.

The subject of immigration is laden with emotion, the Hispanic issue even more so because of the bilingual situation. As yet the Hispanic community is far from uniting behind its interests, although it is not as far away from doing so as some would think.

Today's teenagers are split; many are involved in punk and total rejection of society, but just as many are involved in the preppy tradition of anxiously working for the standard versions of success and achievement. For both groups the competition is fierce.

Competition: the old against the old, the old against the young, the young against the young, the citizens against the immigrants, the immigrants among themselves, minorities against each other and the rest of the population. And region against region, state against state. Competition for federal dollars, foreign investments, and maybe even valuable natural resources like water.

This is who we will be as a people into the mid-1990s. This is the complex, tumultuous human landscape that we have attempted to help you understand better, monitor more accurately, market to more effectively, and employ to better advantage. To do those things, it will be necessary for you to:

■ Insist on more depth, precision, and segmentation in market data.

■ Use more creative reasoning and common sense and refuse to accept stereotypes.

■ See the opportunities for investment in the delivery of goods and services in the areas in which the pressures are building: water management technology, at-home teaching and learning devices that are bilingual and/or upscale, employment programs for the "retired," automated alternatives to entry-level positions, youth counseling for career training and stress management.

■ Seek a diversity of population types in your pool of workers, whether or not it is mandated or enforced by government, because of the wealth of perspectives and innovation such a mix might bring and because of the need to breathe new life into rigid and traditional thinking about products, markets, and services.

CHAPTER 4

Locomotive Technologies

Publications ranging from esoteric scientific journals to daily newspapers are full of stories about strange and wonderful new technological developments. They are the footprints of the army of the scientific and technological revolution now taking place. Our world is being transformed, literally before our eyes, by new technologies that are bringing about radical and fundamental alterations of everything from the mundane routines of our daily lives to international political and economic structures. Every day we wake up to a new world, and by bedtime that world has significantly changed again. It can be argued that never before—not at the time of the Industrial Revolution, not at the introduction of gunpowder, not even with the invention of the plow and the wheel—has technology so powerfully and swiftly changed the world and the lives of the people who live in it.

More specifically, developments in information technology, communications technology, biotechnology, and materials technology are the principal forces, the *locomotives of change,* that are pulling us at so rapid a pace into the future.

■ Starting on April 1, 1982, several dozen newsletter publishers were able to deliver their publications directly to subscribers electronically over telephone wires to which computer terminals were connected.

■ Jean-Pierre Chevenement, former minister of state for science and industry in France under President Francois Mitterand, called science a "passion" and determined that a "gigantic effort" in research was necessary for the future independence of the country.

■ The Japanese electronics firm Fujitsu Fanuc has built a factory in which robots make other robots.

■ A new technique uses a TV camera and a computer hooked up to electrodes in the brain to give blind people the ability to distinguish geometrical figures.

■ A Stanford University scientist has written a computer program that enabled a computer to create a new electronic circuit.

■ ITT Rayonier Corporation announced in 1982 that its researchers had successfully cloned slash pine trees from tissue cultures and were working on cloning hemlock trees.

■ It is estimated that business will be spending close to $100 billion on data communications services by 1990.

■ Currently, business is spending upwards of $5 billion researching home information and entertainment systems, according to a study by Frost & Sullivan.

■ A recent study by SRI International forecasts that the number of automated office work stations will exceed the existing number of electric typewriters by 1990.

■ Genetic engineers have developed a microbe that feeds on the principal component of the controversial herbicide Agent Orange.

■ A newly emerging specialty, rapid solidification technology, is enabling metallurgists to develop totally new alloys with greater strength and more resistance to wear, corrosion, and high temperatures.

■ Laboratory experiments have demonstrated that plastics such as polyacetylene can conduct electricity as easily as metals and hold promise for use in new lightweight batteries.

■ Arnold Penzias, Nobel prize–winning vice president of Bell Laboratories, predicts that people without programming skills will some day be able to build a new computer for each special job and that we then may be able to use computers as we now use paper.

Information Technology

In the brief period of time—little more than a generation—since the computer was first introduced, improvements and changes in information processing have come so quickly that even the experts have a hard time keeping current. The first computers were enormous pieces of machinery; their equivalents today can be carried around in a briefcase or even a pocket. The initial computers were the functional equivalents of stepladders; they raised people up to a higher level of mathematical or clerical performance. The new computers, or those now on the way, can substitute for people and perform such human tasks as thinking, inventing, and counseling.

Computer scientists at Bell Laboratories have developed a computer that can choose routes between two locations. When matched against people, the computer almost always selected shorter routes. Eventually, it is hoped, the user will be able to find in a computerized Yellow Pages not only where a particular store or business is but also the best way to get there.

Boris, a computer program created at Yale, can read stories in English and answer questions about them. It understands the emotional context of words and answers questions such as "How did Richard feel when the coffee spilled?" by responding, "He felt embarrassed." The question raised by this kind of computer program is this: If the computer comprehends human feelings and can react the way a person would, is that computer capable of feeling emotions?

Xerox Corporation scientists have developed computer programs that function as tutors. They diagnose mistakes children make in arithmetic and point out the basis for the errors.

Some of the most significant developments have been in the creation of "smart" machinery—robots. It should be recognized that robots and other intelligent machines are not merely improvements in factory or office efficiency; they are substantively different from the assembly line. The new machinery *controls* processes; it replaces not just human energy but human thinking. There are robot inspectors that can examine as many as 1200 small parts per minute for both surface and internal defects and flaws. Having examined the parts, the robot inspectors decide whether to reject them. Other robots can decide, entirely upon the basis of constant assessment of tool wear, when cutting tools on an assembly line need to be replaced. Researchers at Battelle Institute are developing a goal-oriented control system for manufacturing. An overall goal for quality control, such as maximum allowable variation, is established, and all the elements of the computerized control system are programmed to achieve specific subgoals such that the variation from standard is kept within the specified limits.

Programs have already been developed to diagnose diseases, give stock market advice, provide interpretations of legal and tax problems, and counsel distraught patients when their therapists are otherwise occupied. Pharmaceutical companies are using computers to design new drugs; the computers, their memories crammed with huge data bases of information on chemical compounds, do a multitude of complex calculations on the properties of the compounds and produce graphic representations of their molecular structures. The graphs can be manipulated to arrive at an ideal structure and shape for a specific goal.

Prospector, a computer program developed by SRI International, has been used to locate hidden mineral deposits. In 1982, by using geological maps of a location in the state of Washington and rules obtained from an exploration specialist, Prospector correctly identified the location of previously unknown deposits of porphyry molybdenum.

These and many other developments are creating what some observers are calling the Information Age. In a series of articles in *Sky* magazine in 1982, author Allan Zullo depicted a society in which entertainment, medicine, education, politics—even sports—will be substantially if not radically changed by the ubiquitous computer. The truth is, we don't really know what kind of a new world we are making, any more than Henry Ford knew how the automobile would ultimately transform his world. (One of the unnoticed ironies of our time is that

Henry Ford's monument outside Detroit is Deerfield Village, a loving restoration of a past that Ford, as much as anyone, destroyed forever.) Like any new technology, the computer's impacts are often, if not largely, unanticipated, because new technologies open doors to the unknown. The one thing we do know is that the world will not ever again be the same.

Communications Technology

In 1981 the respected British magazine *The Economist* did a comprehensive report on developments in communications. Significantly, the article was entitled "The Born-Again Technology." Technological advance in communications has taken the somnolent, taken-for-granted businesses of broadcasting, telephone, telegraph, and mail and turned them into telecommunications. And telecommunications has become a wakened giant of immense dimensions with political, economic, and social ramifications that boggle the mind. Even that born-again giant of the old communications, AT&T, no longer calls itself a telephone company. It is, according to its own annual statement, "in the business of transporting and managing information." Now the telecommunications industry, according to Ivan Wolff, a communications expert with the Wall Street firm of Donaldson, Lufkin & Jenrette, includes telephone, telegraph, computers, office equipment, printing and publishing, electronic components, broadcasting, consumer electronics, software, and cable television.

Foremost among the transforming factors is the merging of communications and information technologies. Starting with the transistor, invented at AT&T's Bell Laboratories, microelectronics has made communications quicker, cheaper, and more efficient than ever imagined before. Digital transmission, made possible by cheap little computers, is many times faster than voice can ever be. Automated communications exchanges are infinitely quicker and more accurate than human operators. Satellite communications and optical fibers provide enormous increases in message capacity over the capacity of traditional copper cables. One optical fiber no thicker than a human hair can carry 1000 telephone calls; an equivalent copper cable would have to be thicker than a human body. Also, glass is cheaper and far more plentiful than copper.

Lasers will multiply manyfold the channels available for television, telephone, and data communications. Holography can use lasers to create three-dimensional images. Cable and satellite TV, as well as low-power transmission, will substantially increase the number of channels available, some of which can be used for two-way communications. Inexpensive and widely available computer terminals linked to the telephone and the television set can make of virtually every office or home a self-contained entertainment, information, and education center. Electronic mail and facsimile transmission can make all communications instantaneous and unfailingly accurate. Video-recording technology will enable users to control how and when they will receive transmissions. Beepers and cellular radio will enable anyone who wants it to be never out of touch. Table 4-1 shows the options for sending a 20-word message that were available to a manager in 1981.

The much-talked-about office of the future is changing not only the way jobs are done in offices but the nature of the jobs themselves and, most importantly, the nature of the relationships within organizations. This will require you to consider, for example:

■ How can you justify paying a computer technician more than a secretary when the secretary may be using computerized equipment just as routinely and skillfully as the technician?

■ Who is managing whom when the clerks and secretaries have the know-how to use and access the systems and the managers themselves have not been trained to do so?

■ Given the fact that much more organizational overhead is attributable to managerial and supervisory costs than to clerical and secretarial costs, will it make sense to use the expensive new technology just to make secretaries and clerks more effective?

As powerful as the impact of telecommunications on the office will be, its impact on the home will be even greater. Sony is already making a modular TV set that can accommodate attachments which will turn it into a control device for entertainment, information, and communication. Interactive TV can be used to bank, make purchases, or vote on referendums; satellites and optical fibers expand many times the number of entertainment and information channels available within the home and thereby reduce "the audience" to fragments; a video–telephone–home computer linkup can connect individuals to virtually everything and everybody else instantaneously. From being the hub from which individual family member activities radiate, the home could become a self-contained entity within which more and more individual and family activities take place. The family and its members can create their own environment and direct their own activ-

Table 4-1
Delivery Options for a Nonvoice 20-Word Message Across 500 Miles

Agency	Delivery	Time to Accomplish	Approximate Cost
Hand carry	Physical	6 hours	$250
Airline parcel service (Sky Cab)	Physical	6 hours	$85
Federal Express	Physical	Overnight	$9.50
Postal Service express mail	Physical	Overnight	$8.50
First-class mail	Physical	2 to 5 days	$0.20
USTS's FAXNET	Facsimile	Hours	$2.00 to ?
FAX machine plus phone line	Facsimile	Minutes	$2.00 to ?
Mailgram (fastest)	Message, but in paper form	Overnight	$4.00
Telex (both must subscribe)	Message	Instantaneous	$0.20 to 0.30
Time-sharing service (both must have terminals and subscribe)	Message	Instantaneous	$0.20 (plus perhaps a minimum if this is only transaction)
Postal Service ECOM	Message, but in paper form	2 days	$2.00 to ?
Computer with dial-up capability and access by addressee	Message	Instantaneous	Cost of voice or data call—$0.30 to 1.50

Source: *The Communications Industries*, Donaldson, Lufkin & Jenrette, New York, 1981, p. 28.

ities within it. They can alter time: A video recorder can enable them to create their own prime time; a teletext device can link them to electronic libraries that hold all of history; interactive TV can let them tell retailers and manufacturers what and when they will want to buy in the future.

Telecommunications has already significantly changed the nature of business competition, and it seems likely to continue doing so at an accelerated rate. Holiday Inns discovered that, with its combination of hotels and telecommunications equipment, it could be in the teleconferencing business rather than just supply the places where conferences take place. AT&T, it is feared by banks, may become, among other things, a bank, because banking is increasingly the electronic transmission of data—and that is what AT&T does.

The technology is having a substantial effect upon international relations. The issues range from concern over the economic and military implications of remote sensing by satellites (if a satellite belonging to a superpower detects mineral deposits in a third world country, to whom does the information belong?) to worry about TV programs beamed by satellite into countries whose governments don't want them. Increasingly, governments in all kinds of countries are becoming concerned that the new technology has the potential to erode their control—or hopeful that, by controlling the technology, they can enhance their authority. Telecommunications also means that information-processing jobs can be located anywhere in the world, regardless of where the home office is. So word processing and data entry are now performed in Barbados by low-salaried workers linked to corporate offices elsewhere by satellite and facsimile machines.

Publications are feeling the effects too. Scientific journals are now challenged by electronic data banks that make reports and articles available instantly to interested scientists. Instead of wading through one or more of the thousands of scientific journals (there are more than 8000 in medicine and biology alone), scientists can access data banks for specific items in their fields. Also, they can do so in much less than the 6 months or so it takes research reports to reach print in conventional journals.

A critical question, just now beginning to be debated, is how the electronization of publications affects the First Amendment. In his book *Electronic Nightmare* author John Wicklein expresses his fear that this development has the potential to impair quite seriously freedom of the press. If, for example, newspapers distribute text electronically, does that bring them under the control of the FCC, which is charged with regulating the airwaves and can effectively influence, if not control, program content through its rule-making and franchising powers?

There are obviously many other areas of impact, concern, and promise, far too many to be covered in this brief summary. But the subject is thoroughly covered these days in everything from scholarly books to daily newspapers. There is, however, one more area of impact that needs to be touched on. That is the equalizing and handicapping potential of telecommunications—a yin and yang of promise and threat that are inseparably linked.

The introduction of gunpowder and guns is the best-known historical example of an equalizing technology. The gun effectively eliminates the advantages of size and strength; a 97-pound weakling with a gun can be the equal of an all-pro linebacker with a gun. Telecommunications advances the limits of equality well beyond that.

■ In England, a supermarket chain and Newcastle University have set up a system that enables housebound old and disabled people to order groceries through computer terminals.

■ A talking wristwatch, available for under $100, will enable blind people to tell time without a braille device.

■ Robots now in experimental stages can pick up, hold, and carry objects for paralyzed people upon voice commands.

■ Dr. Harry Levitt of the City University of New York has invented an inexpensive portable computer that will enable deaf people to "talk" to each other over the telephone.

There are hundreds of other developments that will allow people whose handicaps and deficiences have theretofore excluded them from the mainstream to become equal with the nonhandicapped. In addition, there will be an equalizing effect in business. Smaller companies will be able to have the same computing and communications capacities as larger ones—another nail in the coffin of the economies-of-scale concept.

The other side of the coin is the possibility of a society increasingly divided along the lines of access to and skill with the new technologies. If information is wealth and if control of or access to information is power, those who possess that wealth and power will be the new rich, the new aristocracy, the new rulers. Although much of the thrust in both computers and telecommunications is toward making the technology increasingly user-friendly—that is, easier to use by more people— the computocrats and communocrats will be those who determine the design and use of their tools.

Biotechnology

Although biotechnology encompasses a great many scientific areas, the media in recent years, reflecting (if not creating) the furor surrounding genetic engineering, have focused on that one aspect of it. Perhaps no area of scientific endeavor, with the possible exception of nuclear weaponry, currently arouses so much concern, fear, and hostility. In their early years of public awareness, recombinant DNA activities were threatened with severe restrictions ranging all the way from establishment of public oversight groups to outright abolition. Self-regulation by scientists successfully defused the explosive situation. But the fears did not go away. One sees them reflected in the fierce and powerful opposition to anything that might appear to be outside the natural pattern of reproduction, including abortion, test-tube babies, prenatal testing (such as amniocentesis) for birth defects, and genetic surgery in embryos. And one sees them reflected in the periodic recurrence of articles about the possibility of virulent new diseases being created through genetic engineering and escaping from laboratories.

Many if not most people are uneasy with the thought that other human beings, no matter how well trained or careful, are fooling around with life itself. Nowhere is the Frankenstein syndrome more manifest than in public reaction to genetic engineering. But behind the fears and sensationalism, wonders are occurring. One of the most significant areas of development is agriculture. By using genetic engineering, scientists have altered plants to increase yields and dramatically decrease crop losses to disease. They have been able to multiply plant ability to resist disease, withstand heat, and survive for long periods without water. They are developing salt-tolerant strains of food crops that can be grown in previously unsuitable areas. So exciting are the prospects that one respected scientist, Professor Peter Carlson of Michigan State University, recently said, "In fifteen years or so, we'll be able to do anything we want to plant cells." Richard Critchfield, one of the leading authorities on third world development, believes that biotechnology is making possible an agricultural revolution that will be the salvation of the third world. In *Foreign Affairs* in the fall of 1982, Critchfield states that advances in agriculture based on biotechnology are particularly beneficial to poorer, less-developed countries because they are less expensive than energy-based advances, do not disturb the traditional rural patterns of the third world, and do not substitute capital for labor.

Another area of great promise is the development of monoclonal antibody production. Monoclonal antibodies are created when two cells, one diseased and the other the producer of an antibody to that disease, are fused together to create a new cell combining the properties of both. Thus a cancer cell and a spleen cell can be merged to produce a cell that produces an antibody specifically for that cancer. Scientists anticipate that monoclonal antibodies, in addition to serving as specific weapons against diseases of many kinds, will help us to better understand the mysteries of the cell. That, in turn, will lead to greater understanding of how diseases affect cells and, ultimately, how to treat each disease most effectively. The big hope for monoclonal antibodies, however, is in the war on cancer. Researchers expect that they will be able to develop antibodies that can pinpoint cancer cells within the body, attach themselves to the cells, and deliver killing doses of radioactive chemicals or drugs.

One of the most intriguing and promising areas of biotechnological research is the development of microorganisms to perform tasks that range all the way from pollution control to manufacturing. Hooker Chemical Company scientists are experimenting with a microorganism that renders industrial chemical wastes totally harmless. Enzymes are being used to manufacture human insulin. And, perhaps most mind boggling of all, researchers are working to combine microorganisms and electronics to develop molecular switches for computers that would make computers smaller, faster, and much more like the human brain. As reported in the British magazine *New Scientist*, the electronics industry is on the brink of a new era—the age of the "biochip." Chips no bigger than molecules could enter human cells to make repairs or even replicate themselves. A biochip implanted in the spinal cord could enable a paraplegic to move his limbs; another biochip could signal and correct abnormal heart rhythms. The possibilities are boundless.

Some observers believe that the 1980s will be the decade of biotechnology. And the scramble to capitalize on that possibility is on. Japanese companies, backed by their country's Ministry of International Trade and Industry (MITI), are prepared to pour massive resources into establishing Japan as a world leader in the field. It is already the leader in enzyme manufacture and use through advanced fermentation technology. European countries, including Holland, France, and the United Kingdom, are giving priority to national efforts in biotechnology development. It is significant that, in Europe and Japan, the focus of such efforts is on cooperation between industry and government. In the United States, the focus is on industry-academic cooperation. In 1982 the giant chemical company Monsanto entered into a biomedical research agreement with Washington University under which Monsanto will give the university $23.5 million for basic research. Monsanto scientists will work with their university counterparts, and Monsanto will have the right to review all research findings to determine if there are any product possibilities and will have the exclusive right to manufacture and market such products. Other universities and companies are developing similar working arrangements.

So widespread has this form of cooperation become that there are increasing expressions of concern that university research will become too focused on commercial possibilities. Instead of the traditional academic drive for new knowledge, the aim may become new products—and profit. In his book *The Double-Edged Helix*, scientist Liebe F. Cavalieri decries the obsession with recombinant DNA as a science with great commercial potential. Commercial interests, he says, will overwhelm the public interest, and science will no longer be science but will instead be technology.

Materials Technology

The unseen technology is that of materials. It has thus far escaped the kind of public attention the other locomotive technologies have received, but it is no less important.

■ Exciting progress is being made in developing plastics—specifically polymers—that are extremely good at conducting electricity. In addition to being relatively low in cost, uniform, and easy to process, they hold the promise of freeing industries (and countries) from the current dependence on strategic and often scarce metals such as copper, nickel, and zinc.

■ Superconductivity—the flow of an electric current through a substance with no resistance—was formerly thought to be possible only at absolute zero. Scientists have long dreamed of superconductors that would function at much higher temperatures. The Soviet Union claims to have accomplished superconductivity at high temperatures in the late 1970s, and many scientists now believe the claim to be genuine. Superconductivity means no loss of energy; theoretically, a current could flow forever with no loss of power. If, as now seems likely, we can achieve superconductivity at something like room temperature, then according to NYU Professor Irving Lefkowitz, there is no energy problem.

■ In 1982 a group of French scientists demonstrated a technique for placing silicon transistors on glass by using lasers to transform the silicon and bond it to the glass. This technique makes feasible a large-screen TV set that can hang on a wall like a mirror.

■ New techniques in metallurgy offer much promise for more efficient use of existing resources and for better products as well. In a process called *cladding* diverse metals and alloys are joined by atomic bonds created with high pressure. Thus, copper and stainless steel can be bonded together to make virtually indestructable underground cables. Also, scientists at the University of California's Lawrence Livermore Laboratory have created a steel that is more shatter-resistant at very low temperatures and does not require the use of nickel.

These and other developments will create new industries, new international relations, new products, new ways to use and conserve important and scarce resources, new weapons, and exciting new breakthroughs in science and technology.

On the Change Track

And all together, the technologies briefly described in this chapter make up a force for change that is awesome in its power. It has already wrought profound changes; its promise for tomorrow is even greater change. This description of technology may seem to you to be too cosmic, but its implications for you—in your own life, as a manager, as an employer, as an investor—are very real.

The reliance of the industrialized northern countries on strategic minerals from the less-developed southern countries is almost certain to be reduced. The United States, for example, needs to import anywhere up to 100 percent of such minerals as chromium, cobalt, nickel, titanium, and molybdenum, much of it from African countries. If these countries find their markets lost or diminished (and just about all of them, with the exception of South Africa, are barely just getting by as it is), will they collapse? And if so, what would such a collapse do to the precariously balanced world economy? Would the potential of a debtor's cartel or increased terrorist activity be escalated? How would that affect the financial institutions you are directly connected with? What would it mean to your investments?

The new technologies are resulting in industries which tend to be energy- and capital-intensive, but not labor-intensive. Telecommunications and computers, in particular, tend to result in displacement of workers with significantly higher levels of skills. Some experts believe that as many as 45 million jobs in the United States alone could be affected by automation. There is obviously an urgent need to study the impacts of the new technologies on people and to think seriously and pragmatically about the retraining of displaced workers. A study by the Deltak Corporation, which trains data processing workers, predicts that developments in office technology will require office workers to be retrained up to eight times during their careers. Unions in some European countries have negotiated contracts that establish gradual rates for the introduction of new technologies in an effort to protect existing jobs. Gerrit Nijland, a professor of robotics in the Netherlands, has studied worker response to the introduction of robots in his country and has found growing resistance in the form of sabotage. A study done for the Canadian government concluded that women would be disproportionately and adversely affected by the introduction of office automation, since most jobs displaced would be those customarily held by women. What of your own career path—how might it be affected by the new technologies? And what about the future opportunities for your children? Will there be, as some think, radical changes in the nature of jobs and the workplace?

There is an intense and growing competition among countries in the new technologies, a kind of Olympics syndrome, as it were. The competition is not for gold medals, but for economic gain, national security, and prestige. The industries selected are known, quite accurately, as "chosen instruments." Led by President Mitterand, France has poured enormous resources into a coordinated national effort to become a leader in telecommunications. Canada's Prime Minister Trudeau has urged that his country try to achieve a similar eminence. Japan, having achieved a dominating position in electronics, is marshaling its formidable resources for similar accomplishments in computers and biotechnology. Italy is trying to coordinate academic and industrial research and development through a revitalized national research and development council. Yugoslavia is devoting substantial resources to making itself a leader in biotechnology. You can anticipate that more barriers to the flow of technology and scientific information will be erected. The move will undoubtedly spill over to affect markets for high-technology products as countries try to nurture their own industries.

In the United States, concern about declining eminence, both economically and technologically, combined with the awareness that future economic well-being depends upon new-technology-based industries, is fueling discussions and efforts aimed at restoring the country to its position of leadership. Frank Press, president of the National Academy of Sciences and former science adviser to President Carter, called in 1982 for a combined and coordinated effort by government, industry, and academia to ensure that "the nation's premier scientific status prevails." Similarly, concern over the declining number of young Americans undergoing advanced training in science, and what is perceived as the declining quality of scientific education, has led to calls for a coordinated national human resource policy. (See Figure 4-1.) Conceivably, there will be increased entrepreneurial opportunities in early and advanced education and retraining as part of a major national effort to beef up our scientific and technological capacity.

Out of this intense competitive effort is emerging, in a new guise, the old ogre called central planning. But this time it is not based on ideology; it is no longer an issue of left versus right. Now it is based on pragmatic assessment of economic and technological imperatives. And now it is more likely to take the form of coordination or cooperation among the segments of the society rather than exist solely as a government function. In the United States (where it will never be called central planning but may be called industrial policy) it is likely to be indicative; that is, it is likely to take the form of recommending and setting policy rather than be explicit and highly directive, as in the Soviet Union. More likely than not, your organization will be involved in this societal development.

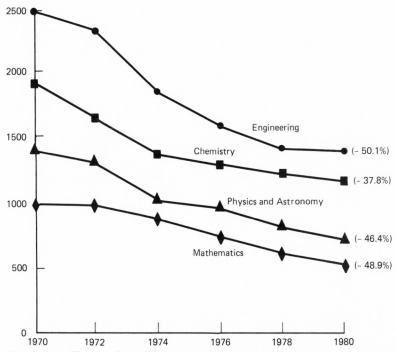

Figure 4-1 The number of doctorates in science and engineering awarded to U.S. citizens by U.S. universities. (*Reprinted by permission from* Nature, *vol. 299, no. 5878, p. 5. Copyright © 1982 Macmillan Journals Limited.*)

Growing concern over the impact of technology on people is reflected in a new discipline, called ergonomics, that focuses on adapting technology to people. There is growing awareness that human considerations are too often lacking in the design of everything from our airports and hospitals to our residences and workstations. Ergonomics could affect your organization, your purchases, and your assessment of the competitive engineering performance of the companies in which you invest.

New technologies are already creating new jobs and new careers, and the future holds promise for many more. Technology management is an example. Early in this decade MIT became the first university to offer an advanced-degree program in technology management. In the computer field we can anticipate a growing demand for computer security specialists. Robotics engineers, metallurgists, information managers, ergonomists—these and other jobs as yet not even thought of will provide new opportunities.

There are, of course, other areas of science and technology which are important for the future. Space and health are two obvious examples. But the four technologies described here are the most powerful forces of their kind that are at work today shaping that future—your future. There is no way any of us can escape the impacts of these technologies. They will profoundly affect everything from the way you spend time with your family to the nature of the products and services your organization will offer. They will have a major effect on where you will be working 10 years from now—and what kind of work you will be doing. They will substantially change the education your children will receive and how they will receive it. They will create new profits and new investment opportunities, and they will bring giants of industry down.

It will be necessary for you, if you wish to have any control over the personal consequences of the technological revolutions, to keep current. Make sure you include in your regular reading at least one good general science publication such as *Science, The New Scientist,* or *The Sciences.*

Just reading is not enough, however. It must be combined with analysis. Keep asking yourself pertinent questions. What does this mean in terms of new product possibilities? How might this change the way I do my job? Can we use this development to improve our market share, and if so, how? Do I have working for me people who know about this and can use it to improve productivity or profitability? What kind of human resource needs for the future does this mean? What are the likely new career opportunities? What possible new investment opportunities does this represent?

Popular literature, particularly some science fiction, often represents technology as evil. But it's not evil. Science and technology are neither bad nor good any more than natural forces such as winds and waves are. But their consequences, particularly the unanticipated ones, can be harmful, and that is why to be a supermanager you must have this enhanced capacity for understanding what technological developments could mean.

CHAPTER 5

The Economic Transition

The paradox of economics: At a time when none of the economic theories are working, all the economists are.

When an economy goes through a major and unforeseen wrenching, one of the first victims is the validity of economic analyses which apparently served well to describe previous conditions. But economists, like generals, are always ready to deal with the past. Current debate over economic theories—Neo-Keynesian, supply side, and the like—are amusing to noneconomist observers, who wonder at what point the "experts" will forego theories for reality.

Reality, as we see it, is the compounded aftereffect of record growth rates, expectations of (and, indeed, attainment of) wide spread affluence, dissatisfaction with the existing tax system, a growing underground economy, massive employment dislocation, mature and saturated markets for many existing products and services, decades of management overstaffing, the push toward conglomeration, foreign competition, the fragmentation of the marketplace, the second law of thermodynamics, a new cynicism regarding the concept of economies of scale, and a host of other factors. Can old theory stand up in a time of new rules? If we look at a spate of recent books—including *New Rules* by Daniel Yankelovich, *The Third Wave* by Alvin Toffler, and *Megatrends* by John Naisbitt—we must conclude that all these respected analysts are either misguided or correct. And if they are correct, this country—indeed, the whole world—is going through a major and manifold economic transition.

The Kondratieff
Wave Theory

The transition theory is, at least to some degree, supported by the economists and modelers who accept long-wave cycles as a pattern of economic evolution. Analyses of patterns of economic performance in industrial countries led to the observation, most notably by the Russian economist Nicolai Kondratieff in 1926, that there are regular and measurable cycles of important interplay between social, economic, political, and technological processes. These cycles result in peaks and troughs about 50 years apart. The data used go back to the beginning of the nineteenth century.

The great economist Joseph Schumpeter was an early Kondratieff disciple; present-day believers in the Kondratieff "wave theory" include Jay Forester of MIT and Walt Rostow of the University of Texas. There is a host of plausible explanations of why economies rise and fall in a long-wave fashion. Forrester, for example, attributes the cycles to the interaction of capital goods and the consumer goods industries. He believes the capital goods sector has become overbuilt worldwide, and he predicts the result will be a protracted period of excess capacity and deflationary pressures. Another explanation is that the cyclical transitions are tied to the worklife experience of a human generation, which is approximately 50 years. In effect, according to this concept, people in an advancing society are bound to commit the errors and achieve the successes of preceding generations.

In the standard Kondratieff wave there is a long period of strong growth lasting about 30 years. The early part of this period (comparable to the 1950s) is quiet; the country enjoys the prosperity that followed the prior trough. The latter part of the growth phase generally incorporates an investment boom, rising inflation, and a lot of sociopolitical activity reflecting the perception that, with affluence, inequities can be addressed and overcome. That could be a description of the 1960s. Then there is a plateau, which can last as long as a decade, often initiated by a *primary depression*. According to some observers, such a plateau occurred from 1921 (a primary depression) to 1929. It is now being said that the current wave's primary depression occurred in 1975 and that we are still in the plateau phase.

The third and final phase is characterized by stagnation for one or two decades. It is usually triggered by a *secondary depression,* which itself is usually triggered by a financial panic. The third phase is typically marked by a high degree of political activism as a result of serious unemployment and poor profitability. Often one of the turning points at the end of the stagnation period has been war.

The Kondratieff wave theory is not overburdened with supporters. But that does not detract from one of its major premises: that the economic order changes with a shift in investments and new directions in technological and industrial development. Wall Street economist George Goodman, writing as Adam Smith, contended in a 1982 *Esquire* article that we can no longer count on the Dow Jones averages as a measure of economic well-being. He pointed out that the average is based on thirty "mature, mostly industrial companies that represent a declining America," whereas, in reality, future action will be with companies like Wang Laboratories. It is significant that American Express has been the latest addition to the Dow, replacing the beleaguered Johns-Mansville.

Such economic indicators as gross national product (GNP), Consumer Price Index (CPI), productivity, employment, personal income, and corporate profitability are serving us less and less well as descriptions of reality. For reasons ranging from the growth of the underground economy to creative accounting and from the changing nature of work to the changing nature of industry, our economic road maps are leading us nowhere. The declining usefulness of traditional quantitative indicators will be treated in greater detail later in this book.

How the Economy Is Changing

If your concern, like that of the rest of us, is understanding economic changes well enough to manage an enterprise or make sound investments, it is important for you to keep in mind that the experts are in all likelihood no less confused than we are. But there are some areas of change in the economy on which there is a broad consensus. That consensus, encompassing people on both the left and the right, labor leaders and managers, economists and technologists, intellectuals and Neo-Luddites, includes key points discussed in the following sections.

Lifting of Barriers to
Resource Maximization.

The new technologies (see Chapter 4) are generating a frenzy of activity in the pooling of expensive research and development projects. Companies once prohibited by antitrust statutes from talking to one another are now finding more lenient government attitudes toward cooperation in discovery phases. Academic institutions are exploring new channels of financing and collaboration with government and the private sector. Companies from different countries are entering into joint ventures. Some major implications you will need to consider are:

■ There will be growing confusion and conflict over control and ownership of technologies and technological information. The result is likely to be a dramatic upswing in patent and copyright litigation.

■ Transborder information flow will be an increasingly contentious issue. The U.S. government has already begun to define national security in both military and economic terms, and it has begun to crack down on the pooling of technical information in the form of professional publications, seminars, conferences, and the hosting of foreign students in U.S. laboratories.

■ Sweeping changes in the tax codes and in regulation (for example, SEC, FTC, and antitrust) will lift the barriers to resource maximization.

■ There will have to be more focus by participating companies on product differentiation and marketing, rather than on returns gained from the protection of the rights to their basic research, because shared research will force that course of action. Some companies that were weak marketing entities will have a major challenge ahead in building greater marketing strength.

The Questioning of
Economies of Scale. Although the points made on the preceding page seem to acknowledge the validity of the economies-of-scale theory, there is a growing question whether conglomeration is always the most effective way to utilize resources. Too many "mom and pop" operations have become unprofitable when absorbed into major conglomerates. And even large acquisitions can prove to be too costly to both acquire and maintain. "Small is beautiful" has become a rallying cry for people who believe that, with regard to provision of jobs, decentralization of control, and application and development of technology, smaller organizations may well have the advantage over larger ones. The implications of this are significant.

■ There is an increasing likelihood that you will see a growing wave of divestitures as conglomeration loses some of its manageability and charm.

■ Government will, in all probability, be asked to intervene by removing the tax incentives that provide both capital to undertake major acquisitions and the short-term bottom-line advantage of write-off of interest on the debt incurred in the stock purchases.

■ There will be a new round of rethinking regarding what businesses a company can really be in and remain profitable.

■ Many more companies will look to joint venture rather than acquisition.

■ There will be accelerated growth in entrepreneurship and small business.

■ Middle-sized businesses, felt by many to be the backbone of the economy and the most appealing targets for takeover, will grow faster and will generally be in a healthier position than their larger or smaller competitors. Because of their vitality, as a group they should, and probably will, be in the forefront of trying to stem the acquisition tide.

A Thrust for Longer-
Range Planning. With the spreading of the corporate ownership base that took place in the 1950s and 1960s, Wall Street became the piper whose tune corporate America obediently followed. Earnings per share, based on short-term (often quarterly) results, became the overriding yardstick of success. The obsession with market valuation, often achieved by sacrificing longer-range development and by accounting practices that add dollars but not quality to the bottom line,

may have peaked. Foreign competitors with longer-range market penetration objectives have sobered up the American game players. General Electric announced in 1982 that earnings per share—formerly the idol to which that company paid obeisance—will give way to emphasis on market share. Analysts themselves are adopting new criteria for evaluating company performance. They are paying more attention and giving more weight to long-term prospects, and they are demonstrating a more thorough understanding of the financial manipulations that modify, but do not necessarily improve, the bottom line. The use of rolling averages of 3 to 5 years duration, rather than annual results, to determine executive compensation is another indication that times are changing. Important implications for you include the following:

■ Reward systems for performance will be reevaluated, and more emphasis will be placed on longer-range duration of positive results.

■ Strategic planning will become a more valued, albeit changed, discipline that will reside, with greater acceptance and effect, at the top levels of management. Strategy also will be a more common topic in boardrooms.

■ Impediments to short-range drains on returns will be weakened when they inhibit long-range creative growth opportunities. For example, rigidly rational approaches to strategies and planning, of the sort that had their heyday in the 1970s, will be increasingly challenged as stifling and conventional.

■ There will be greatly diminished correlations, for several years at least, between the market value of many stocks and the true worth of the companies. Over- and undervaluation will be common, and swings will be rapid and unpredictable.

More Centralized or Cooperative National Economic Planning.

High unemployment, the decay of the country's roads, bridges, sewers, and other elements of the infrastructure, already burdensome taxes, and the presence of foreign competition have driven both theorists and activists on the left and the right to press for more cohesive and longer-range economic programs. National economic planning as a concept has shifted from the ideological (sociological) base of the 1960s to a technological and economic base. Retraining programs to redress massive employment dislocations, joint public and private ventures to revitalize decaying infrastructure, tax or other incentives to leading-edge industries, such as electronics, bioengineering, and materials, and other pieces of what would constitute long-range national economic planning are beginning to fall into place. Progress in this direction seems likely to come about despite the fact that the United States will probably never publicly accept the idea of an overall, centralized national plan. Among the implications you can look for are the following:

■ The formation of new public-private partnerships with a wide and innovative range of types, programs, outcomes, and incentives will increase. There will be lots of entrepreneurial and private sector room for capitalizing on this trend. *Privatization,* as well as co-ventures in the public-private domain, will be welcomed by local politicians, communities, and professionals (if not by unions) as one major solution to problems of bureaucracy and funding, especially in areas of housing, construction, education, health, sanitation, security, and the arts.

■ Political platforms will increasingly include heavy emphasis on the long-range accountability of government and business with regard to provision of jobs, job retraining, and analyses of the impacts of new technologies and foreign competition on jobs. Interstate competition for jobs will get heated, if not vicious, and one of the most critical tasks of the federal government will be to hold the lid down on the heated tempers developing from state to state and region to region. In the process, uneven situations with regard to property taxes, personal income taxes, welfare payments, unemployment insurance, and so on will be looked at from a more centralized perspective, counter to the decentralizing, or states rights, trends of the past several years.

■ There will be growing and heavy pressure to use pension funds as a major source of long-term capital to be directed by and for public and/or employee interest.

Greater Awareness of
International Linkages.
The major economic lesson we learned in the 1970s was that our economy, as large and as powerful as it is, is linked in complex and important ways to the total world economy. When the price of oil shot up, we found our ability to manage our own economy was significantly lessened. When the Japanese automobile industry outperformed ours, we teetered on the brink of economic disaster. When third world countries approached economic chaos, we discovered that we had to keep lending them money or face a dangerous decline in our markets and financial system. Ever-increasing, ever-more-potent international competition for markets and resources will force American business to become more effectively competitive.

Among the things you will need to be alert to are the following:

■ Efforts to improve efficiency through automation, trimming of management and staff functions, and holding down cost increases in peripherals such as employee benefits will speed up. Paradoxically, increased efficiency may not be the answer to better and more competitive performance. As someone has pointed out, efficiency is doing things right, but effectiveness is doing the right things. Innovation, insight, and energy are in the long run more helpful than cost cutting.

■ More attention will be paid to intelligence gathering and analysis. Americans have traditionally been woefully weak in understanding other peoples and cultures. We will no longer be able to afford such ignorant provincialism.

■ Perhaps most importantly, there will be more emphasis on marketing. For an organization to survive and prosper, it will have to recognize that success in a highly competitive environment depends as much on marketing skill as it does on product innovation and quality.

The New Market Era. The United States and the world have become buyers' markets. Executive offices in business and government are increasingly lairs of paper tigers. Selected forces for decentralization and individual control, which are discussed in other chapters, are making the marketplace the seat of decision making. The heightened competitiveness of the world environment adds to the power of the marketplace. Thus, policy decisions from on high are more and more ignored, rejected, or contravened.

The radical slogan of the 1960s, "power to the people," has described reality much more closely than either its opponents or its proponents knew. The Edsel, the Vietnamese war, marijuana, mandatory seat belts, light beer, the Sony Walkman, bicycles, the underground economy—there are hundreds, if not thousands, of examples of how decisions by individuals in the marketplace resulted in unanticipated successes or failures irrespective of what efforts and resources were spent by the companies or government agencies involved.

Entrepreneurship, dropping out, diversity of lifestyle, decentralization, and market fragmentation—these and other forces seem likely to enhance the power of the marketplace in the years ahead. What actions should you be alert to as a consequence?

■ Know and use new techniques to read the marketplace better. Traditional survey research has obvious limits in a time of increasingly unpredictable consumer behavior. Other quantitative indicators, most of which are historical rather than anticipatory, also have limits.

■ Use the new communications technologies available to you to create opportunities for *direct* and *timely* participation in decision making by consumers and constituents.

■ Research *needs* first; new-product possibilities to meet those needs second. Too often, development of new goods and services is unrelated to marketplace needs. (One bit of advice is to have employees keep diaries in which to jot down what happens to them in the course of a week that they *wish* some product or service addressed. This could provide a gold mine of ideas from a huge disposable damp towel for the noontime jogger, to black Band-Aids, to a portable security beeper for those who walk home from a bus or train late at night.)

Let It All Hang Out

If you include the arguments of the long-wave theorists, the observation that we are moving from an industrial to a postindustrial society, and the fact of the shift from a domestic to a global economy, let alone such matters as resource depletion, climate shifts, soil erosion, and stock market irrationality, the evidence that we are in a period of major economic transition is overwhelming.

So we see that, while the traditionalists try to tinker with monetary and fiscal formulas, the people are remaking the economy by doing their own things—bypassing, substituting for, or otherwise rendering obsolete the customary suppliers of goods and services, ignoring tax laws or finding loopholes, starting up their own businesses, reading special-interest publications and watching cable TV, and making sometimes rational and sometimes seemingly irrational decisions about how they will spend their money and their time. That is true of major purchases as well as minor, and housing is a case in point. Housing may be in trouble for the short term, but people need housing. When they can afford it, they will buy it. Smaller, perhaps; shared, perhaps; and many more will rent. The poor will face trouble because they will suffer most from the imbalance between supply and demand. Indeed, housing could become as important an issue as jobs in the 1980s and 1990s.

A number of the issues mentioned here in passing are explored more fully later in this book, including transition itself. Perhaps the most important point to remember is that the economy is presenting us with a new game board, one that is being built without any of the formal blueprints. The savvy players will not try to play the old economic games, with the old economic rules, on the new board. It is a new game, and it seems that the rules have not yet been codified—or if they have been, no one knows where to find them. It has been said that these are times that make beginners of us all, and nowhere is that more true than in the economic sphere. You will have to be flexible, quick to recognize opportunities and hazards, and unwilling to go down while clutching onto outmoded economic beliefs. That can considerably improve your chances to supermanage the new economic game.

CHAPTER 6

The New
Social Context

Much has been written since the 1950s about social trends, but trends may do little other then titillate or anger us unless we can place them in a *context* that enables us to see what they really mean for us.

That overriding social context is one of *relationships*. Relationships between individuals; relationships between individuals and institutions; relationships between individuals and societies. The single most important element in these relationships in coming years will be change. A middle-aged executive commented wryly not too long ago: "When I was a child, children were seen and not heard; father ruled the roost. When I became a father, children were paramount. When I first went to work, the boss's word was law, and you did what you were told. By the time I became a boss, we had to cater to the workers. All my life my timing has been off." Although there are observers who say that they detect signs of a return to past familial and employment relationships, we can never fully return to the past. All such relationships have been altered in fundamental ways. They are still being altered, and it is most unlikely that what they will be 20 years from now will resemble what they were 20 years ago.

Morality

A major element in the changes now emerging is morality, a subject we will discuss at length in Chapter 26. The minimalist, almost anarchic system of ethics roughly defined by "if it feels good, do it" is now locked in struggle with a new emphasis on community standards. Underlying this struggle is the old and never-ending tug-of-war between individual rights and community needs. Christina Hoff, a professor of philosophy at Clark University, asked recently if the emphasis on individual rights has created a society of morally passive individuals who no longer see themselves as having a responsibility for others. She contended in an article in the *Hastings Center Report* (August 1982) that individual humanitarianism has evolved into institutional benevolence performed by paid professionals in large public agencies. Consequently, people can feel "morally exemplary" merely by adhering to an "enlightened" set of moral principles while leaving the actual performance of good deeds to those who are paid for it.

But that may be changing; responsibilities now loom larger. The individual's relationship to society, according to the new focus, must be a two-way one. It must be active rather than passive. The great buffer institutions which have grown up between the individual and society are now increasingly being bypassed or discarded. New institutions are emerging, and individuals are themselves becoming more directly involved in exercising their responsibilities toward society. Environmental organizations, for example, are becoming directly political—not quite equivalent yet in this country to Germany's Green Party but certainly more of a political institution than before. And individuals are more locally involved in ways that range from neighborhood anti-crime patrols to direct political participation.

The Changing Role of Women

Other major changes in relationships are quite obviously related to the changing role of women in modern society. The powerful, if not irresistible, thrust toward equal rights for women has not by any means run its course, even though there has been a softening of some of the more extreme manifestations. The enormously significant issue of equal pay for comparable work has yet to be finally decided. As more women move into management ranks, they may bring other women with them; and we might expect an increasing proportion of management women in years to come.

But it should also be pointed out that there are less publicized negative consequences as well. One of the most serious is the increasing violence, both real and symbolic, directed by men at women. Because the statistical record is inadequate, no one really knows whether wife abuse has increased, but there is reason to believe it has. Date bashing appears to be much more widespread, most noticeably among college students. Date rape (submission caused by a real or implied threat of violence) is being reported much more extensively than ever before. Films, particularly the horror films so loved by teenagers, have a very high level of violence in which the victims almost always are young women. A University of Manitoba study in 1981 showed that men's attitudes toward violence aimed at women is strongly influenced by such films. And violence is a pervasive theme in the lyrics and videos of rock songs.

On yet another hand, men's roles also are changing. Psychologist Dan Mezibov conducted a study of 100 families in the San Francisco area and found that increasing numbers of men were shifting to less traditional father roles; they were participating in child care and becoming more directly involved in all ways with their children. In more than 25 percent of families in which both husband and wife work, the wife makes as much as or more than the husband. It appears that more and more people accommodate to this with little or no difficulty.

Youth and Fragmentation

A substantial change in relationships has occurred among the young. A report on youth issued by the Business Intelligence Program of SRI International in 1981 noted that the most striking characteristic of today's youth is the absence of the unities that made the young such a powerful force for change in the 1960s and 1970s. Today's youth group is as fragmented as any other segment of our society, perhaps more so. Some are pragmatic and materialistic, some are idealistic; some are committed to community participation, some are alienated; some are liberal, some are conservative; and many are escapist. As SRI reported, one extremely troublesome factor is that many reports and studies reveal a predilection for violence—against both institutions and individuals—in all fragments of the young segment. "Many young people today seem to view violence as another, equally legitimate form of expression."

Considering that this was the generation that came after *Brown v. Board of Education*, the group that grew up in an era of massive official and personal support for the ideals of equality, what is most surprising—even shocking—about youths is their rampant xenophobia. Their violence, both physical and verbal, is often directed against "others": whites against blacks, blacks against whites, men against women, women against men. Anti-Semitism is on the rise, as is hatred of immigrants. As SRI points out, youths have gone from a unity based on a commitment to a common ideal—making the world a better place—to fragmentation characterized by "competitiveness, selfishness, even bitterness." Even their music, formerly the most recognizable expression of their unity, now reflects their fragmentation and discord. Rock, for example, is sharply divided into white music and black music, and the division is often marked by violence.

Intergenerational Conflict

The emerging battle line is young versus old—the war between the generations. It is not surprising that young muggers would steal from the elderly; the elderly are generally easy marks. But the high level of viciousness accompanying the robberies reflects, many observers feel, the instinctive hatred some of the young feel toward the old. And the underlying emotion is by no means confined to young criminals. One young writer, Phillip Longman, in *The Washington Monthly* in 1982, presented an intellectualized expression of it. "The old," he wrote, "have come to insist that the young not only hold them harmless for their past profligacy, but sacrifice their own prosperity to pay for it." In other words, the bleak economic future so many of the young feel they face is the fault of the previous generations, and the young are very bitter. Longman says this is a new era, one in which age is a "prime determinant of one's economic destiny."

It is rare to find a young worker these days who believes that he or she will ever collect from Social Security. Many young workers see the program as one more mechanism forcing the young to support the old. And when the old are gone, the young will be left with the bills and without the means to pay them. Significantly, Longman criticizes both the left and the right for the current situation. He obviously believes that youth must have its own political movement. "If there were ever a generation that had reason to take to the streets," he writes, "it is this one."

The older generations, of course, believe that what they have they earned. Most political analysts agree that Social Security was a major factor in deciding the outcome of the 1982 election; the elderly rallied to support the system, and the two parties vied for advantage in positioning themselves on the side of the old folks. Older people have substantial political clout. They tend to have a higher proportion of voters than their successor generations; they are organized into effective pressure groups; and they are fighting desperately for what they perceive to be their very survival.

Crime

Oddly, and unhappily, while crime against the elderly has gone up substantially, crime *by* the elderly has gone up as well. According to *Time* magazine in 1982, major felony arrests in the 55-and-older group increased by 148 percent during the 1970s. In a way, that strange statistic highlights what has become an overwhelmingly important issue for the American people: crime. Crime—and even more important the perception of the level of crime—has become an obsession, particularly with groups such as young single women and the elderly, who see themselves as primary victims. It is affecting how people behave and live, how they relate to other people, and how they view their relationship with society.

Former West Virginia state chief justice Richard Neely, writing in *The Atlantic* in 1982, pointed out what may be the key factor: most people believe that they themselves can do little, if anything, about crime, and they feel that society is not doing enough about it. The perception that society is not fulfilling its part of the social contract is leading to varying degrees of vigilantism. The responses range from moving into walled enclaves to buying guns. Neighborhood anticrime patrols have proliferated; the unofficial vigilante group, the Guardian Angels, which started in New York City, has spread throughout the country with dazzling speed.

It is terribly dangerous for a society when its people lose their faith in its ability to protect them. There is no question that many new societal developments, including the underground economy, reflect dissatisfaction with the failure of society in one of its most fundamental functions. This dissatisfaction is undoubtedly a factor in the failure to get strict gun control legislation, and it has led to an extraordinary increase in the prison population as judges have responded to the groundswell of public pressure.

Crimes against people—murder, rape, robbery—are one thing. Crimes against institutions—shoplifting, embezzlement, insurance fraud—are something entirely different. There is a double standard. Indeed, there may be a yin and yang of attitudes toward crime, two apparently contradictory attitudes which combine to form an individual's overall response. Perhaps because people feel victimized by violent personal crime and unprotected against it, they are able to justify crimes committed against the impersonal institutions that make up society. "To steal from the neighborhood grocer is not acceptable—he's an individual," wrote Roberta Reynes in *Glamour* in 1982, "but people feel it's okay to steal from a faceless corporation."

Religion

Paradoxically, as we noted earlier, there is an increase in the sense of need for a more demanding moral code. It is reflected in changes taking place in religious life in America. The upsurge in religious affiliation has taken place in the fundamentalist Christian churches, those that require an intense personal involvement. The more traditional, cooler, more ritualistic churches have seen a decline. Since the early 1970s, young people have shown a heightened interest in religion, but primarily in what their elders call cults. Starting with the Jesus freaks and the Hare Krishnas, we have seen young people hurl themselves into beliefs and rituals that require intense and even total commitment.

Optimism and Pessimism

The stresses, societal and individual, that we have touched upon in this chapter are reflected in people's attitudes toward themselves, their institutions, their society, and the future. One of the most obvious manifestations is a decline in optimism. We have always believed in this country that we had the resources and the will to do anything; all we had to do was want to do it. We no longer believe that. A decade ago, in the midst of a surge of youthful idealism, we lost a war. We have since seemed more and more unable to solve our most troublesome social and economic problems. There are many prepared to believe the messages of the ecologists and the limits-to-growth people who tell us that the world is finite, that resources are limited, and that some problems can't be solved.

A poll conducted by Potomac Associates for *Psychology Today* in 1981 was one of many which recently showed increasing concern about economic conditions and less certainty regarding the future. Fear that Americans were facing a lower standard of living for themselves and their families was up in this study from 16 percent in 1974 to 32 percent in 1981. Concern about the nation's economic stability increased also, from 24 percent in 1974 to 37 percent in 1981.

Pessimism is also seen in the widespread belief that crime is out of control and in the revival of the antinuclear movement. There is still a strong and persistent streak of optimism in America, but it is weaker than before; and doubt is creeping like a ground fog across the countryside.

Antirationality

Social systems are circular. The pessimism generated by change also provides impetus to change. The faith in rationality which underpins the scientific method and is, in turn, the basis for industrial society, is declining. Rationality, in fact, is under attack, as if people were saying this system no longer works. The concept of expertness is questioned in scientific journals themselves. Science fiction increasingly presents science and technology as the basis for evil, and scientists are portrayed as fools or fiends. In *Star Trek,* it was often the very human, emotional Kirk, and not the detached, rational Spock, who could ultimately outwit the enemy. In *Star Wars,* Luke Skywalker succeeded by turning off his computer and trusting to "the Force." In the phenomenally successful *E.T.,* innocent, trusting children were arrayed against menacing scientists.

The increase in fundamentalist religion and the related attacks on such fundamental scientific principles as evolution also reflect the antirational trend. So, too, does the growing interest in biblical prophecy, as reported by sociologist William Martin in *The Atlantic* in 1982. Perhaps because we are nearing the year 2000, millenialism—a belief that Jesus will soon return—is a growing phenomenon. Hal Lindsey's *The Late Great Planet Earth,* which forecast the second coming, was the number-one best-selling nonfiction book of the 1970s.

Even some scientists reflect the change. Brian Josephson, at 33 the youngest physicist ever to win the Nobel prize, has gone beyond traditional physics, which he says is inadequate now. Today he is investigating altered consciousness and the paranormal and trying to use meditation to gain new understanding of the nature of reality. And in business, too, the rational approach embodied in the concept of management science is increasingly under attack, even by professors in business schools where rationality is most assiduously preached.

The Dilemma of Social Change

The human dilemma is that we are, in the words of René Dubós, both caretakers of the past and builders of the future. Our problem today is that the line of demarcation between the two gets less clear all the time, so that the past and the future blend into each other until our vision blurs. Change is no longer deliberate and gradual. We always face what Daniel Bell called "radical ruptures with the past." In such a turbulent time, some cling to the relationships they know and are comfortable with; others leap willingly into the unknown future. The majority of us experience a sense of schizophrenia; we waver between the old and the new and are not quite sure how to deal with the subjective nature of the real world. In the process, the social fabric is altered forever.

Clearly, all these social forces affect and alter the relationships between individuals and groups of individuals in ways that have major significance for your personal life. Will they disrupt or even destroy the continuity from generation to generation, as some observers fear, or will the bonds of human need and kinship survive or overcome these new stresses? Will the family be strengthened by the increasing interest in stricter standards of morality? Will communities flourish more if the primacy of the individual declines?

As a manager, you can anticipate that the forces described here are bringing about fundamental alterations in the relationships between individuals and the organizations with which they are affiliated, whether as employees or members. A renewed interest in community does not necessarily mean a lessened demand for individual attention and autonomy in the workplace. There is no law that says there shall be no contradiction in people or in life. Indeed, you could assume that submission or surrender of some parts of one's individualism could mean a strengthening of other parts, just as pruning a tree makes the remaining branches stronger.

As a manager of people, you will obviously need to be alert to signs of conflict or xenophobia in your work force. Economic forces, it is true, do override social forces, which means that the current economic concerns are causing a weakening of the efforts to bring about equality in the workplace. But such social forces do not go away, and it would be a serious mistake to think that they do.

Whatever you may feel about some of the social trends, mastering the changes the trends are causing requires looking for the opportunities in them—new markets, for example, or new alliances for the advancement of social or political causes. Above all, you must enhance your capacity, and that of your organization, to observe social change objectively and translate it into intelligence you can use as a basis for positive action.

CHAPTER 7

The Changed Political Climate

One of the major political trends of the twentieth century has been centralization; more authority has moved into the hands of central governments, and more power has been gathered in ever-larger political and economic institutions. In the past five decades, democratic federal governments have assumed substantially greater control over many elements of their societies and economies. Even in the United States, this trend has ranged from land-use policies in various states to rules for hiring and promoting in business. Much of the impetus for the trend came from a perception that the average citizen was a helpless victim surrounded by rapacious and uncontrolled beasts whose size and resources were overwhelming. The federal government was seen as the defender of the weak, a shield against injustice. Since World War II the sense of victimization has spread, and that has led to more emphasis on the federal government as a mechanism for achieving higher degrees of political and economic equity.

As laudable as the centralization objectives were, some observers have been concerned about the potential for abuse. George Orwell's *1984* is the classic expression of that concern. Despite their differing beliefs, Ronald Reagan and Jimmy Carter expressed a similar concern: that government in Washington was becoming more remote from the people whose champion it was supposed to be. It is reasonable to assume that both presidents owed their election, at least in part, to anticentralization sentiment.

Decentralization

At the height of the centralization trend, particularly in the 1960s, there began to emerge a little-noticed counterthrust toward decentralization. In the early 1950s, economist Leopold Kohr, then teaching at Princeton, wrote about what he called "the one and only problem permeating all creation. . . . Wherever something is wrong, something is too big." It took 5 years for Kohr to find a publisher for his book, *The Breakdown of Nations,* because decentralization was not very respectable in those days. But now Kohr and his book have gone beyond a fringe following to wide acceptance. Kohr's contention that the answer is "not union but division" is reflected in the growth of what we call localism. Today's young activists, and even some of the radical remnant of the 1960s, have as their arena not the world, but the community. Kohr is also the guru of a movement that calls itself the Fourth World, fervent believers in communities (and enterprises) small enough to be manageable and thus responsive to individual human control.

A new populism, which has been widely misinterpreted as a swing to the right, has emerged. It is being manifested politically, socially, and culturally. There is a resurgence of state and local autonomy, with smaller governmental jurisdictions resisting federal authority and attempting to assert their own primacy. Within the federal government itself, power is becoming more diffused. The two major parties have seen their hold over their members weakened. A variety of caucuses and ad hoc organizations around and within Congress have resulted in more fragmented authority and a separation of powers. Single-issue pressure groups have further diluted party cohesiveness.

The small-is-beautiful concept popularized by the late British economist E. F. Schumacher (a disciple of Leopold Kohr) has spread beyond its narrow technological beginnings to serve as an ideological base for attacks on massive social programs in health, housing, and education. Political columnist David S. Broder, in his book *Changing of the Guard: Power and Leadership in America,* anticipates development of what he calls a new, leaner, tougher progressivism, one "more in tune with the skepticism about big government." Highly educated middle-class young people have moved in a small but significant way to isolated settlements, many of them in remote deserts. These are not communes; they are almost in the nature of new colonies, the settlers of which seek to escape the ills of large communities and find both independence and simplicity.

In business, in the face of a strong trend toward conglomeration there is an even stronger upsurge of entrepreneurialism. Witness the fact that more and more colleges are offering, and students are attending, courses in entrepreneurship. Witness also the fact that start-ups of new businesses are at their highest ever. And within large organizations there appears to be a growing resistance to overly authoritarian management. The electronic media, which at first glance appeared to have a powerful centralizing potential, now appear to be reinforcing what have been called this country's fractious, privatistic tendencies.

The fragmentation of the media both reflects and encourages decentralization. Some analysts are afraid that the outcome will be destruction of our national unity and identity; others ask, "What national unity and identity?" Writers on the arts comment on how strong populism is in the cultural scene from architecture to drama. Victims appear as heroes in plays; they reflect a pervasive sense that the individual is handicapped by powerful forces beyond his or her control. The hero's victory comes in asserting personal autonomy. Some architects call for a public review process for new construction so that the buildings can reflect community values.

The Ecological Ethic

Historian Barbara Tuchman in *A Distant Mirror*, her brilliant study of fourteenth-century Europe, showed how medieval institutions and value systems crumbled under the massive, inexorable flow of the Renaissance. So too in our time we see traditional institutions battered by an emerging and, as yet, dimly perceived set of new values and beliefs. A major element in this new value system appears to be the ecological ethic, which says that everything in nature is part of an interconnected, finite system.

Politically, the ecological ethic signifies limits. Until recently, the dominant liberal ideology of this country was based upon a sense of abundance, of limitless optimism about the future and our ability as a society to go ever onward and upward and bring everyone along. But over the last decade, beginning particularly with the publication of the Club of Rome's *Limits to Growth*, a sense that there are limits has nibbled away at the prevailing ideology. Today the need for restraint, for nurturing what are now seen as limited resources, is as much a part of liberal as it is of conservative rhetoric.

There is an increasing perception on all sides that massive government social programs, like the dinosaurs, have come to the end of their time. Some believe that such programs just don't work and are therefore wasteful at a time when we can no longer afford to waste resources. Others feel that even if they do work, we have to apply a cost-benefit analysis to determine whether the results are worth the cost. Consequently, there is a solid and growing consensus that we are approaching a new time, one that requires new governmental approaches. There is no consensus on what the new approaches ought to be; indeed, there may never be one.

Struggles for Power

In Washington the executive and legislative arms of the federal government are elbowing each other in an effort to be on top in whatever new arrangement results. And while they struggle, the third branch, the judiciary, quietly like a soufflé, rises to fill the partly empty dish of power. The rise of the judiciary in recent years is, of course, also due to the fact that we are increasingly a litigious society. We have the highest percentage of lawyers in any country. One in every 5000 Americans is a lawyer, which brings to mind the old Mexican curse, "May your days be filled with lawyers." More and more we are settling our disputes and differences of opinion in the courts. The number of civil suits increased by almost 100 percent between 1970 and 1980. Thus, the courts are becoming regulators of our society. While many feel that this provides safeguards against abuses of power by other branches of government, particularly with respect to the rights of the individual, there is concern that it could represent a diminishing of democracy. It is, after all, difficult to hold the courts accountable. It is also difficult to lobby the courts; they cannot be approached except through the narrow and restricted passages of law.

Another political issue is the increasing importance and weight of the state governments. State legislatures, which not too many years ago spent relatively little time in session, now sit for long periods of time. The volume of legislation they consider and enact is enormous. And now much of what the state governments do creates jurisdictional conflicts with the federal government or with the governments of other states. Sometimes state laws conflict directly with federal laws and the matter has to be resolved by the Supreme Court; laws governing abortion are an example. In other instances the individual states deal directly with foreign countries to arrive at trade agreements or other elements of foreign relations. An example is California's joint solar energy project with Israel. And there is the increasingly important issue of disputes among states over control of resources—most obviously and particularly water, which *The Wall Street Journal* has called *the* issue of the 1980s.

This claim to sovereignty by states, and the complexities arising from it, predates Reagan's new federalism. It is part of the tide of decentralization—fragmentation, as some call it—that is acting in powerful ways to slow and even reverse the flow of power and control toward Washington.

The New Shape of Government-Business Relations

What does all this mean for the other institutions in our society and in particular for managers in business? First, it can mean that excessive and overly burdensome central government control may not come to pass. The weakening of central government, and even more importantly the declining belief in an adversarial central-government role, holds the promise of less interference in the everyday activities of business.

But as events of recent years have demonstrated again and again, things are not always what they seem. We can also interpret the coming environment as one in which society backs off a little and says to business: "Okay, you've been complaining that you can do the job yourself. Go ahead. But don't fail." Thoughtful business leaders see this environment as one not only of opportunity but of testing. Business, in effect, has lost some of its excuses: the burden of regulation has eased; taxes have been reduced; labor has become weaker; the nation has made a commitment to restoring economic vitality and leadership. But those very things bring with them an increased responsibility for business. Business will almost certainly be held accountable for how well it responds in the public interest, and not just in its own.

Furthermore, public willingness to accept an easing of the regulation of business does not extend across the board. Survey after survey reveals that the public overwhelmingly wants a high level of government regulation of business activities that directly affect health and safety. That includes food, pharmaceuticals, toys, and any industries intimately connected with what people eat and drink. And we cannot assume that current attitudes toward other industries are permanent. As noted above, much depends on how business performs.

On the more positive side, business will have, in the years ahead, a great opportunity to capitalize on its increased freedom. Innovation, growth, efficiency, effectiveness, profitability—all can be enhanced if the new freedom results in an unleashing of the competitive, productive spirit that created what became, in the twentieth century, the most beneficial economy ever known. Privatization is a spreading idea based on a belief that many social services could be provided better through the private sector. There have been some successes, notably companies that provide day care and alternatives to the Postal Service. There can be many more if you are alert to the potential opportunities. Education is one field in which opportunities abound. There is a need for more people better trained in fields ranging from tool and die making to electronic engineering, and there is a widespread perception that the public education system is failing to do its job properly.

Decentralization can simplify the business environment, but it can also add complexity. Dealing with fifty state governments and their myriads of regulatory agencies is very different from dealing mostly with Washington—not necessarily better, not necessarily worse, but different. Whatever one may think of them, the elected and appointed people in the federal government are, at least at the upper levels, almost universally bright, able, and energetic. There is more variation in state governments. And however burdened and short of time people in Washington are (a congressman once told us he could allot no more than 6 minutes a day to read newspapers), their information resources are many times better than those available to regulators and officials in state capitols.

The insurance industry, which has always been regulated primarily by the states, has found that it is necessary to try for some kind of uniformity of regulation in order to avoid having inordinately complicated and expensive government relations. It does so by helping to promulgate and support a national association of insurance commissioners through which uniform legislation and regulation can be encouraged. Now managers in many other businesses will have to come to grips with the staffing, associations, and information systems they will need as Potomac fever subsides and power moves back to the states. In general, political and societal decentralization may render bigness, uniformity, and economies of scale counterproductive. A more fragmented political structure, more fragmented media, and a more sharply segmented society can tend to work against large and centrally controlled organizations. They may be less capable of addressing segmented markets and other institutions than smaller organizations. It may be necessary for business itself to decentralize more to be able to respond more productively to the new political environment.

Although advances in information and communications technologies make continued central control of government relations feasible, reality may require you to consider the advantages of more local autonomy. Politics is a personal thing. There is as yet no known mechanical or electronic substitute for a skilled, knowledgeable, effective individual who can meet and talk with a legislator or regulator in a human context.

If your organization is a very large one, do not be lulled into a false sense of security. The populist tide in this country is far stronger than has heretofore been recognized. If yours is a small firm or a new one, you may have more friends in Washington and in your state and community than you realize.

CHAPTER 8

The International Economic Battleground

Since the end of World War II we have seen an extraordinary increase in the number of nations. Colonialism has ended; the imperial age is gone, perhaps forever. But in recent years we have also seen a decline in the number of democratic governments as most of the new countries have tumbled into the authoritarian pit. At the same time there are strong pressures toward decentralization within both democratic and nondemocratic countries. Separatist and sectional liberation movements are thriving even in developed countries with strong national identities. The Soviet Union is losing its grip on the eastern bloc; and some well-informed observers believe that western corporations should begin to treat with eastern bloc countries on an individual basis, meet their needs for trade, and bolster their economies to aid in the loosening of their economic dependency upon the Soviet Union. All of this leads to an international precariousness the result of which is increasing uncertainty and unpredictability in political and economic relations.

Another factor further muddies the situation: heightened economic competitiveness. There was a time when the United States dominated the world economy; it bestrode the world like a colossus. Then the resurgent economic machines of other countries, particularly Japan, came up almost unnoticed on the blind side of the complacent Americans. And now our automobile industry is no longer number one, our steel industry is no longer number one, our electronics industry is no longer number one. From some perspectives, we look like an obsolescent and rundown machine indeed.

A Conference Board report in 1981 showed that foreign-based transnational corporations were growing much faster than those that were U.S.-based. Of the hundred largest such corporations, 67 were U.S.-based in 1963. In 1979, however, only 47 were U.S.-based. Of the 500 largest industrial corporations in the world, the United States had 300 in 1963. By 1979, the U.S. figure had dropped to 219. In a further manifestation of decline, U.S. companies in industries such as pharmaceuticals, computers, advertising, and autos are forming joint ventures with companies in other countries. Some companies are moving manufacturing facilities out of the United States—to Mexico, for example, where U.S. companies have opened border plants that employ over 250,000 people.

The success of the Japanese economy, sometimes known as Japan, Inc., has inspired a number of other countries that hope to make themselves more competitive in international markets. The Japanese system is based upon cooperation between public and private sectors to advance the larger and longer-term interests of the nation. Resources are directed to areas of activity that hold promise for achieving high levels of market penetration. In that way, for example, the Japanese came to dominate the microchip memory market. They did not invent memory chips, but they made them better and they marketed them better. They had help from Japanse banks and from the Japanese government, through the Ministry of International Trade and Industry (MITI). Now other countries are following Japan's lead. Many governments are encouraging research and allocating resources toward new technologies in the hope of establishing positions of dominance in world markets—and for reasons of national security and prestige. Consider France in biotechnology and Canada in information technology.

Interdependency

Paralleling the growth of competition has been the growth in international interdependency. All countries are affected by what happens in any one of them. An economic crisis in the United States can be devastating in Europe and the Americas. Currency and interest rate fluctuations have worldwide consequences. The developed nations depend upon less-developed nations for vital resources, and the less-developed nations, in turn, are almost totally dependent upon market prices in the developed countries. The United States, for example, imports more than 90 percent of nine essential minerals and more than 50 percent of another eleven. It is significant that economic weapons are coming to be used more than military ones in political disputes. Russian aggression in Afghanistan and Poland generated economic reprisals, such as trade embargoes, by the west. The disputes between Argentina and the United Kingdom and the United States and Iran involved such nonmilitary weapons as asset freezes and credit restrictions.

The struggle over control of resources could well be the dominant economic factor for the rest of the century. The long, painful, and so-far-unsuccessful effort to get a law-of-the-sea treaty agreeable to all countries in the world is directly related to the availability and control of strategic minerals and other resources. It is significant that the elements of the proposed treaty that deal with traditional aspects of national sovereignty—such as rights of passage of shipping—were the easiest parts of the treaty to get agreement on. But the parts dealing with retrieval and ownership of undersea resources remain the stumbling block.

Great sums of money are now being devoted to materials science research throughout the world in an effort to break free from dependence on unreliable and potentially unreliable sources of necessary raw materials; the lesson OPEC taught us will never be forgotten. Breakthroughs in materials science are now occurring. But the road from innovation to production is a long one, and in the meantime interdependence is changing the political and economic alignments of the world. Power is no longer a matter merely of size and strength, nor is it necessarily related to the relative degree of economic development. Small and even minimally developed nations, through control of vital resources, can exert disproportionately great economic power. And they can force profoundly significant alterations of international relations. Just as the Vietnamese war demonstrated how a small and seemingly weak country could defeat a superpower that was, in effect, handicapped by its own size and strength, so the smaller countries can translate economic clout into political clout as well.

The North American continent illustrates vividly the kinds of changes that can take place. For more than 150 years the United States dominated the continent while Canada and Mexico trod warily in its enormous shadow. The United States defined the relationship, and the other two countries could not do much more than be resentful. But now there is a shift toward a more equalized relationship. Canada and Mexico have resources the United States has great need for—oil and water, to name just two. And even though they are not currently in as much demand as they may be again, both countries are exhibiting a more militant nationalism; they are demanding more internal control over their resources and how and under what terms they will be traded to or allowed to be owned by the United States. In this country awareness of our potential dependency upon such resources is leading to a growing acknowledgment of the sovereign rights of the other countries. We even hear talk, from both left and right, of establishing a North American Common Market.

Controlling Information

In addition to the interdependence of nations that has developed, advances in communications technology have resulted in the creation of individual and institutional interrelations—social and economic networks that transcend national and political boundaries. America's IBM and Japan's Matsushita get together to produce and market small computers; Japan and the United Kingdom form a joint venture to produce jet engines; in advertising, Young and Rubicam from the United States and Dentsu of Japan combine to create international advertising; Ford Motor Company proudly advertises that it makes a "world car," constructed of components manufactured in different countries. Even terrorists, it is reported, are linked in an international network that supplies support in the form of training, weapons, and personnel.

This tendency for people and institutions to come together on the basis of commonality of interest rather than political identity is one of the factors that, along with separatism, is leading toward a weakening of nationalism. But it is the new technology that provides the means. Governments are increasingly concerned about controlling the transborder flow of information. Satellite TV broadcasts, for example, are particularly troublesome to the governments of countries in which television broadcasting is under tight governmental control. The potential for computer-to-computer communication also troubles many governments; it may be one reason why the effort to get a universal computer language has at best lukewarm support in many countries.

The third world's efforts, supported by the Soviet bloc, to establish a "new world information order" is really a thinly disguised attempt to allow national governments maximum control over information flow into and out of their countries. But even governments in developed Western countries appear to have a secret yearning for the same kind of control. That may explain why there has been so little real opposition to this outrageously Orwellian proposal.

For the future, perhaps the most worrisome aspect of efforts to control transborder information flows is the potential impact on scientific development. Science requires unobstructed flows and exchanges of information. Scientists learn from other scientists; their experiments must be validated or refuted by other scientists. All the geniuses of science have acknowledged that they were standing on the shoulders of their predecessors. But now two political factors threaten to disrupt this essential circulation system of science.

One is the increasing tendency of governments to view information, particularly scientific and technical information, as a national resource. In the United States scientists are being asked to voluntarily refrain from publishing certain kinds of information—cryptographic, for example—on the ground that it may jeopardize national security. Admiral Bobby Inman, when he was deputy director of the CIA, made a point of telling scientists that almost any kind of scientific and technical information, even if it had no obviously direct military implication, could be connected to national security. A further complication is that basic science is increasingly linked to commercial development. In consequence, scientists and researchers may now fear that publication would give others an opportunity to capitalize on potential commercial rewards.

The second political factor is what we call the Olympics syndrome in science and technology. There is a growing nationalistic cast to science that is imposed by governments and grows out of a view that advancement in science and technology is necessary for political, economic, and military strength. And it is seen as increasingly necessary for national pride and honor. Thus third world countries, many of which urgently need to press ahead with development in agriculture and basic industry, aspire to participation in space exploration and India mounts a scientific expedition to the Antarctic. Developed countries, on the other hand, think it necessary to have their national efforts in as many areas of science and technological development as possible. In the United States, for example, Congress has already mandated that 1 percent of the huge federal R&D budget must go to small companies on the ground that most technological innovation comes not from the industrial giants, but from the small entrepreneurial businesses.

International Trade

One of the remarkable economic and political developments of the post–World War II era has been the growing domination of international commerce by giant transnational corporations working closely with the great international banking institutions. This internationalization of business has had, and will continue to have, many insufficiently understood consequences. One is the parallel internationalization of labor. Unions are increasingly thinking in terms of standardized contracts, including pay and benefits, worldwide (although recent economic difficulties have forced national unions to refocus on their own issues). The potential impact on the economies of countries which currently benefit from lower labor costs could be substantial. For one thing, it could render those countries less competitive. For another, it could mean that many companies, which are ever more aware that they need not be rooted wherever they happen to be located at any point in time, would move facilities to more amenable locations. Both governments and unions hope to reduce that possibility by stricter regulation of all aspects of transnational corporations.

Another little-noticed phenomenon has been the growing significance in international trade of invisibles—services such as banking, insurance, advertising, consulting, and education. Now amounting to more than 25 percent of the total dollar volume of international commerce, trade in invisibles is in an even more confused state than trade in resources and manufactured goods. As this trade increases, we are likely to see more efforts to arrive at standards and agreements— and more attempts by many countries to develop their own national industries.

Hazards and Opportunities

Out of all this and many other factors—such as the emergence of China as a market and a potential competitor and the nuclear war threat (not just on an east-west basis, but also on a north-south basis as developing countries seek to establish their own nuclear arsenals)— we can develop a picture of an international arena that is increasingly complex, obscure, and full of both hazards and opportunities for business. Simultaneous factors such as growing nationalism and growing separatism, seemingly contradictory, require managers to develop a greater capacity for reading the environment in which they are operating and a sensitivity toward emerging trends that can bring about quick and radical change in that environment. This means that the kind of environmental scanning managers do in this country needs to be done wherever else their organization does business.

If you are a manager in a technology-based enterprise, you have to be concerned about potential effects of nationalized science and technology and control over the flow of scientific and technical information. In today's competitive era, lead time on technological development may be the deciding factor in profitability and even survival. For many years we exported our technology; now we may find that, having cast bread upon the waters, we're going to end up hungry instead of well supplied.

American science and industry have depended upon talented immigrants. It is possible that the Russian model may become more widely adopted, and more countries may prohibit emigration of scientists and technicians. American managers need to encourage development of home-grown talent. Farsighted employers will support, privately and through public policy, programs aimed at getting more young people trained for careers in science and technology. They need to resist the temptation to eat the seed corn by raiding campuses for talented teachers in the sciences and technologies. And they need to find ways to help benefit more from the existing pool of talent, as by retraining and recycling technologists to enable them as well as their organizations to be revitalized.

One thing you will have to watch out for is the possibility of hasty and ill-considered government actions aimed at maintaining or restoring American technological and commercial preeminence. No such actions, whether in the form of tax reform, resource allocation, or protectionism, should be taken without careful study by both business and government of the potential long-term consequences, which could very well be counterintuitive. But at the same time, you should encourage a search for ways to bring about more joint business-government focus on the farther margins of planning.

The issue of natural resources is a thorny one. Developed countries rightly pursue technologies that promise freedom from dependence on supplies from politically unreliable and unstable countries. We cannot afford to become so dependent on those countries that they have a profound and perhaps pernicious effect on our important political decisions. But those same less-developed countries represent necessary markets. Thoughtful managers will implement courses of commerce that bolster infrastructures of the developing nations rather than impoverish those nations further, especially in the areas of health, communications, education, and agriculture. In that way the expanded markets will be better capitalized and more politically and economically stable.

Perhaps above all, American managers need to free themselves of provincialism. Greater success will accrue to those who understand other countries, other cultures, and other people. That means, for example, a need to speak languages other than English well enough to have an empathy with people in other countries with whom you are doing business.

American institutions will, of course, benefit by a greater global awareness in their management ranks. Ambitious and promising young managers should seriously consider breaking away from the tradition of a very different past. They should experience, in addition to advanced business school training, the people, languages, cultures, and countries with whom we are so increasingly interdependent.

PART 3

The People Side: Who Manages Whom, and for What?

People stiffen in the attitudes they adopt to make themselves suitable for the jobs and lives other people have laid out for them.

V. S. Naipaul
A Bend in the River

CHAPTER 9

Who Are the New Employees?

It is not uncommon to hear, "The pendulum has swung back. All of those 1960s radicals are now seeking middle-class jobs, the house in the suburbs, the proverbial two-point-something kids, and designer clothes. We knew it would happen." But has it really? Are today's employees in the 25-to-40 age bracket unchanged in the wake of their former idealism, lifestyle, and activism? We doubt it. Yes, Jerry Rubin has embraced mainstream American employment, but is he the employee he might have been in another era?

Several things have happened since the late 1960s that wishful thinking and surface appearance cannot erase. Five are overriding factors:

■ The introduction of two-wage-earner households

■ A broadened social awareness and search for "meaning"

■ The explosive growth of the service economy

■ The economic, demographic, and technological challenge to middle-management positions

■ Being forced to live in a time of rapid change and future uncertainty.

Today's young workers are immersed in this legacy of the late 1960s.

Two-Wage-Earner Households

One of the most significant changes of the recent past is the explosive presence of married women in the work force. This has had a decisive effect upon women, their male counterparts, and the work force itself. Three major areas of impact are relocation and promotions, the notion of sole breadwinner, and child rearing.

More companies are experiencing difficulty in recruiting talent from remote locations because of the now common problem of spouse relocation. The same thing is true with regard to corporate transfers. When two people are tied to independent careers, it is difficult to move one and provide for continuity and success in the transition of both. The woman who is recruited for a senior job in Boston but cannot accept because her husband is an officer of a company in Chicago and the man who is asked to accept a promotion in San Francisco but cannot because his wife has a tenured teaching position in Florida are now becoming more the rule than the exception.

One possible solution is regional cooperative job pools. Companies within a defined geographic area could pool information about positions they have open in an attempt to secure jobs for a spouse upon the hiring or promotion of a targeted employee. Thus, when a manager says, "I'd love to accept that transfer, but my wife has an executive position in a local insurance company," the answer might be, "We know of several comparable positions for her here, and we would be glad to arrange interviews." While this tack is probably the wave of the future, it is still not a panacea. Never again will geographic transfers be as easy as they once were.

A second consideration regarding working wives is the relative economic independence now enjoyed by their husbands. The need for that next promotion—the one that would mean a lot more work and a salary increase small in comparison with the tax bite and inflation—becomes greatly diminished. Wanting time to spend with one's spouse outside work, and having pooled finances, decreases one's desire to move up for the sake of earnings alone. And although it is true that in times of economic downturn money and position are important, the longer-term trend is in the direction of independence.

Employers have to offer promotions with new thoughts in mind; the new job must be intrinsically more enjoyable and satisfying, and there must be benefits other than straight salary increases. Expecting that each move up must command more hours out of an employee's day will be unrealistic. And many of the promising employees who turn down promotions will have to be viewed as making decisions just as acceptable to the organization as if they had eagerly jumped at the opportunities.

Another factor to consider in the two-wage-earner household is the greater sharing of child-rearing responsibilities and a variety of housekeeping chores. It is more common now for the father to take some time off to pick up the ill child from school because the mother is away at a conference or meeting with a client. And the husband will be increasingly drawn into the mundane position of staying home to wait for the washing machine to be repaired or going to the bank to straighten out the error in the account because the wife may be employed in a position that makes finding the time for such tasks difficult for her. (Service companies that recognize this will be more successful if they change their hours of operation to accommodate to the new household reality.)

Flexible hours have come to be a good idea for men as well as women as a result of these changes in work force composition. For that reason, flexibility of work schedules, and even work at home, is not a fad but a fundamental and long-lasting shift in work patterns out into the future. Managers that resist such flexibility will find themselves having a difficult time with many of their subordinates, and they will face difficulty in finding adequate replacements. The rigid nine-to-five, 5-day-a-week work schedule is no longer the sole choice.

Broadened Social- and Self-awareness

Many social researchers are prone to label eras with phrases that can capture a whole mood for ease of communication. Thus the decade 1965–1975 was considered the me decade, and the young people the me generation, because the focus was on individualism and self-awareness. As campus unrest subsided and many young people took their places in the work force and began marrying and having children, they were described as changing their focus to family and community. That, according to many, created a shift to the we decade from 1975 to the present.

Nothing could be further from the truth; in fact, one could argue the reverse. Though the earlier activism focused on individual lifestyles and concern for self, there was also much concern for the plight of others in society, for the reshaping of institutions and societal programs to address the needs of those who were somehow disenfranchised, and for general refocus on societal priorities and progress. When it was found that society could not change as quickly as many would have liked, that the deck was still stacked against those who did not play wisely and well, and that much of the so-called liberal agenda had failed to deliver the expected outcomes, the young people moving into the work force began to attend more to themselves and leave the general social struggle behind. What was blossoming, and is now in full bloom for many, is indeed a me decade.

New-marriage rates are deceiving. Divorce has become, and remains, a permanent partner of marriage in the society we now inhabit. Community participation has become splintered, and so that activity is highly individualized and personalized. One can now select from any number of community interests ranging from cleaning up dump sites to the PTA and stick pretty close to one's self-interest.

Life-threatening considerations that extend beyond the local community, such as fear of nuclear war, are among the few remaining issues that inspire mass activism across the broad range of the public.

So "me-ism" is alive and well and thriving, but the "search for me" has been translated, in a Maslovian sense, to "search for meaning." The difference between "me" and "meaning" is that the first evokes a sense of isolation, the second a sense of interaction with the greater society—a sense of purpose, of involvement, of achievement, of satisfaction because of a highly personal definition of what one's role in life ought to be.

It is this marriage of a history of social awareness with the turning inward toward self-fulfillment that creates a new individual coming into today's work force and populating some of the middle-management ranks. And the same attitude is now pervading the ranks of senior management.

To have a "meaningful" job is the current idea of "making it." To have a "meaningful" life is also considered a must by many. Thus, becoming a parent is one of the possible roads to achieving self-fulfillment and societal meaning. Engaging in a series of professional and personal interest networks, from associations to informal discussion groups to community action organizations, is considered meaningful use of time to achieve self-satisfaction. Working for less money at a job one believes to be of social merit or becoming one's own boss in an entrepreneurial venture is also considered self-actualization.

If you are a manager, you will be faced with accommodating a work force seeking this now-expected form of compensation: meaning. Flexible work hours and other support for employee time to do volunteer work or join professional networks are becoming more common. Stress-management programs are increasingly employed to deal with employee struggles to find a happier, healthier life. Job restructuring to provide meaning in work is no minor task, but it is a necessary one to satisfy today's and tomorrow's employees. And despite the feeling that, in tough economic times, money takes precedence over other forms of compensation, talented and capable up-and-comers will continue to seek other sorts of benefits from their work, such as more time off, paid-for attendance at interesting conferences, and health counseling, exercise, and maintenance programs.

Seeking self-fulfillment and meaning may also work itself out in transitory stages. The advent of professional contracts of about 5 years' duration might be one solution management can live with and still accommodate today's and tomorrow's high achievers.

Explosive Growth of the Service Economy

In the early 1970s the United States crossed over the line into an economy in which a majority were employed in the service sector.

Many positions are now in the information component of the service sector. The younger workers of the 1980s will never know the concepts of piecework and productivity that earlier generations used as yardsticks of work done.

A service economy, by one definition, is an industrial economy in which more layers of intervention are placed between the producer and the consumer. These can take the form of finance, advertising, public relations, research, law, accounting, marketing, data processing, and so on. In light of the above discussion about search for meaning, many new workers in these burgeoning fields feel out of touch with or lack a sense of what they are actually producing. Productivity has become a brand new field of study because, in a service economy, it can no longer be measured as it once was.

How can one measure the productivity of a data processor? Or a market researcher? Or an employee benefits supervisor? The talk switches tracks, and the vocabulary now breaks down into "production workers" and "overhead." It is hard for young workers to enter a work force and be tagged as overhead. Conceptually, that runs head on into the notion of self-actualization and meaningfulness.

Thus, a dilemma faced by managers is how to construct jobs and compensation schemes that help alleviate the stressful condition. Because of the structurally inadequate feedback loop from units of production to middle-management tasks, direct contribution to the decision-making process becomes a real employee benefit. The 1980s will mark the first decade of widespread employee participation in decisions regarding job design, work schedules, intercompany relations, and goal setting. By accommodating to this transition, you will be one up on those who, because of their rigid clinging to hierarchical and traditional reporting schemes, are left with dissatisfied and underproductive employees.

Hence, the realities of a service economy will require a manager to:

■ Allow for greater employee participation in planning and decision making

■ Accept flexible work hours and even work-at-home possibilities (since many service workers do not have to be at a particular facility in order to carry out their tasks)

■ Restructure jobs to allow for a sense of achievement and productivity

■ Recognize that many good people will not remain with the company for more than 5 to 10 years before moving on to other areas in which to test their talents and potential contributions.

Economic, Demographic, and Technological Challenges to Middle-Management Positions

Traditionally, organizational structure has been described as a pyramid with a few people at the top and many at the bottom. The truth of the recent past, however, is that U.S. corporations have more closely resembled footballs: few at the top, few at the bottom, and many crowded around the middle. We are now moving into an era in which the Mae West, or hourglass, shape will be the predominant configuration. (See Figure 9-1.) The reasons are economic and technological. A new reality has hit American business. There has been a growing realization that the bloated management ranks in corporate America—a product of affluent times, more educated workers, world dominance in many markets, predictability of costs and profits—are now an extra weight born by a weary swimmer.

The Japanese have shown how much more effective and efficient—in respect to morale, productivity, cost, supervision, and quality—an organization can be with fewer managers. The world has shown us that we cannot utilize resources cheaply and at our whim and that management overhead is now a serious impediment to deployment of dollars elsewhere. Technology, too, has come along at a time when its most

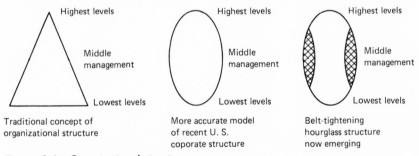

Highest levels

Middle management

Lowest levels

Traditional concept of organizational structure

Highest levels

Middle management

Lowest levels

More accurate model of recent U. S. coporate structure

Highest levels

Middle management

Lowest levels

Belt-tightening hourglass structure now emerging

Figure 9-1 Organizational structure.

cost-efficient application is the elimination of many middle-management tasks, or at least the time needed to undertake them. No longer is technological obsolescence merely the lament of the elevator operator. It is now air traffic controllers, data gatherers, meeting organizers, market researchers, graphic artists, legislation trackers, and many, many others who find that computers are taking over many of their tasks and either distributing access to their skills to a broader number of people or concentrating the skills in few hands.

And all this comes at a time when many major companies are closing down operations, when government can no longer act as employer of last resort, when tenure is blocking access to jobs in higher education across the country, when certain industries (such as car manufacturing) are trimming thousands from their management ranks, and when a sizable bulge in the population pipeline is in the age group with expectations of entering, or staying in, middle-management positions. Because of the tremendous pressures on middle-management positions, the drop-off and dropout rate is likely to be of significant proportion into the 1990s and will create three important new phenomena on the American scene: increased entrepreneurialism, a vast army of "hads" (a new addition to the haves and have-nots), and an educated and ambitious new class in the underground economy.

A serious question managers now have to face is, "Given the pressures, how do I keep my best and brightest employees and not lose them to other enterprises that are less stifling and more rewarding?" A second question is, "How do I keep *myself* afloat in this time of turmoil in the management ranks?"

Aside from strengthening stress management and outplacement counseling programs, perhaps the key lies in a concept now called *intrapreneurialism*—encouraging innovation and linking compensation to initiative *within* an organization. Jobs are being restructured and reporting procedures are being reexamined with an eye toward how really bright people can not only have ideas but take the responsibility to champion them and see them through to reality. Promotions can be based on initiative rather than avoidance of initiative (as has too often been the case in the past), and the intrapreneurs rather than the bureaucrats will eventually rise to the top. Encouraging intrapreneurialism will be one of the most critical opportunities to confront management in the next several years. It would behoove you to be acquainted with the issue, to research the various methods other companies are already exploring, and to press for consideration of intrapreneurialism within your own organization—for your sake as well as that of those who may work for you.

Time of Rapid Change
and an Uncertain Future

The most significant legacy of the 1960s is the lingering thought that change is ever-present. The future is not assured, even if one works hard to try to see that it is. The value of one's savings in the future is questionable. The quality of one's environment in the future is questionable. The ability to retain a job and/or an income in the future is uncertain. The lifestyle ultimately selected by one's own spouse, one's child, or one's parents is unknown. What one's neighborhood may look like in the future, who one's friends will be, who will own the store on the corner, what career one will be into, what new technology will invade the home and the office, what one's knowledge may be worth— all are uncertain. Of course, it could be argued that they never were certain. No matter. The most important, overriding factor about today's employees is that, as many studies show, they do not believe they have significant control over their own long-term future.

Thus, many will reach out to informal and formal support and interest groups for a sense of affiliation beyond the job and home. It will be important for you to encourage employee participation in external interests because these will act as safety valves for stress buildup and fears of the future.

The restructuring of jobs to provide a sense of continual learning and acceptance of responsibility will help instill vital skills in times of

Workplace Changes

Driving Forces	Flexible hours	Work at home	Support for networks	Stress management	Restructuring of jobs	New recruiting and promotional considerations	New compensation schemes	Professional contacts
Two-wage-earner households	√	√				√	√	
Broadened social and self-awareness	√		√	√	√	√		√
Explosive growth of service economy	√	√	√	√	√		√	√
Economic, demographic, and technological challenges to middle-management positions				√	√	√	√	
Time of rapid change and an uncertain future			√	√	√	√	√	√

Figure 9-2 Responses to change in the workplace.

change and uncertainty. The employee who will be least able to cope with change will be the one most sheltered and isolated and least exposed to new knowledge and a full range of responsibility.

Recruitment and promotion have to be considered in the light of a highly uncertain future. Here again professional contracts are a good tool for both management and the employee. At least certainty can be guaranteed for some length of time without commitment made too far out.

Unions will surely take on a new look as their membership becomes more fragmented because of fear of what the future holds, and that fear will cause each individual to examine his or her own priorities in a context separate from the union's long-term strategy. Immediate self-interest reigns when an individual begins to fear that postponing rewards means losing them forever.

New compensation schemes such as a cafeteria approach to benefits (allowing individual employees the opportunity to select different combinations of benefits to suit their own needs at various times) will gain acceptance. That will be especially true as the computer capability and the economics of tailored benefits combine with the employee's own uncertainty as to long-term needs.

The matrix in Figure 9-2 depicts the driving forces discussed in this chapter and the kinds of workplace changes you can anticipate as part of the effort to respond.

CHAPTER 10

Where Will You Work?

The Industrial Revolution brought with it a radical shift in work patterns. Whole waves of population moved to urban centers, where industry was centralized and jobs were both specific and limited as to location. During the nineteenth century, people from many different areas and even foreign countries flocked to U.S. downtown cores of activity; they settled in or near the cities and towns that offered the new industrial opportunities. Infrastructure developed to support the massive infusion of people. Mass transportation, schools, hospitals, shopping, bridges, highways and streets, traffic control systems, and all the necessary systems and functions grew to accommodate the inflows.

In the twentieth century the cities became the hubs of massive wheels whose spokes were the multibillion dollar networks of rail and highway systems that supported the commuting of daily workers from surrounding neighborhoods and suburbs. Over the years, the pattern of worklife settled into something like an eight- or nine-to-five, 5-day week for most of American society.

During a typical weekday, workers with a variety of ethnic, neighborhood, training, and educational backgrounds would meet at a central location, work together, and socialize with each other during breaks (but not exclusively then) and during trips to and from the factory or office. The stereotypical professional or managerial office worker was a middle-class male with a wife who stayed home and raised children. (And, of course, the stereotypical clerical worker was an unmarried female.) The stereotypical shop or factory worker was blue-collar, male or female, and lower-income.

Then, of course, there were the policemen, teachers, shopkeepers, sales clerks, librarians, electricians, and plumbers—white-collar and blue-collar, many of them unionized—who also had fairly standardized workweeks. Most of them also worked on-site away from their homes and neighborhoods.

Cars, buses, and trains consumed billions of dollars worth of energy in moving these masses of people from home to work and back again each day. Countless hours were spent on traveling between home and work. In today's environment, with our new and growing awareness of the costs and limits of resources, we have come to recognize that two of our most valuable resources—time and energy—were not properly taken into account in those many years of shuttling populations to and fro, to and fro, day in and day out.

The Transformation of the Economy

Perhaps we would have gone on forever squandering those resources, were it not for some developments of profound and lasting significance.

In the late 1960s our economy became transformed. The proportion of workers in the service sector began to inch upward toward a majority. Today, in the early 1980s, almost seven out of ten workers are employed in the service sector. Services now account for about two-thirds of our GNP. And the single largest component of those services is the handling of information: gathering, storing, retrieving, manipulating, and communicating it. Information regarding finance, planning, security, health, education, population, marketing, product development, investment, human resources, whatever.

The information-handling element in the industrial sector also increased substantially. Between 1960 and 1980 the ratio of managers to workers increased by 50 percent. A substantial part of the increase took place in staff functions such as planning. Coupled with the shift from making things to generating information was the microelectronic revolution manifested in two major technological thrusts: information processing (computers) and information transmission (communications). Some hailed the new age as the postindustrial or information economy, and its foundation was believed to be the marriage of two locomotive technologies: communications and computers. The titanic AT&T–IBM clash heralded this wave of structural change in our economy. Communications and computers were seen to be Siamese twins, inseparable and integral parts of the key element in the postindustrial era of information management.

In the early 1970s energy became a critical economic issue for reason of both cost and availability. And communications technology began to be seen as a new, energy-efficient alternative to transportation.

At the same time, businesses were decentralizing their operations; they were relying heavily on computerization and communications to tie their operations together.

At the same time, rural America was growing in attractiveness. Urban blight, suburban malaise, and a host of other factors made living farther away from downtown centers more attractive.

At the same time, many industries began to automate their production functions in successive waves, the culmination of which is now occurring in robotics. Export of undesirable production jobs was also a widespread practice. And the decline of many heavy-manufacturing sectors, like autos and steel, led to plant closings. Millions of factory jobs, which drew workers into central industrial locations, were eliminated. Those declines in the manufacturing segment of our economy will not completely reverse if and when the economy fully recovers. They have been occurring over a long period of time, and the change marks a fundamental shift in the structure of our economy.

At the same time, family and lifestyle behavior and values were changing. Women were working; fathers began to be involved more with their families and communities, and time became a valuable commodity. Time spent commuting was seen as an expensive price to pay for a job. More young married and empty-nest families moved to downtown areas from the suburbs, spurring the *gentrification trend*. Others went further out to rural areas and sought new employment opportunities, at lower pay, for a slower-paced, more close-to-home lifestyle.

Work at Home

The handwriting is now clearly on the CRT. For technological, time, energy, value, and economic transition reasons, commuting to centralized locations to do work on a 7- or 8-hour-a-day basis, 5 days a week, may be losing its economic value and rationale for a segment of the work force that, while still in the minority, may someday be a majority.

Yet in spite of all the technological, economic, and social forces cited above, managers have been slow to embrace the possibilities of work at home. Why? The basis for resistance seems mostly fourfold:

1. **Fear of the novelty or newness of the idea.** Familiar patterns of work are much more comfortable from an organizational perspective, and anything new is often resisted.

2. **Fear of losing management control.** Being able to see an employee at his or her desk gives at least the appearance that work is being done. The employee can be monitored, counted, and reached easily, and the manager can be seen as managing work flow.

3. **Concern about losing the benefits derived from face-to-face interaction.** There is a sense that the employee must mingle with others in the workplace in order to get creative ideas, develop a sense of belonging to the organization, facilitate communications among workers, and observe the overall workings of the enterprise.

4. **Skepticism about the impact of working at home on the employee's family and home life, and vice versa.** This includes concern about invasion of privacy on the part of the company, interruptions that are likely to occur at home, the possible development of sloppy work habits, and questions of security and safety of machines or information removed from the workplace on a regular basis.

Directions for the Future

It is likely, however, that the tide, although still low, is inexorable and that work at home in the service sector will be commonplace in the future, much as flexible work hours have become a more accepted practice. What, then, can you do to take advantage of the work-at-home potential, and meet the challenge of all the economic and social forces shaping this likely future, while avoiding the problems raised above?

You should recognize that work at home offers attractive savings. Less workplace space would be necessary, and there would also be a diminished need for support services such as telephones, cafeteria, secretarial support, interior design and construction, furniture and equipment and supplies, and parking facilities for on-site workers. It should also be recognized that if a sizable number of potential candidates for work-at-home jobs would opt for that alternative (and this might be found out by something as simple as a survey), productivity might actually improve. In a speech delivered in 1982, James Robinson III, chairman and CEO of American Express, claimed that between 1976 and 1979 productivity in goods increased by 10 percent. Productivity in services, however, increased by 20 percent. That was especially true, he said, in information-related businesses because of the revolution in computers and telecommunications. Thus the bottom-line argument, often the prime mover in getting organizations to accept a new practice, could certainly be advanced by managers who wish to initiate more work at home.

The theory and practice of management has already been going through an evolution, which can be seen as forming the basis for accommodation to work at home. Workplace democracy has so advanced that many workers now have more control over the design of their jobs and the decisions which affect their work. Foreign competition has forced American management to review the efficacy of many intervening levels of supervisory personnel. Flextime (flexible working hours) has proved to be manageable, despite early fears of the possibility of a management nightmare. Assignments and deadlines can be given, monitored, and judged irrespective of where and when they are acted upon, so long as interim checks and balances are instituted. Pagers are available to contact vital employees who may be mobile and not at home. The sophistication and range of these devices are improving all the time. Even in the absence of this peripheral technology, the telephone is still a fine solution, provided certain core hours are spent by the employee where he or she is reachable. And telephone-conferencing technologies are also developing to accommodate more flexible requirements for remote group discussions. Moreover, the presence of an individual at a desk is no more evidence that a job is getting done than is standard dress code or a properly filled-in time sheet. The more progressive managers of tomorrow's enterprises will be comfortable with the fact that, if it is done well, it matters not where a job is done. The trappings of a traditional setting, when no longer necessary, become cosmetic.

There is evidence, mostly anecdotal, that social and work-related interaction is a necessary and beneficial force for creativity and organizational solidarity. It also satisfies some of the belonging needs on the part of people. Unexpected feedback from coworkers, whether of a personal or professional nature, is sometimes a valued adjunct to employee development. Of all the resistances to work-at-home schemes, this cluster of concerns perhaps has the most merit and deserves the most careful consideration. The challenge to managers is how to achieve these interactions and still allow a work-at-home mode. One solution is the splitting of workweeks between at-home work and on-site work (say, 2 days home, 3 at the office). That would allow for a rotation of workers in and out and still permit the cost savings mentioned earlier. Another solution, somewhat similar, is to have employees, especially those working on long-term projects, report to work one day a week or one full week out of the month.

There may be merit in any one of these schemes, but as the difficulties in adopting such changes as flextime have shown, no solution will be a real one unless it is undertaken with the advice and consent of the affected workers. Perhaps the most important managerial task at this juncture would be to open up discussions and considerations of alternatives with employees, and even to be willing to consider experimental approaches, before adopting any long-term organizational policy.

The sociological impacts of work at home on the individual, family or household, and corporation have not yet been adequately explored. It is important to surface issues of privacy and security, but, once again, these are not necessarily insurmountable. As already noted, a lot of work at home is now being done by professional employees, and somehow the problems have managed to work themselves out. However, not to dismiss this issue lightly, it might make sense for a group of organizations to sponsor a joint intensive and independent study. Potentially sloppy work habits seem to be no more than a minor concern. Again, a job is done if it is done; and under any method of work, employees must be held accountable by management for their productivity and achievement.

There would, of course, be a variety of other issues to consider. Insurance is one of them. How can an injury be determined to be work-related when a good deal of work is performed off-site? Magazine subscriptions, the routing of memos, and mail delivery can present distribution problems and attendant cost increases. In the long run, however, these appear to be relatively minor difficulties that can be worked out through positive and creative approaches.

Despite common misconceptions, the work-at-home mode need not apply solely to office workers. The factory of modern times would also be a candidate. Alvin Toffler points out in *The Third Wave* that when Western Electric shifted from producing electromechanical switching equipment to electronic switching gear, the work force at its advanced manufacturing plant in Illinois was transformed. Fully half of the 2000 workers now handled information instead of things. According to one Western Electric official, 10 to 25 percent of the work done at the plant could be done at home. A senior manager of the Hewlett-Packard factory in Colorado Springs reported that perhaps 25 percent of the 1000 people in manufacturing there could work at home. By Toffler's estimate, fully 35 to 50 percent of the entire work force in the advanced-manufacturing sector could, in 1980, have been doing most if not all of their work at home, provided the choice was made to organize production that way.

The ranks of organizations that are allowing employees more latitude to work at home are swelling. From Weyerhaeuser to McDonald's, the landscape of workday and workweek is changing. Technology supports the shift. Energy costs practically demand it. The growing importance of time argues for it. The transition of the United States economic system allows it. The problems and concerns that are raised are solvable. It remains for managers to conclude that it is an idea whose time has come.

CHAPTER 11

The Dual Realities of Unemployment and Underemployment

Perhaps the most serious problem resulting from modern technology is the displacement of labor. It is a problem made more serious by the unwillingness of our leadership in government, business, labor, and the media to accord it the attention it warrants. And this applies not just to the United States. Even so knowledgeable and astute an observer as Jean-Jacques Servan-Schreiber, chairman of France's World Center for Computer Science and Human Resources, sounded almost too glib and superficial when he told the Congressional Committee on Science & Technology (in May 1982), "More than one-third of the male and female workers in our countries will have to change jobs by the end of the '80s." How? With what help? From whom? And if, as Servan-Schreiber went on to point out, there are 50 million jobless people in the developed countries by 1990, on what basis will the fortunate employed be selected?

We in the United States and other developed countries are becoming the victims of our triumphs—in particular, the *bourgeoisification* of society. Never before in human history has there been a social revolution of such magnitude. Starting in this country with the GI Bill for World War II veterans, the doors of higher education were thrown open to the entire society, and we indulged in an orgy of education. Now close to 50 percent of all high school graduates go on to higher education. That was fine as long as the economy continued to expand and the age of affluence seemed endless. Indeed, there was perhaps nothing more symbolic of the entitlement era than access to upward economic and social mobility. But if, as some believe, we have come to the end of the entitlement era, it is because the second of those doors is closing. Education no longer guarantees anything. And just as we did not plan for accommodating all those eager people with their bachelor's, master's, and doctor's degrees—we just made room for them when the time came—so we are now neglecting to plan for *not* accommodating them.

We are now paying the price of that failure to plan. There were so many young people, and we unthinkingly expanded the managerial and professional ranks for them. We changed job titles; we created new jobs; we built staffs of adjunct workers to "interface" with each other; we added layers of intervention between production and consumption—and between production and management. But economic growth has now slowed, and economic competition has become brutal. Business in general, and American business in particular, has discovered that if it is to go faster, it must first become slimmer. Technology is giving us smarter machines, too, a further complication.

Facing Up to Reality

It is becoming increasingly apparent that dealing effectively with the unemployment and underemployment that results from all these developments is much more difficult than anyone had thought. It is also becoming apparent that we may have to learn to live with (1) a higher constant level of unemployment than had been previously considered acceptable and (2) regular periodic upswings in unemployment affecting not only lower-level workers but middle and upper management as well. But above all, a growing number of people will have to lower their career and economic expectations. The United States Department of Labor forecasts that in the 1980s one of every four college graduates will have to take a job that does not require a degree—and that seems at this point to be a conservative prediction.

As early as 1978 the College Placement Council predicted that there would be an oversupply of almost one million college graduates before the end of the 1980s. But even that number is misleading, because many graduates who do have jobs—some social scientists estimate as much as 80 percent of them—are working below their potential. Even worse for their well-being and that of society, they are working below their level of expectations. Today, people with bachelor's degrees are holding jobs and doing work formerly the domain of high school graduates; the jobs haven't changed, only the credential requirements. People with MBAs now have jobs that formerly required only a bachelor's degree. And now that academic and research opportunities have diminished, PhDs are being hired instead of MBAs. This is another displacement phenomenon, whereby people with more education replace those with less, even if the jobs themselves are unchanged.

The effects of technology, it should be pointed out, are not by any means all negative. Indeed, the new technologies, particularly information and communications technology, will create new, higher-level jobs. And they will upgrade existing jobs and make them more interesting and rewarding; for example, word processing has the potential for radically changing the job of clerk-typist. Even robotics, so dreaded as ultimately replacing hordes of humans in increasingly higher-level jobs, will create new jobs that call for new forms of knowledge and skills.

But without proper long-range planning, both the positive and the negative consequences of the technological revolutions will occur uncontrolled. It is important that we understand the possibilities so that we can fully appreciate the need for some kind of control, some logic, some plan. In 1981, *Newsweek* reported on a study of 674,000 workers displaced from New England's old mills between 1958 and 1975. Only 20,000 of them were employed in high-tech industries; more than 100,000 went to lower-paying trade and service jobs; and most of the rest dropped out of the labor force or went into jobs not covered by Social Security. A 1981 study on the potential impacts of information technology on employment of women in Canada concluded that the jobs likely to be rendered obsolete are those traditionally held by women. It predicted that one million Canadian women would be displaced by 1990, with a 30 to 40 percent reduction in employment in jobs such as bank teller, telephone operator, and clerk-typist.

And, as Nobel laureate Arnold Penzias, vice president of Bell Laboratories, pointed out recently, we are well on the way to developing a computer that doesn't need programmers. We already have robots that can run factories that make other robots—in effect, reproduce themselves. We already have computers that can diagnose and repair some of their own breakdowns. Is it any wonder that fear of technology, the Frankenstein syndrome, is coming to dominate the minds and conversations of so many young adults?

Some observers now feel that if we are to begin to deal effectively with displacement, we must shift our focus from getting people back to work to *managing unemployment*. This requires acknowledging the existence of a permanent gap between the number of jobs and the number of people looking for work.

Compounding the problem is the issue of immigration. A 1982 study by the Population Reference Bureau projects net annual migration into the United States at 795,000 to 970,000 during the 1980s, about half of which will be illegal. Others put the figures much higher. Some estimates of illegal immigration put it at more than 1.5 million people per year. And although it is part of the thoughtless rhetoric of some people that all those foreigners are coming here to go on welfare, the fact is that they come for jobs. They are the most fervent believers in the American dream; they come to make more money than they can make in their own countries; they come to prosper and to see their children prosper. And in the process, they take whatever jobs they can get and unwittingly exacerbate the unemployment situation.

As a consequence, they are increasingly objects of fear and hatred. Xenophobia is rampant. After a generation of almost total public commitment to racial and religious equality and the eradication of bigotry, prejudice is making a comeback. It appears to be based largely if not entirely on economic concerns, and it is not by any means confined, as many would like to believe, to the lower economic and social elements. As stated earlier, in 1981 *The Humanist* magazine, which has a liberal, educated, well-to-do readership, devoted an entire issue to the subject of illegal immigration. The points it made included these: The United States is already overpopulated; our first duty is to our own citizens; workers have most to lose from uncontrolled immigration; in effect, keep them out or send them back. Some observers are predicting that unless unemployment is drastically reduced, we will see class warfare breaking out in this country, perhaps beginning with large-scale attacks on immigrant groups. Not too long ago, a congressman

stood up in the House of Representatives and said that the problems of
the American automobile industry were the fault of "those little yellow
people," and apparently nobody was outraged.

A Culture of Despair

There appears to be developing what Martin Peretz, writing in *The
New Republic,* called a "culture of despair." Peretz was writing about
what he described as the "flotsam of a society"—the unemployables.
Although his focus was on what has now popularly come to be called
the underclass, that culture of despair is spreading slowly upward, like
a fungus. It is swallowing the faith of many in, and frightening others
away from, the American dream of limitless opportunity and fair return for effort.

The times are making people not only unemployed or underemployed—which is bad enough—but unemployable, technologically obsolete. You can get away with telling a person almost anything, but
never that he or she is useless. One has to wonder how long this
situation will go on before something terrible for all of society happens.

In his science fiction spoof, *The Restaurant at the End of the Uni-
verse,* British writer Douglas Adams describes how a mythical planet
uses an end-of-the-world hoax to load all of its middlemen—
management consultants, hairdressers, marketers, personnel officers,
public relations executives, lawyers, security guards, etc.—onto a
giant space ship and send them away forever. According to Adams,
this group then became the first humans on earth. There are some who
are beginning to wonder if that is as farfetched as it appears to be.
Members of the middle class are beginning to fear that perhaps Marx
was right and that they *are* superfluous.

We have now reached the point where almost seven out of every ten
workers are employed in the service sector, as noted in Chapter 10. The
service sector, by and large, is still labor-intensive and therefore has
become, to some extent, the employer of last resort. But a great many
service jobs are low-paying and dead-end; indeed, it is just those jobs
that many of the illegal immigrants are taking.

And, of course, there is entrepreneurship. As never before, people
are starting their own small businesses. Even though the failure rate
for new small businesses remains very high, people still try. Sometimes they feel that's all they have available to them, but not always.
One of the manifestations of the increase in middle-class, middle-
management unemployment is the enormous increase in consultants.
If you don't have a job, if you can't find a job, if you don't want to or

can't afford to invest a lot of money in a franchise or some other high-cost new enterprise, you can become a consultant. This may be, in fact, the age of the consultant; after all, it is a way to avoid saying you don't have a job.

Coming to Grips with the Problem

It is impossible to overemphasize the importance of coming to grips with the unemployment-underemployment issue. In both societal and institutional terms, no issue has more profound implications for our society. And because it is an issue which has such serious consequences for society as a whole, individual attempts to deal with it must be seen and considered in the context of the whole. Here are some of the questions managers must examine:

■ Are we overemphasizing credentials in writing job descriptions, simply because there is a surplus of credentialed people? Are we therefore hiring overqualified people whose bitterness will adversely affect not only their performance but the entire organization?

■ In considering the purchase of new technologies, such as advances in office automation, are we fully exploring the ultimate costs to society, which must eventually be paid by us as individuals and as organizations?

■ Should we examine new approaches to employing people, such as job sharing, which could enable us to control or reduce costs without drastic personnel cuts?

■ Would investment now in job retraining, perhaps jointly with others, enable us to reduce the ultimate costs to ourselves and society of dealing with a permanent high level of unemployment?

■ Will the situation eventually get so bad that government will require businesses of all kinds to maintain or increase their levels of employment? (Following enactment of the 1981 tax reform bill, which contained specific incentives for businesses to expand and create jobs, there was much anger in Congress at the fact that many large companies were instead taking advantage of the incentives to buy other companies, a practice that adds neither capacity nor jobs.)

■ Instead of firing or demoting surplus staff, can we find uses for them that will result in gain rather than loss for the organization? (For example, some companies now use executives as part-time consultants or public relations representatives.)

■ Will a large, disaffected element from middle America—those who have been the infantry in the army of the faithful—embrace the neoliberal ideology, which calls for far more direct government control of business?

■ What ways, if any, can we find to elicit loyalty from middle-management people who are afraid they may be replaced by technology?

■ Are we sufficiently alert to signs of declining morale in management?

■ Are we sufficiently alert to, and prepared to respond to, signs of racial, religious, or ethnic hostility within our organizations?

If thoughtful planning is to help America deal with the explosive unemployment-underemployment issue, it must begin with questions such as these. Above all, you must understand that individual personnel decisions are pebbles thrown in a pond; they send ripples throughout society.

CHAPTER 12

What Will Your Compensation Be?

Compensation used to be such a simple matter; people worked and they got paid. But not anymore. Increasingly, compensation is more than pay for work. Now it entails benefits, entitlements, and expectations as well. Employee benefits—remember when they used to be called fringe benefits?—now average more than 30 percent of total payroll. That includes health insurance, retirement plans, paid vacations, and so on. More and more companies are also providing—for some or all of their employees—annual physical examinations, exercise facilities, free or subsidized lunches, child-care facilities or allowances, education reimbursement, financial counseling, therapy, biofeedback facilities, dental and prepaid legal insurance, retraining, and a host of other, previously unthought of forms of compensation.

Some of the manifestations of the internal and external factors complicating compensation include the following:

■ In 1982, in a landmark case, 1500 women nurses struck a San Jose, California, hospital demanding equal pay for work that was comparable to what men were doing.

■ According to a report in *Business Week* in May 1982, more and more corporations are making accommodations to the scheduling needs of managers who are mothers—part-time work, flexible hours, maternity leaves, etc. The 1981 tax law triggered a rush by corporations into providing day care for employees' children, since the law established that employer-provided care is not taxable income to the employees.

■ In 1982, Xerox Corporation's British subsidiary, Rank Xerox Ltd., encouraged some of its middle managers to work as outside consultants part time while continuing on part time at the company. In many cases the managers ended up earning more money while the company saved substantially, particularly in benefits, taxes, and overhead.

■ In 1982, General Electric and the International Union of Electrical Workers concluded a 3-year agreement that the union leaders hailed as providing "historic" gains for employee job security. GE will give a minimum of 6 months' notice of plant closings or worker transfers and a minimum of 60 days' notice of the installation of robots or other labor-saving machinery. Dismissed employees will be entitled to education and retraining reimbursement and company assistance in finding new jobs.

■ The British civil service unions told the government in 1982 that their members would not work with any new technological equipment without official assurance that such equipment would not result in any job loss.

■ Ford Motor Company began an experiment in lifetime guaranteed employment for the more than 3000 hourly workers at its Livonia plant in May 1982.

Some of the impetus for all the changes came from the entitlement mentality, a widespread feeling among both workers and managers that forms of compensation originally intended as rewards are now entitlements. Even more significantly, perhaps, the nature of the relationship between institutions and employees has changed profoundly. Particularly in the last two decades, the emphasis has shifted from the organization to the individual. Instead of individuals accommodating themselves to the organization, more and more the reverse has been true; organizations have felt compelled to take into account the needs and circumstances of the individuals in their employ. As individual values with regard to compensation have changed, there have been corresponding (if sometimes lagging) changes in compensation systems.

Responding to Changing Needs of Workers

Foremost among the compensation changes, and the one that seems most likely to influence such changes in the future, is individualization. This has been most strikingly manifested in response to the increasing feminization of the work force. Fifty-two percent of the labor force is now female; well over half of all married women work. One relatively new benefit, flextime, enables women with young children to have work schedules that accommodate their family needs. Another significant change is in the number of single-parent families, which are generally headed by women. There are now almost 7 million of them, approximately 21 percent of all families. The book (and subsequently a hit movie) *Kramer v. Kramer* dramatized how single parents faced with rigid and nonunderstanding employers may sacrifice advancement and income for family well-being. Recognizing that, many forward-thinking managers are becoming more flexible about work schedules and times in order to keep good people.

A substantial increase in two-income households has encouraged the spread of cafeteria-style benefit programs that enable individuals to choose and vary their benefits program, as, for example, to have less health insurance (perhaps already provided by a spouse's coverage) and more vacation time.

A female floodtide into the work force has also generated the issue of discriminatory discrepancies in pay. Some jobs—nurse and secretary, for example—have traditionally been female ghettoes, and pay scales have been low. Now women are demanding that they be paid, not according to traditional wage scales for those jobs, but comparably to what men in other but reasonably similar jobs earn. This is a thorny issue; comparable work is not necessarily easy to define. But indications are that the courts and the regulatory authorities are moving in that direction, helped along by technological developments that are changing the very nature of traditional jobs.

An equally large factor in changing compensation is the issue of job security. In 1981 Douglas Fraser (then United Auto Workers president) announced that his union would concentrate on job security; it would seek a "guaranteed right to employment." White-collar workers in the hard-hit U.S. auto industry also have demonstrated growing concern about job security. *The Wall Street Journal* reported in 1982 that salaried workers at General Motors were considering joining a union "for protection from unexpected job loss."

While some workers and managers are looking to contractual protection against job loss, others are seeking job security through requiring employers to provide or pay for job retraining for displaced workers. A House Education and Labor Committee report in 1982 predicted lingering unemployment for hundreds of thousands of workers unless there are substantial increases in retraining programs.

Another new form of compensation focuses on the worker's physical and mental well-being. Employers have become aware that the cost to them of preventing illnesses and accidents is less in the long run than the cost of health insurance and is better for the employee as well. Providing regular physical exams and exercise facilities is only one example of what is now being done on a large scale by both big and small firms. Coming along, and likely to assume more importance by the early 1990s, are such health-related steps as genetic testing to protect susceptible workers from hazardous substances, general improvement of the work environment to remove or diminish potential hazards (ranging from fluorescent lights to electrical and magnetic fields, all of which may be carcinogenic), stress reduction, weaning from cigarettes, treatment for alcoholism, diet counseling, and mandatory vacations (for workaholics).

Linking Compensation to Performance

There is likely to be much more emphasis in coming years on linking compensation more closely to performance. One of the strongest criticisms of top management in recent years, as epitomized in the *Fortune* 1982 cover story on "The Madness of Executive Compensation," is that management pay seems too removed from how well or how poorly the company has done. An obvious example is International Harvester, which, in the late 1970s, gave its CEO compensation worthy of a rajah at a time when the company was plummeting toward disaster. Another is the popular practice (among top management, that is) of providing "golden parachutes"—large sums of money paid to senior people in the event of a merger, a takeover, or some other cause of job loss. (It has been increasingly difficult to reconcile this practice with the substantial layoffs occurring in business. It could be argued that managers, who are paid more than workers, should take greater risks.)

One complaint about linking compensation to performance is that, when it is linked, it is usually to short-term performance—quarterly or annual earnings per share. To encourage a longer-term perspective, such as that characteristic of Japanese industry, top management must make a greater effort to tie at least part of compensation to success in long-term planning and management.

Achievement and Self-worth

Academic theorists and human resource managers in public and private organizations generally agree that serious problems of productivity, morale, and loyalty cannot be addressed effectively by traditional forms of compensation alone. An article by human resource researchers Ann Howard and Douglas Bray of AT&T, published in *Wharton Magazine* in the summer of 1981, pointed out that the giant communications company was seriously concerned about a decline in managerial motivation and a growing resistance to the traditional hierarchical structure and systems of the organization. New managers, the authors said, want emotional support; they want individual treatment; and they want a more direct and obvious relationship between accomplishment and reward.

Psychologist Daniel Yankelovich, one of the most astute observers of the social scene, denies that, contrary to conventional wisdom, there has been a decline in the work ethic in the United States. People *do* want to work, he asserts (and he cites survey results to support his claim), but the traditional reward system militates against them. Why, he asks, should workers try harder if (1) they don't have to and (2) they believe that others will be the beneficiaries of their efforts? Noted economist Lester Thurow asks similar questions. How can organizations get commitment from workers when, according to him, almost 50 percent of the work force either quits or gets laid off every year? He sees one answer in changing CEO compensation to reflect, not current profits, but long-run profits.

Unions, too, are breaking away from traditional compensation demands. *The New York Times* reporter William Serrin, in an insightful analysis of the professional football players' strike in 1982, described the strike as a struggle over workplace power, not merely compensation. In particular, it reflected an awareness of how technology is altering the workplace. In the case of the football players, television technology was the key; the strike focused on the introduction and use of the technology. Serrin reported that Jack Golodner of the AFL–CIO predicts more such confrontations as the rapid introduction of new technologies in all industries makes significant impacts on earnings and compensation.

What Lies Ahead

You can anticipate that alterations in concepts and forms of compensation will continue at the dizzying rate of the recent past. Among the possible new developments are the following:

■ The emergence of new kinds of insurance. Kidnapping and ransom insurance on executives is one example. *The Financial Post* reported in 1982 that more than 250 Canadian companies have taken out such insurance in the last few years. Canada also saw in 1982 the introduction of job insurance for executives; it pays up to 2 years of a fired executive's salary.

■ There is likely to be an increase in worker ownership. This ranges from employee stock ownership plans (ESOPs) to co-ops owned and managed by the workers; from companies like General Electric (which spin off unprofitable business units in a joint-ownership arrangement with their managers) to Sweden's socialist government's proposal for a tax that will fund worker purchase of major corporations.

■ Working at home will accelerate. Although work at home is not generally perceived as a form of compensation, many who do work at home feel quite strongly that it is. According to *Business Week,* as many as 15 million American workers may be working at home by 1990. For handicapped people, single parents, mothers of small children, loners, and many others, the right to work at home may indeed be a valued form of compensation.

■ Everyone will look for ways to reduce taxes. Many small businesses already pay some or all of their employees "off the books."

Others, big and small, provide noncash services and benefits (cafeterias, low-priced employee stores, etc.) that are, so far, nontaxable. The rapid and wide growth of the underground economy and the equally wide acceptance of barter have created a mind-set that skirting the law is socially acceptable. A Louis Harris poll in 1982 indicated that as many as 30 percent of all U.S. households had at least one member working in the underground economy. According to Harris, this included upper- and middle- as well as low-income families.

■ More workers and employers will opt for part-time and odd-hour work. More than 20 percent of the civilian work force already works part-time or at other than standard nine-to-five daytime hours. Many people want to or need to work part-time or at odd hours, and many companies are accommodating their preferences.

In the years ahead, mastering human relations changes will require that managers recognize the need to be flexible and sensitive when it comes to compensation. It is not merely a matter of finding out what people want and giving it to them. The needs and desires of the new workers and managers must be reconciled with the viability of the organization. If compensation comes to involve granting more power and control to individual workers, does that ultimately harm the organization? It does not have to. The effective managers, understanding the new needs of the new workers, will learn how to share control so as to enhance the acceptance of, and therefore the authority of, management. The consequence can be greater organizational strength.

PART 4

Where Today Clashes with Tomorrow: Exploding Old Myths

One of the cherished fundamental laws, unchallenged for centuries, is "The bread always falls buttered side down." Once in a little village in eastern Europe, a man's slice of bread fell buttered side up. The startled fellow dashed off to inform his rabbi, who was skeptical at first but was ultimately persuaded. The rabbi, in turn, feeling himself inadequate to deal with such a tradition-shattering event, went to ask one of the great Talmudic scholars what it meant. The scholar pondered for several months before he was able to provide the fearful people with an answer, which was: "The bread must have been buttered on the wrong side."

CHAPTER 13

The Trap of Relying on Traditional Economic Indicators

In the space of one hundred and seventy-six years the Lower Mississippi has shortened itself two hundred and forty-two miles. That is an average of a trifle over one mile and a third per year. Therefore, any calm person, who is not blind or idiotic, can see that in the old Oolitic Silurian period, just a million years ago next November, the lower Mississippi river was upward of one million three hundred thousand miles long and stuck out over the Gulf of Mexico like a fishing rod. And by the same token, any sane person can see that seven hundred and forty-two years from now, the Lower Mississippi will be only a mile and three-quarters long, and Cairo and New Orleans will have joined their streets together, and be plodding comfortably along under a single mayor and a mutual board of aldermen. There is something fascinating about science. One gets such wholesome returns of conjecture out of such a trifling investment of fact.

Mark Twain
Life on the Mississippi

Let's look into the office of a manager, J. B. Smith. As we glance past Smith's desk, we see a shelf on which are stacks of materials and printouts containing data from the Census Bureau, the Bureau of Labor Statistics, the various econometric modeling services Smith's company subscribes to, and 3- to 5-year company plans based on expected increases in CPI, GNP, interest rates, and exchange rates. Smith may be in planning or in marketing or in R&D or even be in human resources or public affairs.

It really doesn't matter who or what Smith is. The point is that all of us who inhabit American institutions have come to base our analyses of the world in which we live on increasingly large amounts of quantitative data. It comes to us from government surveys, consulting firms, computerized systems (both in-house and contracted for), and scores of data collection outfits that watch everything from the performance of the stock market to new housing starts to third world debt.

The major problem with all this, however, is that the weight and solidity of the documents containing all those numbers lead us to believe that the numbers are real and not just symbols representing parts of reality. But any objective look tells us that events develop *in spite* of the data, *regardless* of the data, or *counter* to the message we get from the data. The process of quantification requires the deletion or distortion of all unquantifiable material. This results in the paradox that, at a time when our tools for quantifying are advancing at a dizzying pace, the world we are measuring is increasingly irrational and unmeasurable. Thus, many traditionally collected numbers are less—rather than more—able to explain, predict, order, shape, and otherwise guide our impressions of the real world in which real people live, produce, and consume.

Flaws in Census Data

Data from the 1980 census, for example, are a primary basis for shaping the most important public socioeconomic policies in areas such as education, housing, health, and welfare. The data also provide a seeming wealth of material for market research, corporate planning, lobbying, and other activities in the private sector. Yet there were serious reservations about the accuracy of the 1980 census data even before the count began—reservations that seem to have been borne out by the results and by the legal and judicial tangles that will continue for many years. The inability to determine the number of illegal aliens with any accuracy, the lack of cooperation on the part of a sizable segment of the population (rich and poor alike) suspicious of authorities, the almost nomadic lifestyle of a substantial portion of our people, and the uncertain reliability of the census takers themselves— all make many of the data questionable.

In addition, sweeping social change has rendered some of the census groupings misleading. For example, income breaks no longer classify middle-class households as they once did. For many people, income fluctuations (both up and down) as great as several tens of thousands of dollars over a period of just a few years make such class boundaries less clear, as is also true of blue-collar–white-collar distinctions. Can marketers and planners really feel confident of these gross macrostatistics about a society in such a state of flux?

And what about census predictions? Recently, the Joint Center for Urban Studies of MIT and Harvard issued a report, titled "Regional Diversity: Growth in the U.S. 1960–1990," which stated that usually where the Census Bureau predicted a slowdown in recent rapid population growth, the opposite happened. And most Census Bureau predictions of increases where population growth had been slow were wrong also.

One frequent demographic development of recent decades is that migration patterns have replaced birth and death rates as the major determinant of population growth. Much of the migration is internal, but a good deal is a result of immigration. How much do we really know about the sociocultural orientations of these new Americans? How many managers, in how many organizations, can move from a personal gut fear of the tide of immigration, both legal and illegal, to a rational approach to delivery of goods and services to this ever-growing segment of our society? Gross statistics offer little guidance here. It will take intuition and nerve not only to recognize the potential of these changed markets, but to devise new ways of getting the data needed to lift the cloud of ignorance regarding them.

The Underground Economy

Another factor of major importance not adequately dealt with in presenting available data is the underground economy. Ever since economics professor Peter Gutmann stated that $200 billion escaped inclusion in official estimates of regular U.S. economic activity in 1976, the "underground," "irregular," or "subterranean" economy has received increased attention from people concerned about the accuracy of economic data. Estimates of the size of the underground economy range from Gutmann's revised 1980 figure of 13 to 14 percent of the legal U.S. economy to economist Edgar Feige's figure of 33 percent for 1978. In a study challenged as being too conservative, the IRS estimated hidden income in the late 1970s to be more than $150 billion a year. Even that low figure exceeds the GNP of most countries of the world.

Clearly, official statistics on income understate the true dimensions and growth rates of the U.S. economy. Should Smith be manager of a stereo manufacturing company planning for inventory and sales on the basis of official income statistics, he or she could wind up well off the mark.

Estimates of inflation are also likely to be substantially overstated because of the enormous direct-to-consumer activity in the underground economy. Overstatement is probably also true of estimates of unemployment. Several years ago, when New York City was considering adding a numbers game to its lottery, the operators of the illicit game protested that this could endanger their work force, which they claimed was 500,000.

What kinds of activity take place in the underground economy? They are believed to involve 15 to 20 million people, who include self-employed professionals (lawyers, doctors, artists, architects, etc.) who do not declare all their income, household workers, anybody who pads deductions and underreports interest, dividend, rental, and royalty income, moonlighters paid off the books, illegal aliens paid in cash, those who collect tips or take bribes, barterers, those who work and continue to claim unemployment benefits, people who pad expense accounts, peddlers, flea market sellers and buyers, and criminals (in narcotics, prostitution, fencing, smuggling, embezzling, gambling, and so forth).

The really intriguing aspect of this is that, once out of the office, Smith is very likely to shop at a flea market, pay cash to someone to mow the lawn, pay the housecleaner off the books, tip the barber and the cab driver, get a hot TV set from a cousin's brother-in-law, overstate charitable contributions on his tax returns, and let the kids receive money for babysitting that is nowhere reported. But once in the office, Smith forgets all those human interactions that make up so much of the real world and falls back on the many traditional and inadequate economic indicators to provide a far too insubstantial foundation for establishing policy and setting goals.

Problems with Other Measures

Serious doubts are surfacing about the Consumer Price Index—in particular, whether it might actually cause the inflation it is intended to measure. Few of us have monthly changes in all the components of our living costs, yet the CPI is used in cost-of-living adjustments, wage settlements, and Social Security benefit measures as if we did. The resulting increases do push up the inflation rate and cause a vicious feedback loop.

There are also serious doubts about what productivity really is, especially in an economy in which more and more people work in jobs not directly related to the production of goods. Yet we use numbers that purport to show productivity increases and decreases from year to year for the country and even for our own organizations.

The Bureau of Labor Statistics gives us inadequate information regarding such important work force indicators as career and job turnover per employee per lifetime.

Econometric models are used to generate projections of interest rates, employment trends, and supply and demand curves; yet we know that the models are based on more or less subjective assumptions. Because assumptions differ, so do the outputs of the models, leaving the purchaser of the single model with a biased projection and the purchasers of several models with a range of outcomes that often dictate radically different responses.

What Can You Do?

Where does this leave managers in today's enterprises? Are all the quantitative data useless? Should all decisions be made on the basis of intuition and instinct? In a time when we are increasingly presented with ever more data, such questions may be heretical. But they have to be asked, or we will convince ourselves that New Orleans and Cairo will soon be nestling side by side. So quantitative indicators should never be accepted uncritically. We recommend that you do the following:

1. Seriously examine the groupings in which information has been traditionally delivered and may no longer be adequate. For example, if standard breaks allow market analysis for the 35-to-44 age segment and we know that the leading edge of the postwar boom is now entering the 33-to-35 age group, we cannot state that over the next 3 years there will be equally large growth in the entire 35-to-44 age group. To cosmetics companies or baby food manufacturers, for example, women aged 35 are very different from women aged 44. The same is true of market research that ends the age breaks at 55 or over or 65 or over. The former is truly out of sync with today's population (some 55-year-olds are remarrying and starting new families), and today's 65-year-olds behave very differently from those 75 and over. If your organization relies heavily on market data and gross economic assumptions of this sort, a careful analysis of such traditional groupings is in order.

2. By all means, supplement the data with personal observations and knowledge to enrich your understanding of what the traditional bodies of data tell you. We are all somehow involved in the underground economy and therefore know intuitively that GNP is not an adequate depiction of the economic health of the country. So too we know that behind some of the valid indicators of economic malaise are real people, whose particular circumstances are not necessarily reflected in the impersonal gross data. One example is the growing number of middle-class, middle-management unemployed who have been squeezed out by plant closings, corporate belt tightening, reorganizations, and technological changes in the workplace. These people, reared on a particular set of values and expectations, suddenly find they must now live by their own wits, without acceptable jobs and salaries and also without employee benefits and workplace affiliations. These people do have potential for marketers of products such as generic drugs, mail-order discount insurance plans, and do-it-yourself publications.

3. Remember that there is also an army of underemployed people who are even more hidden by the statistics. These are people whose jobs are the least satisfying aspects of their lives, unchallenging and unrewarding. Such qualitative factors can make them a good market for leisure goods and services that are stimulating and rewarding and that appeal to a need for status and success. Regardless of age, income, or career, they could well be among the prime buyers of home entertainment technologies as well as designer clothes and sports gear.

4. Understand that certain types of surveys measure conditions that no longer exist. Sometimes it takes several years for these surveys to mirror the present, let alone the future, if they ever do. Consider, for example, strategic analyses that define one's business in terms of traditional competitors. They cannot help one anticipate that in today's environment a Citibank could be in the data processing business, a Xerox could compete with Kodak, a Holiday Inns could be into satellite communications, a Control Data could be involved in agriculture, and a Japan could dominate the automobile market. Other examples are advertising studies which still have a narrow view of prime time in an ever-expanding TV viewing time frame (including late night, daytime, and videotapes played anytime), and media analyses that have, until recently, virtually ignored the expansion of publications and TV options for readers and viewers.

5. Accept the fact that strategic information encompasses far more than economic and other traditionally quantified data. Critical challenges, whether problems or opportunities, are showing themselves in the form of social, political, or technological diversions of historical trend lines. Limiting the scope of planning to a reliance on traditional economic indicators can truly be damaging to the organization one is managing and planning for. If you are a senior manager, you would do well to encourage your people to undertake a wide range of reading, to explore antiestablishment literature, to become a part of community activities, to broaden their contact with professional groups outside their own field, and to engage in periodic sessions specifically designed to unearth newly learned emerging issues of potential strategic significance to the organization. It is critical that the environment offered in the organization be one in which people can challenge traditional data, offer new insights, and suggest new avenues of study and investigation.

CHAPTER 14

Wrongly Defining One's Business

We're not in the transportation business; we're in the railroad business.

In 1930, in his *The World in 2030 A.D.*, the Earl of Birkenhead predicted transatlantic jet air transport. He expected that it would be operated by the steamship companies, who were in the business of intercontinental transport. But the companies thought they were in the steamship business, and consequently they are now reduced to the small business of Caribbean cruises.

The Financial Services Sector

In 1968 John R. Bunting took office as president of First Pennsylvania Banking & Trust Company, Philadelphia's biggest and oldest bank. Earlier, while still vice president and economist at First Pennsylvania, he had felt his bank would never be able to compete head-on with Bank of America, Chase Manhattan, or any of the other money-center giants. "We may never be the biggest bank," said Mr. Bunting in 1968, "but in a few years we will be one of the four or five most influential *financial institutions* in the country."

Amendments to the Bank Holding Company Act in that same year, 1968, allowed banks to form holding companies that could engage in other bank-related activities. In an industry as conservative as banking was then, the change was viewed as radical. Citibank was first, with Citicorp. But Bunting, too, went right to work. He created First Pennsylvania Corp., a holding company. He acquired, one year later in 1969, Associated Mortgage Company, which had a nationwide mortgage loan portfolio of $1.5 billion. In 1971 he purchased two consumer loan concerns, a real estate investment trust, and an investment advisory company that served individual and commercial clients more aggressively than did traditional bank trust departments.

Unfortunately for Bunting, he was forced to resign in July of 1979 because he had begun an investment strategy in 1976 that was designed to benefit from projected declines in interest rates. When rates reversed in 1977, the situation continued to deteriorate. In 1980 the FDIC was forced to step in and rescue the bank. But Bunting's vision of the future of financial institutions remained pretty much correct. In March 1982 another in a series of liberalizing laws took hold in the banking community. This one permitted more branch banking and allowed bank holding companies to buy up to eight banks in the next 8 years. Again, it wasn't just the major money-center banks that took advantage of the change. On April 20, 1982, *The New York Times* reported that two of Pennsylvania's largest bank holding companies, the Pittsburgh National Corporation and the Provident National Corporation, agreed in principal to merge into a new holding company, the PNC Corporation, which would start up with assets of $10.2 billion. Several decades ago, all that would have been revolutionary and unthinkable. A little more than a decade ago, Bunting was viewed as a maverick. Today, such news is ho-hum in the financial world.

January 1, 1981, marked another turning point in the new era of competition in banking. The Depository Institutions Deregulation and Monetary Control Act of 1980 went into effect. Banks and thrifts were now allowed to offer interest-bearing checking accounts. A 6-year phaseout of Regulation Q, which put a ceiling on the interest rates that financial institutions could pay on deposits, was effected. Thrifts, no longer limited to making home mortgage loans, could fill up to 20 percent of their loan portfolios with consumer loans and corporate bonds. They were also permitted to offer credit cards and trust services. Although bankers had been talking about deregulation for years, the need for loosened regulations wasn't seen as urgent until depositors started yanking out their cash and putting it in money market funds, whose assets zoomed. At the same time, interest rates rose to record highs and became highly unstable.

Still, many bankers saw themselves in a losing situation in terms of competition with the unregulated interstate "branches" of Sears in retail credit, Merrill Lynch's money market funds and Cash Management Account, and American Express's traveler's checks and credit cards.

The late 1970s and early 1980s marked a time of such incredible turmoil in the financial services industry that no one was willing to predict the strange new world that would emerge when and if the turmoil subsided. Competition in banking has become what it never was before. Inflation, tighter monetary policy, saturated markets, the growth of international banking, and new technology have all begun to take their toll. And as banks move further into nontraditional banking services, they find themselves confronting new nonbank competitors that are now moving into areas previously reserved for banks.

Prudential, the nation's largest insurance company, entered Wall Street in 1981 by buying Bache Group, the eighth largest brokerage house. Walter Wriston observed, "The Pru-Bache deal is nothing more than an extension of the trend toward nationwide financial department stores as opposed to local boutiques."

In late 1980 the Equitable Life Assurance Society of the United States began offering a money market mutual fund. In 1981 it began competing with big commercial banks in providing cash management services to corporations. The company already employed an electronic clearinghouse network to collect premiums automatically from the bank accounts of about 300,000 policyholders, and it ran a cash management system for its own use that handled as much as $100 million a day.

Sears, Roebuck and Company acquired Dean Witter. American Express acquired Shearson Loeb Rhoads. Stockbrokers began selling insurance. And on February 11, 1982, *The Wall Street Journal* reported that the term "financial supermarket" might one day literally apply to Kroger Company. The article read:

> Kroger plans to study the idea of offering financial services ranging from insurance to investments in its food stores. Most supermarkets offer check-cashing and some have automatic bank teller machines, and Kroger wants to know how far the concept can be extended.

In less than two decades the entire financial services industry has been reconceptualized, has been reorganized, and has faced competition it would never have expected (even in its wildest imaginings). It has not been alone in any of these developments. There is no industry left that has escaped the kind of transition the financial sector is undergoing. Indeed, one wonders what the term "financial industry," or any industry, means today.

What's in an Industry?

Citicorp expects to muscle in on America's $13 billion–a–year data processing market. It will use its Financial Information and Services Group (FISG) subsidiary, which is a sort of hybrid between a traditional correspondent banking department and a data processor. FISG provides credit and access to money markets, as a traditional correspondent banking department would. But it will also sell Citicorp's financial automation expertise to its customer banks and financial institutions. Citicorp has also asked the Federal Reserve Board to let it sell computer hardware.

Xerox was once a commercial photocopier company, and Kodak was a camera and film company. Today, technology has moved the two products closer together in the marketplace, and Xerox and Kodak are in the same business. Now Kodak finds that it must face stiff competition not only from Japan but also from domestic companies once thought of as being in other lines.

Holiday Inns installed some satellite communications on its properties for its internal purposes. Once having made the major investment, it decided it might go into the telecommunications business. Merrill Lynch joined with the Port Authority of New York to develop a commercial telecommunications satellite park in that city. Again, Merrill Lynch's initial need was for its own communications network. The investment was such that a joint venture looked promising as an income generator for both organizations. The Mattel Company found it could use its electronic circuits for more than toys, and it went into the home security business. Grumman Aircraft found there was a market for its elaborate software, and it is now selling computer programs.

As agriculture becomes a bioengineering industry, it is seen as a major area of opportunity by companies that are not limited by definitions of their businesses. Laboratories across the United States are working on ways to produce more food with less energy on smaller areas of land. Some of the most promising prospects here are related to genetic engineering, although it may be another decade before genetic research will be truly viable for large-scale commercial application. Dow Chemical, Monsanto, Du Pont, and Stauffer are among those now involved in genetic research as both defensive and offensive long-term business strategies. Nitrogen fixation and plant growth regulation are subjects of near-term focus. Monsanto already has a successful regulant on the market. Hydroponics is already being used commercially; Whittaker Corp. of Los Angeles is hydroponically raising lettuce in a 1.8-acre plastic greenhouse and expects to produce 3 million heads a year. And data processing has become an integral part of all of this work. Indeed, Control Data is involved in agricultural experimentation. Shell, Atlantic Richfield, ITT, and other corporations have been buying up seed companies, thereby ensuring themselves a place in the future industry that agriculture will become.

Gulf + Western has taken a hand in developing electric cars. Newspapers cried foul when AT&T proposed an electronic Yellow Pages up-to-the-minute update, potentially depriving newspapers of ad revenues. GE, which received the first patent ever granted for a new life-form, could just as well stand for Genetic Engineering. The list is endless. It seems as if everyone is getting into everyone else's business.

And, of course, the greatest war of them all is the monumental AT&T–IBM clash on the business battleground of the future: information management. The computer, information, and telecommunications melding has progressed to a point where, as in financial services, everything is seen as overlapping everything else.

Law and regulation are bowing to the irresistible forces of the marketplace, particularly as new and powerful competitors demand an end to what they see as officially countenanced, if not protected, monopolistic practices. In becoming more lenient through the years, legislative and regulatory decisions have increasingly opened the doors to competition. (Some call them doors; many others call them floodgates.)

The Impact of Technology and Foreign Competition

Technology quite clearly has been the major force behind the merging of industries and businesses. Foreign competition has had a major role to play as well. Foreign banks, for example, were not under the same restraint as domestic banks. In early 1981, Willard Butcher, chief executive officer of Chase Manhattan Bank, lamented, "Britain's Midland Bank comes in here and buys up Crocker, the fourteenth largest bank in the nation. I want to know why *I* can't buy Crocker." And the success of Japan has plunged the west into a long period of intense soul searching regarding restraints on the competitive and long-term positions of its own businesses. In the United States the mood has shifted more clearly to one of freer, more open competition domestically and, long term, greater viability on the international scene. Both Sears and General Electric, for example, have formed world trading companies along the Japanese lines. In 1982 Edward Telling, Sears' chairman and CEO, said his trading company would participate in exporting, importing, third country trade, and so-called counter trade or barter. He further stated, "We can no longer fail to recognize that the largest trading companies exporting goods from America are all foreign-owned and based." He added that Sears' size and financial resources qualify it to become a "truly significant" international trader.

So, rapidly advancing technology, eased regulatory restrictions, foreign competition, marketplace receptivity, and the need to maximize return on resources have inspired competition across traditional competitive lines. That leaves us to speculate about what lines of business today's companies will be in tomorrow. General Motors is today the world's leading manufacturer of computers; it produces more than 25,000 microprocessors a day for its cars. The chips now regulate some engine functions. Will GM add nonauto functions? The capacity is there. Will that make GM a computer company? AT&T has stated in a recent annual report that it *used to be* a telephone company but now it is in the business of transporting and managing information. Will AT&T become a news publishing great? Few companies, even now, can afford to persist in believing that they are *only* what they have been traditionally thought of as being.

What Must Managers Do?

And where does all this leave today's manager? It used to be that managers could ask, "What business do we want to be in?" but in the future the overriding question for managers will be "What business or businesses do we need to be in?" To be able to answer the second question correctly will require an enhanced ability to see and understand the new dimensions of markets, a keener sense of how to match resources and markets, and, above all, a new boldness in breaking away from the conventional wisdom of the past.

Perhaps there are four major issues you will have to consider in analyzing the competitive environment:

1. Traditional competitive analyses can be, if not carefully scrutinized, practically worthless. New competition and displacement of products and service by new concepts and technologies can be overlooked and can thereby impair survivability. One new tool is technology assessment, which you can use to determine what new competitive products and services could develop out of technologies now available.

2. Innovation in and entrance into virtually any attractive field once seen as reserved for other companies is a possible avenue for exploration by almost any company.

3. Conversely, a much more ordered and strategic assessment of one's own organization's strengths and weaknesses has to be undertaken frequently to avoid entering businesses just for the sake of seeming to be progressive or, even worse, just to get on the bandwagon. New business avenues should be considered if they truly make sense and fit with the organization's long-term strategies and planned-for capabilities. Rushing headlong into businesses that drain resources and talent and meet with saturated markets or better management by the competition could debilitate the original and traditional strengths of a company.

4. Trade association memberships have to be continually reviewed to see if they truly reflect the fields of enterprise one's organization is involved in. And associations have to be encouraged to maintain a high level of understanding of what businesses their constituents are in and how changing needs can best be served.

CHAPTER 15

Believing that Dollars Solve Most Problems

Our defense budget is to be increased to $1,500,000,000,000 over the next five years. That's $34 million every hour for the next five years. Will it make us more secure? Rear Admiral Gene LaRocque, after a seven-year stint in strategic planning at the Pentagon says "No." It will "distort our society and decrease our security."

Franklin Stark
National Vice Chairman of the Campaign for U.N. Reform[2]

It is the same in just about every activity in the world today. Big systems command big dollars. Yet these systems seem increasingly beyond the control of the people who pay for them; they seem to go on despite their own ineffectiveness. Indeed, their original goals may have become, in more cases than we care to admit, ever more remote.

At an ever-spiraling cost, Social Security promises less security today than in the past, and there is growing fear that it will offer none in the future. The rest of the pension system in the United States, even with more than $700 billion in assets, gives cause for concern as well. Unfunded pension liabilities are a time bomb, particularly as a number of large companies face bankruptcy or failure. The pension guarantee fund set up under the pension reform act of 1974 could be unable to cope with the crisis. Many, if not most, municipal and state pension plans are actually unsound. That raises questions about their ability to meet future obligations at a time when taxpayers are balking at increases in taxes.

Health care costs have risen at a horrendous rate; they now represent more than 10 percent of the GNP, and no slowdown is in sight. Yet many poor people have difficulty getting access to quality health care. Employers are increasingly burdened, if not handicapped, by the costs of health insurance. General Motors, for example, pays more for health insurance than for steel—more than $3000 per employee per year. Those out of work, having lost their employee benefits, fear the impact of catastrophic illness or accident. And in spite of all that spending on health care, Americans do not live as long as people in at least ten other industrialized nations in which expenditures are significantly less.

The imprisonment of a criminal in the United States costs many thousands of dollars per year, in many cases more than the annual cost of an Ivy League education. On the average you could support a middle-class family of three on what it costs to maintain one person in prison. Costs to build, renovate, and maintain prisons run into the tens of billions of dollars. Yet there has not been any appreciable change in the crime rate, which continues to be the highest for any developed country.

The dramatic increase in cost per student in the public education system has not resulted in a corresponding increase in achievement test scores. Parents and employees lament the fact that today's students are deficient in basic reading, writing, and math skills. Perhaps even more critical is the widening gap between the technological literates and the increasing number of people left behind by today's complex technology. And our society is increasingly aware that we lack the familiarity with foreign history, culture, language, and geography necessary in a world that is increasingly international.

Looking to Alternatives to Money

Americans have always believed that any problem can be solved, particularly with money. Using money, the supply of which seemed unlimited, was the quick and easy way, and thus it tended to inhibit the creative development of alternatives. Using money was also less controversial than new ideas or approaches, and everyone came to believe that it was a panacea. (The same attitudes afflicted managers within organizations. Many of those who did try to counter traditional practices of substituting dollars for thought found themselves out of favor with those above who had stakes in the preservation and expansion of their budgets.)

Faith in the availability and power of money was held most strongly by liberals. Ironically it is the liberals, now influenced by environmentalism and the limits-to-growth theorists, who are looking hardest for ways to adapt to a time when the pie is no longer expanding. Morton Kondracke, writing in *Public Opinion* in 1982, analyzed an emerging "neoliberalism" that attempts to combine traditional values of liberalism—compassion, equity, opportunity—with today's "unpleasant" economic realities. The new liberal agenda includes a better planned and directed allocation of money as a substitute for just more money.

Massachusetts Senator Paul Tsongas is one of the neoliberals who agree with this new direction—away from "more" and toward some centrally or locally determined notion of "more effective." Tsongas would have government *do less* in the way of public spending and programs but *intervene more* to guide private investment into sectors where it is needed, such as alternative energy sources, the cities, and basic research.

One of the student leaders of the 1960s, Tom Hayden, is among those who would like to see an even bolder agenda—a program of "democratic economic planning." Hayden wants a partnership of government, labor, and business, the use of existing pension funds instead of increased taxes as the major source of capital, and emphasis on decentralization and community and employee participation.

Dealing with Society's Needs

In August 1982 a *Newsweek* cover story detailed the dangerous deterioration of America's infrastructure—roads, bridges, sewers, rails, mass transit. The decay is most acute in older industrial cities, but it is also threatening booming sun belt towns and rural communities. The cost of needed repairs around the country could run as high as $3 trillion. Historically, the pattern has been for the federal government to build major public works and leave them to the states and cities to repair. However, some municipalities are beginning to realize that they can no longer afford the maintenance, and some novel alternatives to increased funding are being found.

Cincinnati has, when feasible, adopted a policy of "planned shrinkage" of its physical plant even to the extent of declining federal grants and using its own limited funds to maintain what it already has. Says the *Newsweek* article: "As the national budget debate increasingly becomes one of guns vs. butter vs. asphalt, planned shrinkage may become the public-works policy of the future."

The public is more and more reluctant to increase taxes to alleviate major problems, even when decisions are made locally, because it has lost confidence in those who spend the money. Psychologist Daniel Yankelovich, in the June 1982 issue of *Psychology Today,* writes that the steady erosion of social authority has several major causes. One is the perception that no one in power is capable of dealing with society's problems. Nothing undermines social authority as much as public doubt that those in charge, whether at the national or local level, know what they are doing. And there is growing suspicion that those in positions of authority often act in bad faith.

In business the doubt and suspicion carry over to corporate social responsibility programs. The Reagan administration's new federalism includes reliance on the private sector to help make up the shortfalls of federal funds. Critics argue that although the problems of the 1980s bear scant resemblance to the problems of the 1950s, the beneficiaries of corporate giving have remained essentially unchanged over the 30-year period. James Hathaway, writing in *Business and Society Review,* suggests that nonspecific charities like United Way should be cut, charities that handle specific problems should be judged on the basis of essentiality, education funding should be based on severe quality control standards, and community development contributions should concentrate on providing employment and an adequate tax base. He believes corporate contributions in general should be made to organizations working on social problems whose solutions are essential to business survival.

Here again, then, are the increasingly popular themes of redirecting money rather than spending more money, of quality control, of containing overhead, of recognizing that problems haven't disappeared despite years of continuous funding. In response, new and innovative approaches are emerging. *The Flint Voice,* a biweekly blue-collar newspaper in the decaying industrial city of Flint, Michigan, recently proposed "seven ideas to save Flint." One of them was neighborhood food co-ops.

City governments have become more willing to experiment with sharing authority and speak of new public-private partnerships. The result has been an increasing diversity among cities as creative local solutions have been applied to counteract federal funding cutbacks. Another positive sign has been an upswing in participation by middle-class citizens in public affairs. And there are signs that major corporations really are redirecting and refocusing their contributions, even though they make clear that they can in no way totally replace government cutbacks. (More on this in Chapter 22.)

The International Experience

Internationally also the more-money approach has fallen on hard times. The number of countries rescheduling their external debts has grown alarmingly. Banks have known for some time that throwing good money after bad will not solve the long-range dilemma of overextended credit. One novel tack has been a turn toward barter. According to the Department of Commerce, almost a quarter of world trade is now done through some form of barter. *The Economist* reported in 1982 that France and Algeria have agreed on barter deals, as have Romania and South Africa. The Reagan administration has talked with Zaire, Chile, Peru, and Bolivia about swapping food for strategic minerals.

Did large influxes of money in the past several decades solve the problems of oil-exporting countries? In almost all of those countries, dreams of sociopolitical stability and respectability, a solid middle class, and real technological advance have remained unfulfilled. And the vision of forever unlimited money, now shattered by the decline in oil revenues, is replaced by the reality of declines in agricultural activity, increases in budget deficits, debt, and unemployment, incomplete megastructures, disaffected and disenchanted populations, domestic inflation, and economic stagnation. Many observers believe that the major influx of money in the span of a few decades caused the majority of problems now experienced by oil-producing countries.

Developing New Strategies

Most developing countries have been criticized for placing too much emphasis on money and too little emphasis on long-range solutions. It has been suggested, for example, that food aid has made it unnecessary for third world policymakers to concentrate on the fundamental problems of underdevelopment. Often cited now, even by those who were involved in food aid programs, is this Chinese proverb: "Give a man a fish, and he will live for a day; give him a net, and he will live for a lifetime." Many who lobbied for increases in foreign aid have now stepped back to observe a system that only succeeded in getting dollars transported from the developed countries to the administrative, bureaucratic, and military elements in underdeveloped countries. The new approach, now espoused by many long active on behalf of developing countries, is to replace dollars with education, decentralized technology, regional cooperative facilities, and local control over resources.

In the United States many observers, both black and white, are now saying that the welfare system traps blacks in permanent poverty. They argue that blacks need to push for programs that stress opportunities for independence and earning power rather than for more taxpayer transfer payments.

Traditional national security expenditures are also being questioned. A critical mass of interested experts, both within and outside the military establishment, is organizing around alternative methods—less costly and much more innovative—to provide long-term security in a changing world. A 1983 Heritage Foundation report criticized the appetite of the United States military forces for high-tech, supercostly weapons systems. While not advocating a defense cutback, the conservative think tank did cite the squandering of funds on weapons that are irrelevant to the probable combat needs of the country. In 1982 the Military Reform Caucus of Congress boasted fifty members, twenty six of them Republicans.

One suggestion gaining adherents is the idea of bolstering our unarmed forces working for peace (volunteer programs, networks of overseas technicians, religious missionary workers, and even a uniformed "army" trained to make and keep peace.) Constance Holden, in *Science* for May 1982, reported that the proposal to establish a national peace academy, which has been floating around Capitol Hill for years, is gaining support. Some claim that a peace academy (which would also provide a national focus for conflict resolution) might have helped resolve the Iranian hostage crisis.

Localities, tired of crime, are coming up with innovative alternatives to the law, order, and judicial systems. Ranging from Curtis Sliwa's Guardian Angels to experiments in prisoner employment programs, many of the alternatives have had encouraging results and widespread public acceptance. Mediation and arbitration are on the rise, and they have proved to be more effective and less costly than traditional litigation. The corporate community has been very much involved in devising some of these alternatives to litigation, especially those for resolving consumer and environmental disputes.

In education, too, the more-money syndrome is being countered by a range of new strategies across the nation. Libertarians call for a voucher system that would allow parents to determine for themselves the education they wish to purchase for their children. Courts support the rights of qualified parents to teach their own children. The private sector has begun to work more with academic and vocational schools to instruct, provide apprenticeships, donate equipment and materials, and even bring education within its own doors. Financial institutions, R&D firms, and hospitals are among those that have begun awarding degrees. Some companies have spun off teaching institutes that grant degrees; an example is the Wang Institute. Quality control has become a more serious exercise in many states. Among the reforms are requiring students to pass stringent tests before being graduated and having teachers pass equally stringent tests before being allowed in the classroom.

Individual responsibility for one's heath—in the form of diet and exercise and education about early diagnoses—has been touted as an alternative that is less expensive and more effective than traditional money-intensive approaches. Many corporations have begun to establish "wellness" programs to cut their high health costs. New York Telephone estimates it saves several million dollars each year through wellness programs. Some businesses are working with doctors and hospitals to save on insurance costs; for example, they get discounts in exchange for steering employees toward participating health care providers.

Many companies are joining together and wielding their collective medical purchasing power to cut costs and exercise control over providers. In Michigan, such a coalition successfully lobbied for a state law restricting hospital expansion. Near Chicago another business group monitors hospital use by employees and identifies physicians who hospitalize patients for longer than average times or who seem to provide unnecessary services. California has introduced price competition into public health services for families on welfare.

Prevention. Quality control. Alternatives. Personal energy. Longer-term perspectives. These are the new kinds of "money" being used to counter problems we face as a society. They also serve well to remind us that, as managers of society's organizations and as individuals, the challenge rests with us in creating these new solutions. During the energy crisis that followed the Arab oil cutoff in 1973, a search began for alternative forms of energy. If we look at money as a form of energy, we can begin to explore and develop alternatives.

Within the Organization

Increasingly, the budgets of public and private organizations are coming under scrutiny, and effective alternatives to dollars are prized in today's cost-conscious environment. Too often the availability of money within the organization, as in the larger society, masks the need to create long-term and more appropriate solutions.

In advertising, for instance, big budgets in the past have encouraged hiring big names to represent a company in advertising its products and services. The need to establish ongoing credibility as well as cut costs has prompted a new approach to the public: advertising by a company's own executives. People like Chrysler's Lee Iacocca and Frank Perdue of chicken fame are examples of what has come to be known as "integrity advertising."

Many R&D firms and academic labs, faced with reduced funding, are learning the advantages as well as the pitfalls of joint ventures and cooperative research endeavors.

Venture capitalists and acquisition-minded companies are learning that the managerial know-how of those running a potential acquisition target is worth more than all the dollars pumped into glamorizing the acquisition, integrating it into the larger conglomerate, and providing it with advanced management systems.

Costly interior design programs, although aimed at improving employee morale, have not improved attitudes as much as plants and wall hangings brought in from home have. A commentator in a recent *Architectural Record* noted, "We dream up efficient-looking, modern-looking offices, and the staff bring endless plants and miles of macrame to try to 'humanize' them."

Thus in almost every organizational activity, alternatives to more money are being found. The successful executives in coming years will be those who understand this fundamental shift in perspective and the opportunities inherent in it. Those managers will rise to the challenge through initiative and innovation. They will master their tasks not by creating expenses, but by creative thought and experimentation. Instead of devoting their energies to getting and keeping ever-larger budgets and staffs—the ancient and honorable practice of empire building—these managers will stimulate the creative talents of their people to blaze new trails through the petrified forest of organizational custom.

CHAPTER 16

Confusing "Bigger" and "More" with "Better"

Money, as we have noted, is no longer automatically seen as the most effective solution to a host of problems that confront organizations and society. "More," "bigger," and "higher" (in technology, education, organization size, and aspirations) also are being challenged, and the results have been new approaches to setting policy, doing business, achieving goals, and creating opportunities.

In *The New City States* (a 1982 publication for the Institute for Local Self-Reliance), David Morris, the director, writes that cities in the post–World War II era were addicted to growth but, as time went on, became disturbed by projections of the costs entailed. A 1974 study of Madison, Wisconsin, for example, estimated that a new housing development would cost $16,500 an acre for sanitary sewers, storm drainage, water mains, and local streets. Not included was the prorated cost of new schools, fire stations, arterial streets, wells, landfills, and so on.

Morris states that cities, as they gained sophistication in the planning process, began to reevaluate the accepted practice of courting big corporations to locate branch plants in them. He quotes from Neil Pierce's *Washington Post* article in May 1977:[3]

> When new industries are attracted from outside, they bring the well-advertised benefits of new jobs, orders for local suppliers, and a fresh infusion of money into a community. But there can be severe drawbacks. A firm with highly specialized labor requirements may bring its most highly paid workers with it. The jobs left for local residents may be few, menial or both. But local taxpayers will have to pay for new schools, roads, and other services for the newcomers. Capital investments to attract new firms have virtually bankrupted some communities—and even then they face the possibility that a big multinational firm may later decide there's even cheaper labor in Mexico or Taiwan and desert the area as rapidly as it came.

Corporate Giantism

There is an increasing awareness in all parts of the world that small enterprises, long neglected in favor of larger ones, may be the key to long-term economic health and growth. For the first time in several decades, public and institutional support for small, growing companies has caught fire in Britain. At the center of the action is the London Stock Exchange's new Unlisted Securities Market (USM), which was specially designed to raise money for small companies and their owners. USM's performance has been impressive. Significantly in what has been considered since World War II to be a declining industrial power, most of the volume is accounted for by small investors.

The great French historian, Fernand Braudel, interviewed by *Forbes,* comments:[4]

> If I were ruler of France . . . I wouldn't worry too much about the larger firms, because to give them money is to prevent society from reforming itself. Instead of spending on the multinationals, I'd spend it on the small enterprises, because they're the ones that find the new solutions. . . . What succeeds is five or six people. In science as well as production, I favor small enterprises.

Latin American countries will have to create four million new jobs a year to satisfy their growing populations. The strategy adopted by a number of countries is to stimulate the development of small business and so boost job creation. Colombia, for example, has instituted a number of programs partly funded by the Inter-American Development Bank. IDB-financed programs involve everything from management training to setting up revolving credit funds for small business clients. These programs are supported by the public and private sectors. Both agree that the investment required to produce one job in a large company is an amount sufficient to create twenty-five jobs in small business.

Management studies and articles provide evidence that small business firms in the United States account for a large share of major innovations in technology, that their rates of growth generally outpace those of major corporations, and that they have generated much if not most of the growth in employment during the past decade. Congress has enacted legislation channeling R&D funds and incentives to small business. Berkley Bedell, Democratic congressman from Iowa and chairman of the House Small Business Subcommittee on Energy and Environment, wrote in *The New York Times* in November 1981 that to concentrate R&D efforts among large centralized institutions virtually assures that we will be dependent upon those who have the greatest stake in maintaining the status quo—which will only exacerbate our current technological problems.

The 1970s saw two parallel developments in business size. Entrepreneurial activity exploded on the scene in the late 1970s; new businesses are now starting at the rate of 600,000 a year. But corporate giantism also reached new heights. The 1980s opened with one of the biggest and most publicly embarrassing conglomeration contests: the four-way Allied–Bendix–Martin Marietta–United Technologies imbroglio.

Edgar Bronfman, chairman and CEO of Seagram (himself involved earlier in a costly and embarrassing merger fight), commented on this transaction in the September 29, 1982 issue of *The New York Times:*

"Maybe there's something wrong with our system when these four companies line up large amounts of money in order to purchase stock, when it doesn't help build one new factory, buy one more piece of equipment, or provide even one more job." Bronfman goes on to observe that when two would-be borrowers are seeking credit, the cost of money goes up. High interest rates have been called the biggest barrier to economic recovery; they put a new home or a new car beyond the reach of many potential buyers. If the interest on money borrowed for corporate takeovers—specifically to purchase the common stock of another corporation—were not tax-deductible, takeover activity would be sharply curtailed. Banks would have billions of dollars to lend more creatively; the supply of credit would increase; and interest rates would probably drop.

In the wake of numerous highly publicized mergers and acquisitions comes the countertrend that had been predicted by those who decry the inefficiencies of bigness in business. Many companies are deconglomerating, divesting themselves of divisions and subsidiaries. One reason is that the high cost of money and depressed equity markets at the beginning of the decade forced companies to look for alternative ways to generate cash. Another is that the units being sold were often poor performers that drained strength from the organization. A third is that, with industry lines growing fuzzier and competition coming from unexpected and uncharted directions, companies have felt the need to retrench, slim down, and concentrate on what they do best. A fourth, and one much to the point of this chapter, is the inefficiencies of scale. Many "mom and pop" companies bought up by major conglomerates in the 1960s and 1970s have failed to generate the same sort of returns after being acquired by the new parent. That is because smaller, family-operated, and closely held companies operate by different sets of rules—interpersonal, financial, client-related, and otherwise. Here is a sampling of the differences that we have identified as key over the past several years:

■ Small companies demand more above-and-beyond-the-scope-of-duty work from managers and clerical employees. They are able to get this free as a result of shared goals, commitment, knowledge of the organization, and direct relationship to the top. Once the company is acquired or grows much larger, lines of reporting are more rigid, personal interaction from bottom up diminishes, work becomes professionalized rather than personalized, and the expectation is for direct and adequate remuneration for work performed. Thus, hours of commitment and work decrease while pay increases.

■ Small companies more closely control costs on a voluntary basis. Costs are more easily isolated and identified than in larger organizations, and employees who incur expenses are seen as diminishing the worth of all others. (That is not a directly recognizable fact in large organizations).

■ Duplication of effort is much less likely in smaller organizations. More is known of what each worker is doing, and resources are used more sparingly.

■ The spark or genius that resided within the original founders and builders—and the know-how that accompanied the entrepreneurial thrust—are not fostered, appreciated, exploited, or recognized once the smaller company is acquired or expands. Thus, the acquired business often switches to a more professionally oriented management style characteristic of the parent company. Field relations, market savvy, flexibility (or stubborn rigidity, as the case may be) tend to deteriorate. The business ceases to grow at the expected rate; and even if it does grow, returns are not commensurate with the new effort, risk, and breadth of undertaking.

■ Similarly, the vision that drives company founders makes acceptable the often long and difficult struggle to create or penetrate a market. A big corporation's concern for the short-term bottom line often dims vision.

■ In smaller units, employees are willing to trade off pay for a sense of direct contribution and personal growth in the accomplishment of the organization's effectiveness. Once a large, more bureaucratic form is overlaid on the smaller, these psychic rewards are removed and the trade-offs evaporate.

■ The mistaken assumption that bigger is better often obscures the reason for the original success of the smaller enterprise: it served a target market with a high-quality product or service as opposed to the mass-marketed, mid-grade product delivered by most larger organizations.

■ Economies of scale, like most economic concepts, works better in books than in the real world. Too often the money is saved at the cost of human spirit.

Not all of these distinctions are true of all cases, but enough of them are true enough of the time to lead to an inescapable conclusion: big is not always better.

However, to be balanced in our assessment, it is necessary to acknowledge that there are cases in which mergers and acquisitions, both horizontal and vertical, can better serve the customer by reducing prices and can better help the company by ensuring access to the necessary components in the production and delivery of goods and services. Recent trends have been toward a more sensible ground: merger guidelines are being relaxed when relaxation is in the public interest or supports public policy goals, and managers are deciding in many cases that empire building is no longer a sufficient reason for mergers or acquisitions.

Big Technology

Much of the debate about big versus small or centralized versus decentralized has centered on energy in recent years. The Canadian Alsands Consortium's decision in 1982 to abandon a $13 billion oil sands development in northern Alberta seriously threatened the stability of Canada's economy and forced the government to reassess its economic strategy. Disappointed by the cancellation, Alberta's prime minister was subsequently quoted in *The Wall Street Journal* as saying, "Perhaps this isn't the era of the large project." Noting that the Alaskan pipeline and U.S. synthetic fuels projects were running into trouble, he wondered if it was time to reexamine our views and perhaps recognize this era as one of smaller is beautiful. The late E. F. Schumacher, author of *Small Is Beautiful: Economics as if People Mattered,* might have appreciated that rueful acknowledgement of one of the key concepts of the decentralizers by a high government official.

The relatively new information industry, a major growth business for the future, is already facing the issue of big versus small. Stephen McClellan, President of Computer Industry Analyst Group, believes that accelerating technology and customer sophistication are driving the industry toward specialization, by far the most important trend in the industry. Writing in the June 1982 edition of *Datamation,* McClellan says it is now advantageous to be a "small" company, with annual sales of around $1 billion or less. Large size is a burden; it invariably leads to tardy decision making, slow product development, and diffused market emphasis. Smaller companies, he maintains, can more easily specialize, offer more exciting work environments, and attract the most creative people. They can grow faster, and their stock prices often rise more rapidly than those of larger companies do.

In long-established industries, such as agriculture, many mistakes have been made in the pursuit of "more is better." Observers point out that many of the major famines, for example, have actually taken place when there has been moderate to good availability of food. Starvation has been more a political matter of distribution than a technical matter of availability.

Richard Critchfield, in the Fall 1982 issue of *Foreign Affairs,* says the third world is undergoing a quiet agricultural revolution that differs from our own in three fundamental ways:

■ It is 50 years later than ours and therefore uses recent advances in biotechnology to increase output. Biotechnology, unlike mechanical technology, does not demand the same substitution of capital for labor and hence can be more rather than less labor-intensive.

■ Peasants are involved. Their culture is highly dependent upon a village—the basic economic unit.

■ The vast populations are beyond our own experience.

In this analysis, as in many others like it, the author concludes that the newest scientific knowledge can be most helpful when based on a small-is-beautiful model that actually allows for decentralization and labor-intensive solutions. In other cases the new technologies have been attacked for their destructive impact. *The New York Times* reported in June 1982 that two decades after the green revolution arrived in the Philippines its miracles in high-yield cereal and vegetable production have lost their luster and a nationwide search is being conducted for indigenous varieties of rice, corn, and vegetables that have become scarce. Government figures show that in two decades 75 percent of the country's rice lands were switched to high-yield seeds requiring heavy doses of chemical fertilizers and pesticides. The country was able to become self-sufficient in rice, but small farmers have gone into debt keeping up with the cost of fertilizers and other farm chemicals. The green revolution did increase yields, but it contaminated the environment, decreased the supply of fish (the waters were chemically poisoned), and disrupted the rural economy. The seed-retrieval program seeks to rebuild the national genetic pool of plants geared to small farmers and find medicinal plants and special trees useful in increasing the incomes of small farmers.

This battle between the adherents of "big" high technology and the Schumacherites, Neo-Luddites, and other foes of uncontrolled technological development will be a fierce one in the coming decade. No doubt, technology will continue to be instrumental in many positive developments, even those of the small-is-beautiful school. On the other hand, there are some charming stories that depict the mix of primitive, small-scale solutions with high-tech applications. Here are two such examples:

> Couriers for Lockheed Missiles and Space Company had to spend one and one-half hours carrying printouts from a computer back to the designers 20 miles away. Designs done one day did not arrive until mid-afternoon the following day. Carrier pigeons now make the trip

in 20 minutes, delivering early the following morning. The pigeons
can carry a day's work—microfilm of 30 or 40 blueprints—at a cost
of about $1.50.[5]

Scientists in Paris have transformed trout into the world's first
bionic pollution detector. The olfactory lobes of a fish's brain display
changes in electrical activity as a fish senses chemicals. With a tiny
transmitter sitting atop electrodes in the fish's head, and a personal
computer to analyze the frequencies composing the signal, researchers can distinguish pollutants well below the recommended minimum
levels permitted in water.[6]

Making Things
Manageable

During the first half of the 1970s, attention was given to the topics of
complexity and high technology; some of it grew out of studies of the
effect of high-technology industries in less-developed countries. E. F.
Schumacher prompted a host of synonyms for his basic concept, including "appropriate technology," "intermediate technology," and "technology as if people mattered." These words appeared quite a bit in
print, in speeches, and at cocktail parties. But since the late 1970s, it
seems, they have been used less frequently. That might give the im-
pression that the era of small-is-beautiful has waned.

On the contrary, a new spirit has emerged in the United States from
the 1970s; it is characterized by a search for independence and simplicity. People are changing their ways of living, either in their present
homes and neighborhoods or, as data from the 1980 census indicate, by
joining a widespread national migration to new and scattered developments that are distinctly different from central cities, the suburbs, and
prime agricultural areas. In a sense, a significant segment of the population is rebelling against the imperatives of large and complex high-
technology environments. Among the factors contributing to this
search for simplicity and independence are the threat of unemployment, the desire to create small businesses that reflect and satisfy
individual identity, economic uncertainty that causes grave concern
for such basics as housing, food, clothing, and medicine, energy shortages, remote and centralized decision making in government that does
not reflect local needs or interests, a desire for safety and protection
from exposure to such spin-offs of high technology as nuclear hazards,
food additives, and toxic chemicals, the inability of existing technologies to keep up with basic needs such as the problems of waste
disposal, and a desire for creativity in the arts and crafts.

Leopold Kohr, author of *The Breakdown of Nations,* is one of a group of intellectuals who believe that, when something is wrong, it is be-cause it is too big. Aggression, brutality, and other diseases, he wrote,[7]

> [emerge because] human beings, so charming as individuals or in small aggregations, have been welded into overconcentrated social units such as mobs, unions, cartels, or great powers. That is when they begin to slide into uncontrollable catastrophe. The problem is not to grow but to stop growing; the answer: not union but division.

Kohr and others, like John Papworth (founder of the British periodical *Resurgence*) and Ivan Illich, believe that progress and indeed survival depend upon the ability of our institutions to shrink enough so they can be manageable and more adequately responsive to human control.

Rory O'Connor notes in *The Atlantic* for May 1982 that these theo-rists share a vision of a future fourth world, a concept of a multicellu-lar, power-dispersed organic existence, in which people can determine the pattern of their own lives. They are fighting a common enemy—giantism. Doing so, they organized an Assembly of the Fourth World in England's Great Hall, which was to host believers from all over the world. The three-day assembly, however, turned into a fiasco, mainly because it was—you guessed it—too big.

The 1980 annual meeting of the World Future Society carried the same theme throughout its many sessions: "Thinking Globally, Acting Locally." The underlying belief was that, although we must envision ourselves as a global community, small-scale and personalized solu-tions are perhaps the long-range route to progress and survival.

Remastering Your Enterprise

Whether focused on business, political, military, or social institutions, analyses of ills seem often to turn up some of the same problems, and one of them is runaway growth. This is a critical fact to be acknowl-edged by managers and administrators of all of our institutions. Per-haps, having acknowledged it, managers can get on with the business of remastering their enterprises, their work forces, their communities, and their lives. Have you taken a fresh look lately at whether you are truly achieving economies of scale in all of your or your institution's undertakings?

In looking at your organization and its ability to respond positively and effectively to the changing environment, you must also examine your own beliefs and predilections with regard to size. Are you a victim of a culture that equates bigger with success, or are you free to evalu-ate the alternatives to growth objectively?

CHAPTER 17

Misunderstanding the New Meaning of Success

Walter Sampson, senior vice president of a giant corporation, has just returned home from the annual marketing conference, which he had planned and run, and it was the best one ever. His most recent performance review was exceptional, as were the raise and bonus he received. He has been to Europe twice this year on combined business-vacation trips, and his days are filled with meetings and gourmet lunches with important people. Yet Walter feels there is something missing in his life. He admires his son's backpacking, hitchhiking tour of the Mediterranean. He is in awe of a friend who spends afternoons coaching inner-city teenagers in track and field. Inwardly, he greatly respects the carpenter he has retained to renovate his kitchen, a man who uses his hands to create something real. Tonight Sampson is leaving for a talk he must make to a sales group in Atlanta. He is not keyed up about it; he has made the same speech in five other cities recently. He packs his bags, and he puts in a copy of Battalia and Tarrant's *The Corporate Eunuch,* the preface of which begins:

> This book is about the American corporate manager who has made it many rungs up the success ladder, who has achieved a position in which he has status, money and power, but who still feels restless and unfulfilled. This book is about how to make a success of *success.*

Several blocks away lives Eve Patterson. An extremely bright and capable young woman, she has, at age 35, already owned her own boutique, managed a travel agency, been married and divorced, and become a regional sales representative for a well-known electronics firm. She is now marketing manager for that company. She has a history of leaving every career opportunity just when it looks as though she is becoming very successful at it. Now she feels that somehow she will manage to rationalize herself out of her present position to begin anew somewhere else. Eve's problem is that she has a fear of success, and she doesn't know why. In her doctor's office recently she noticed and was intrigued by an article listed on the front cover of an issue of *Cosmopolitan.* The title was "Triumphing Over the Fear of Success."[8] Eve opened the magazine and read:

> Put succinctly, *success* simply means getting what you want. The difficulty comes in knowing what that *is.* . . . Mrs. A.J. Stanley, author of *What Constitutes Success,* said "He has achieved success who has lived well, laughed often, and loved much." Pollster Daniel Yankelovich [reports] in his book *New Rules* that whereas in the past the purpose of self-fulfillment was the improvement of one's social position (and money and status), today 66 percent of Americans consider success to mean improvement of the *self.* The attitude that what's best for your career is most important has changed. People are more

concerned about enjoying their environment and having good relationships. Social psychologist Maxine Schrall has come up with a
term for this antimaterialistic drive toward success: "lateral
mobility."

Eve read on until she reached a passage that struck to the heart of
her own feelings. In exploring fear of success (FOS), the author wrote:

> Nobody will ever argue that success doesn't bring confrontation with
> ever more demanding tasks. *Some* concern over one's ability to keep
> performing would be rational and understandable. What's inappro-
> priate—and therefore typical of FOS victims—is that even though
> they may become TV producers or heads of corporations, they see
> themselves—the real person hiding out behind the important job—as
> incompetents. Frauds. These are the FOS victims who get to the top,
> then suffer from intolerable anxiety.

Not everyone feels that the song "Is That All There Is?" was written
for him or her. Not everyone has severe anxiety upon reaching a high
level of career achievement. And not everyone dreams of dropping out
of the rat race in favor of early retirement, farming, or being a tour
guide. But almost everyone has probably paused at least to consider
how one's view of success has changed at different times and in different places. Success is, for most people, highly elusive and amorphous.
For some it is power; for others it is the avoidance of pressure. None of
this, of course, is new. What is new is that the affluence and economic
expansion of the past three decades have forced more people to face
their feelings about success. And the economic contraction of recent
years has forced even more people to reconsider its value.

The Failure of Success

More than ten years ago, Richard Huber wrote *The American Idea of
Success.* The first chapter was titled "Money . . . Status . . . Fame." That
may have said it all on the surface. But the questions delved beneath
the glitter and glamour to explore not just the character attributes and
clichés that figure in becoming the classical success, but also some age-
old dilemmas:[9]

> As actors in the drama of life, we must play many roles. There is
> scarcely time to shift the scenery before we shift identities. The
> tough-minded breadwinner by day, at night becomes the loving hus-
> band and father. When our actions conflict with our beliefs, when we
> don't practice what we preach in playing our conflicting roles, the
> consequences can be psychologically disturbing. ("The Failure of Suc-
> cess," Chapter 22)

Henry David Thoreau wanted to be his own kind of self-made man at Walden Pond. He tried to live as self-sufficiently as possible, building his own shelter, growing his own food, and providing his own fuel. By simplifying the necessities of life and avoiding its superficialities, he gained precious leisure. He found freedom to enjoy nature, to read, meditate and write. ("A Different Drummer," Chapter 25)

Thoreau didn't much care about his image to the outside world. Others do. Berkeley Rice, senior editor of *Psychology Today,* wrote in September 1982 that there has been an explosive growth in the executive image industry. Listings in the *Directory of Personal Image Consultants* had grown from 37 in 1978 to 206 in the 1982 edition. In one course Rice attended, his classmates, mostly men, ranged in age from the mid-30s to the mid-50s and in status from middle-level manager to senior vice president. Many confessed insecurity about their positions—honest and painful admissions of hidden feelings of vulnerability and inadequacy. The common factor of their insecurity seemed to be change, resulting in the need to reestablish one's credentials and reputation. Wrote Rice, "After all, like Willy Loman, . . . image may be all they've got."

The Pain of Success

Writing on a similar theme in the Spring 1982 issue of *Business and Society Review,* Jay Rohrlick (Wall Street psychiatrist and author of *Work and Love*) observed that many people seek psychiatric help at high points of personal achievement. The stress of success is an overlooked but very powerful cause of psychic pain. Success—being promoted, becoming a partner, coming into wealth and power and fame—can bring with it anxiety and depression often on a par with feelings caused by serious failure. Moreover, people who have made it through individual ambition and drive are, in a sense, neglected. Most of us are initially unsympathetic with a successful person's complaints. ("I only wish I had your problems.")

Dr. Howard Hess, corporate psychiatrist for Western Electric, maintains that people are promoted to their level of pain rather than to their level of incompetence, as the Peter principle has it. They reach levels of success for which they are emotionally unequipped or which stir up sufficient inner conflict to hamper their functioning. Among the factors in success trauma are guilt, loss of peer acceptance, loss of approval by supervisors, fear of increased expectations and responsibility, identity confusion, and addiction to success.

Some people are fearful of achieving because, once rewarded, the positive response diminishes or disappears, and what they are left with is a new, higher level of baseline expectations.

University of California psychologist Richard Berry reports he is seeing many more cases of 25- to 35-year-old professionals who seek help because they have "made it and don't like it." He believes this indicates a trend toward psychological setbacks occurring much earlier than the well-reported mid-life crisis of those in their forties. Berry reported that many of today's relatively young career people made job choices on the basis of market demand and job security without considering their own personal interests. Looking for income and prestige, and selecting the best offer in the job market, they gave no thought to their own needs. This conflicted with the value system of the 1960s that encouraged "doing your own thing."

With greater public awareness of the pain and emptiness that can sometimes come with outward success, less extrinsic pressure is placed on today's individuals to succeed. Society as a whole—and friends and relations—are more willing to accept individual variations in the definitions of success. Andrew Carnegie once remarked, "You can't push anyone up the ladder unless he is willing to climb himself." In a ground-breaking study in 1981, AT&T found that scarcely 30 percent of its current generation of younger potential managers expressed a desire for advancement. Of managers with 20 years at the company, as many as one-third deemed advancement as "not important." Only 36 percent of these older managers said they would give up more personal time for career success.

Inflation has played no small role in this reassessment of success. In an age of affluence and easy credit, it was not very difficult to keep up with the Joneses—or, for that matter, the Astors. But in trying, many people found that the security they thought they had gained was really something else. *The New York Times* reported, on December 20, 1981, that falling into debt has become "as American as apple pie." According to a survey released by a former commissioner of New York City's Department of Consumer Affairs, the profile of a typical debt-ridden person has changed dramatically. No longer are problems of overextended credit and the inability to keep up payments confined to the so-called lower class. Instead, now more and more of those seeking counseling to avoid defaulting are the affluent and the skilled.

Success and Health

The impact of economic stress on health has not gone unnoticed. In this time of organizational retrenchment, the number of white-collar deaths has risen dramatically, and white-collar absenteeism is up.

Fear of job loss has permeated all levels of organizations, and even survivors, though spared, often find themselves overworked and over-pressured at a time when they can no longer be sure of their jobs. The feeling that for many they are newly expendable is raising for the first time the question of whether their careers have truly brought them success.

Congress asked M. Harvey Brennan, professor at the Johns Hopkins School of Public Health, to determine the correlation, if any, between economic recession and health. His study indicated that, when unem-ployment rises 1 percent, first-time admissions to state mental hospi-tals increase 4.3 percent for men and 2.3 percent for women, suicides go up 4.1 percent, murders go up 5.7 percent, and state prison popula-tions increase by 4 percent. Over a 6-year stretch following a jump in the jobless rate, 1.9 percent more people die of heart disease, cirrhosis, and other stress-related chronic ailments.

Carin Rubenstein, drawing from the *Psychology Today* survey of "Beliefs about Health" in the October 1982 issue, reports that "like so many Gatsbys in jogging suits, Americans are chasing an ideal of perfect health. Many of us, in fact, now spend more time thinking about our health than about love or money." The survey findings sug-gest that many Americans, feeling powerless to effect changes in their private lives, see physical health as their last bastion of personal con-trol—something that they themselves can influence.

Health has become a status symbol. Good health is chic, as are many of the things one might do to achieve it. Reviewing Jane Fonda's *Work-out Book,* Charles Krauthammer wrote sarcastically in the August 16, 1982 issue of *The New Republic* that, given the phenomenal success of the book and the current fitness craze, it could be that Fonda has finally found the basis for American socialism: body worship. He con-tended that it is clear that the fitness craze has little to do with gender and much to do with class. Exercise is the new middle-class hobby.

Thus, for many, status is not only wearing designer clothes on the tennis court, being photographed in the marathon, vacationing in As-pen, or being seen on the golf course with the right people. It is also working, often very hard, to keep one's body fit through exercise, proper nutrition, reduction of stress, and altered lifestyle (giving up smoking and drinking, getting enough sleep, etc.).

Status Shifts

There have been other shifts too. Status was once inextricably linked to one's possessions—how many, how big, how costly. But consumption is no longer synonymous with achievement. Camillo Pagano, a top

Nestlé executive, said at an International Advertising Association Conference in 1982 that advertising sometimes creates "cultural insecurities" by promoting consumption as a "global objective." He maintained that advertising is out of touch with today's highly sensitized consumer, who is seeking a new kind of message—one that concentrates on the product's intrinsic quality, its value. We are witnessing, according to him, the fading out of the consumption model that had previously driven society.

Peter Kerr reported in *The New York Times,* on September 23, 1982, that "downsized" homes were selling far better than other types of new housing. No surprise, given the economics of the times. But Kerr's commentary provided an intriguing insight into the accompanying value shift that prevents status from also being downsized: "In the decadent '60s and '70s you had larger and larger homes being built. . . . Now you see just the reverse." The use of "decadent" is particularly revealing.

There are many, especially those influenced by the ecological issue, who view much consumer behavior in the past as decadent, wasteful, unnecessary, and not truly reflecting success at all. There are now many others who, while not making such negative judgments about the past, feel that material possessions are not necessarily modern measures of success.

The Manager's Challenge

The biggest challenge facing today's managers is to cope with their own feelings about success in a time of rapid social and economic change. Obviously, managers must first explore their own inner feelings about success, either with very close family members or friends or, if that is not acceptable, with an impartial professional. There is a good possibility that such an exploration will lead to the belief that one *is* truly successful, in one's own terms. But there is also a possibility that one could find a different destiny more suitable, and that could be the most important change to master in life.

Within the organization, managers must deal with the new definition of success that might be embraced by subordinates, coworkers, and senior executives. Some of the new definitions do include sacrifice or further advancement. Many people still fit the traditional model of seeking acknowledgement through promotion and salary increases, and they are even willing to be ambitious and dedicated in order to achieve that sort of success. But others, among them some of the best and the brightest, are marching to the beat of a different drummer. Human resource policy and management counseling must take those differences into account. Only by doing so can managers help both themselves and their organizations to benefit from the changed visions of success.

And what of marketing? As Nestlé's Pagano pointed out, the significant change in values requires an equally significant change in marketing. New approaches are needed. Health is an obvious one. Leisure, education, conservation, skills acquisition, and personality development are logical bases for redirected marketing approaches. They are examples of the new kinds of symbols of successful living.

The most important point we want to leave with you is this: The new definition of success is not new, and it is not a single definition. Questioning the meaning of success is not limited to dropouts, because it is very much on the minds of some of the country's most notable achievers. It is not a leftover mind-set of the 1960s, because it goes back in American writing to the last century. Perhaps it is that, in the 1980s, we have a much wider, perhaps almost universal, acceptance of the fact that some who *look* as though they have succeeded may indeed have failed—and some who are only modest achievers may have been the most successful of all.

CHAPTER 18

Why Do We Believe in the Decline of the Work Ethic?

One of the profound social transformations resulting from the Reformation was the spread of what has now come to be called the work ethic. The idea that work was a legitimate expression of worship, that it was a road to salvation, made possible a great many developments in western civilization, including the Industrial Revolution and all of its ramifications. The work ethic not only made possible enterprises of great moment; it helped keep them from going awry. It provided the solid underpinning for such characteristics of our time as mass production, capitalism, specialization of labor, income-earning women, and multibillion dollar corporations.

There is now a substantial body of opinion that there has been an erosion of the work ethic in western society—in particular, in the United States. It is based on a number of recent phenomena:

■ An apparent change in attitudes toward work has taken place particularly among younger, blue-collar workers, who appear to question the validity of an ethic that glorifies work, while advanced technology and social support programs blur the connection between effort and reward.

■ Opinion polls seem to show that workers no longer care about their jobs. Of the people surveyed in a 1955 Gallup poll, 40 percent said they enjoyed work more than leisure; by 1980 the figure had dropped to 24 percent. The drop was almost entirely among younger people. According to Opinion Research Corporation, American workers, including middle managers, are more dissatisfied with their jobs now than at any time since the 1950s.

■ The savings rate in the United States, consistently about 5 percent, is relatively low compared with that in most other industrialized nations. This is taken as a manifestation of a *carpe diem* attitude, the antithesis of the work ethic's emphasis on deferred gratification and reward.

■ A drastic decline in the rate of productivity growth has occurred in American industry since the middle 1970s. This is probably the most critical factor in our ability to compete effectively in the international economic arena. Concern over productivity declines is manifested on two levels: (1) the overall effect on the U.S. economy and (2) the impact on an individual organization such as an automobile company.

■ A host of behavioral changes can be taken as reflections of a people less driven to work hard, sacrifice, succeed (as success has traditionally been defined in western industrial society), contribute to the general welfare, and deny themselves the pleasures of the flesh and of idleness.

Self-realization

The relative decline in commitment to work as an expression of faith, as a duty to God, quite naturally leads to questions: "Who, then, am I working for? And why?" It is this shift in focus that perhaps led some observers of American society in the 1970s to use terms such as "the age of narcissism" and "the me generation." People were now working for self-benefit, whereas under the traditional work ethic they put other people and even posterity ahead of themselves and the present.

We have seen people concerned, even obsessed, with questioning. How am I feeling? Am I fulfilled? How fully am I expressing myself? How well am I using my time to benefit me? And, for that matter, who am I? This questioning both causes and is caused by the desire for instant gratification and a concomitant lessening of concern for society. The guilt over self-indulgence that the work ethic fosters fades as a consequence, and work for the sake of working no longer makes sense.

It also leads to new expectations from work, to what Daniel Bell, Daniel Yankelovich, and others have called the psychology of entitlement. If a place in Heaven is no longer sufficient to justify or compensate for a life of drudgery, what is? Money? Yes, but not entirely, particularly for those already making a good living. Thus we have seen growing focus on what has come to be called the quality of worklife (QWL). What it seems to mean is humanizing the workplace. And beneath that, what it means is treating each individual worker according to a high standard of individual dignity and worth. At the very least, this implies that the end of work is not work itself, nor is it merely for the good of the organization or the society. Work, in this perspective, has as its end the gratification of the individual.

Well, we can't all be cowboys or professional athletes or famous artists. Jobs like those provide plenty of self-gratification. For the rest of us, whose jobs are often if not always dull and seemingly meaningless, the gratification has to be added. From that comes the demand for QWL—a shorter workweek, more benefits, more individualization of treatment, participation in decision making, and so on. And since the 1950s, management has largely accepted the underlying premise: the work ethic has eroded, and the workers will have to be made happy instead.

Do Workers Really Want to Work?

The problem is that all this is not necessarily entirely correct. As social psychologist and pollster Daniel Yankelovich pointed out in a brilliant article in *Psychology Today* (May 1982), the work ethic is alive and well; the fact is, it's underemployed. His analysis of survey data supports a belief that the work ethic is, if anything, growing stronger. He cites a 1980 Gallup study showing that 88 percent of working Americans feel that it is personally important to them to work hard and do their best on the job. Such studies, he feels, suggest that "there are large reservoirs of potential upon which management can draw to improve performance and increase productivity."

A 1980 United States Department of Education survey of 58,000 high school students showed that almost two-thirds of them held part-time jobs. Almost universally, they understood the need to work for what they wanted and were willing to do so. A UCLA survey of incoming college freshmen showed almost identical results. In *The Soul of a New Machine,* his 1982 Pulitzer prize–winning book, author Tracy Kidder describes how a group of young engineers routinely and eagerly worked 60- to 80-hour weeks creating a new computer. Kidder compares them to the medieval craftsmen who built "temples to God . . . the root of work that gave meaning to life." And certainly the extraordinary increase in entrepreneurship in recent years demonstrates that Americans are not unwilling to work hard.

So it is possible that American management has been fighting the wrong battle, and maybe with the wrong weapons as well. There is, to our knowledge, no documented correlation between worker happiness and productivity. And there is certainly no evidence that focus on QWL increases either worker happiness or productivity. There are already signs that some rethinking is going on. In a 1982 speech Richard N. Clarke, chief executive officer of Celanese Canada, criticized the emphasis on gaining productivity through making workers happy. His contention was that a company should first concentrate on growth and productivity, and "this will establish a workable and meaningful foundation for individual satisfaction."

The idea that the best way to make people happy is to let them be part of a thriving enterprise is being abetted by technological developments that promise increased productivity regardless of the emotional state of people. Take, for an example, computer-aided design and computer-aided manufacture (CAD/CAM). *Fortune* not too long ago called CAD/CAM the new industrial revolution, saying it had "more potential to increase productivity than any other development since electricity." Even allowing for journalistic hyperbole, CAD/CAM, robotics, and other technologies do seem likely to make industry more efficient. But not without costs, as noted in earlier chapters.

The issue of productivity itself is not anywhere near as simple as, unfortunately, most discussions about it are. It is not merely a matter of dividing output by number of employees. For one thing, the expansion of management ranks since the early 1960s to accommodate the

new educated generation has substantially altered the ratio of managers to workers. And the argument can be made that managers don't
produce anything. The Japanese have a much lower ratio of managers
to workers and a much slimmer management structure than we have.
A typical large Japanese industrial firm may have five layers of management between worker and CEO; a comparable American company
could have as many as fifteen. There is dawning recognition that we
may have too many managers. As a consequence, many companies are
trimming management ranks. It remains to be seen what effects that
will have on productivity.

The bureaucratization of business has undoubtedly been, on balance,
deleterious to productivity. The efforts to avoid responsibility, to seek
the no-fault decision making that characterizes a bureaucracy, are
antithetical to efficiency. The hiring of lawyers—AT&T just prior to
its breakup had 1000—symbolizes the CYA (cover your ass) mentality
that has reduced management vigor. And, of course, the enormous
costs in time and personnel of compliance with regulation have to be
considered.

In sum, you cannot address the issue of productivity with any hope of
effectiveness unless you take into account the complex interactions of
structural changes here and abroad, a changed and changing
sociopolitical environment, and most particularly, whether the decline
of the work ethic is a myth or a reality.

It is obvious to any objective observer that most people are willing to
work hard. The apparent shirker at the plant or office more often than
not slaves enthusiastically at home finishing furniture or weeding a
garden or repairing a car. People starting their own businesses put in
12 or more hours a day, 7 days a week. Adult education is thriving as
never before, as people work hard at learning new subjects and new
skills. Japanese executives open factories in the United States and
praise the commitment and quality of the workers they employ.

As Yankelovich points out, perhaps the fault is not in the work ethic
of the workers but in management and the existing reward system. He
feels that workers in too many cases don't have to make greater efforts
on the job because they are cushioned against accountability, and they
believe too often that others, not themselves, will be the beneficiaries
of greater efforts. Most Americans, it appears, are willing to work
harder and better; indeed, as Yankelovich says, their self-esteem demands it.

The System Is
the Problem

Managers need to question their own ready acceptance of the myth
that the work ethic has declined. (Indeed, any simple, easy answer to a

complex problem should be looked upon with suspicion.) Instead, managers ought to examine what in the current system may be contributing to the problem. For example, are such procedures as annual salary reviews, automatic increases, and linking of both pay and raises to job classifications counterproductive because they weaken the link between performance and reward?

As more and more people are involved in service rather than production, as more and more people work with information rather than goods, their work seems ever more abstract. (Have you ever tried to explain your job to a child?) For most of us, the higher the degree of abstraction in the job, the more we are troubled by the lack of concreteness and the more we need to find meaningfulness in what we do. Managers have to help those who work for them find it; they have to help individual workers satisfy their need for self-esteem, for knowing that they have done a real job well. That requires a closer link between job and reward, a greater degree of individual treatment, and a clear and pervasive understanding that the individual is accountable for performance.

CHAPTER 19

Overmanaging

A society should be at least as good as the sum of its parts, but our society is not. Our reliance on management has produced a society that is less than it could be. We are collectively much less than we are individually. Management suppresses and limits, diminishes the quality and quantity of our human responses.

Richard Cornuelle
De-Managing America[10]

When Tenneco acquired Houston Oil and Minerals Corporation, it shortly began to face an unintended by-product of its action. Houston Oil's key people began, and continued, to leave. The best exploration talent left to join better-paying and less-structured independent producers or to become entrepreneurs themselves. In reporting on this in 1982, *The Wall Street Journal* attributed it to Tenneco's rigid, formal structure. The hierarchy in a huge corporation, noted reporter George Getschaw, produces a frustrating and impersonal system. Small companies, on the other hand, provide freewheeling explorationists the opportunity to express themselves professionally without oversupervision and unnecessary bureaucracy. The ability to generate ideas, move on them quickly, and see their impact on the bottom line is important to such people.

In recent years much has been made of the difference between American and Japanese management styles. Bureaucracy has been faulted in both environments, but for different reasons. The Japanese stifle inventiveness at certain levels of development—as in schools, for example, because of the requirement to show respect for the authority and knowledge of the teacher. But in the workplace the Japanese system entails telling the worker what the objectives are and then delegating to him or her the responsibility for deciding how to achieve them. In the United States, some argue, there is more emphasis on process than on objectives, and innovation is frustrated by limits imposed on the ability to be inventive and productive.

Gene Amdahl was once IBM's most brilliant designer. IBM was slow to exploit his ideas, so he left to form his own company. Some say that if he had been in a Japanese firm, Dr. Amdahl might have realized his dreams without having to leave the company. Amdahl has become symbolic of the inability of mavericks to succeed in large American corporations, even those supposedly in the vanguard of technological development.

The Weaknesses of
Formula Management

Stanford's Richard Pascale is one of the foremost analysts of the differences between the U.S. and Japanese systems. He believes that the Japanese are distrustful of master strategies and concepts because they view them as limiting peripheral vision, which can enable one to pick up changes in the customer or technology or competition. Consequently, they regard our management by strategic formulas as one of our major weaknesses. Their success in the high-quality small-car market, for example, did not result from bold insight by a few big brains at the top; it happened because senior managers were humble enough not to take their initial strategic positions too seriously. In Japan, middle and upper management view their primary task as guiding input from below rather than steering the organization from above along a predetermined strategic course. The Japanese, therefore, have not been strategic planners; they have been strategic accommodators. They have supermanaged by accepting the fact that there *is* change and accommodating themselves to it rather than, like American managers so often, resisting it.

Pascale is not the only observer to fault American corporations and business schools for relying too greatly on the analytic approach that leads to theories and abstractions that, when rigidly applied, stifle entrepreneurship, innovation, and productivity. Two professors at Harvard's Graduate School of Business—William Abernathy and Robert Hayes—also are outspoken critics of American business for excessively valuing analytic detachment over insight that comes from hands-on experience. Indeed, in early 1982 Harvard's Graduate School of Business reduced the students' workload to allow more time for working with corporations in the field.

Standard MBA programs are coming under attack today. Future managers, many believe, are being schooled too much in accounting, analysis, and arrogance. Some say they are people who are taught to count rather than taught that people count. Others disagree and argue that business schools are graduating well-rounded managers. In any event, the MBA degree has become as common and necessary a credential for entry-level managers today as a bachelor's degree was in the 1940s. Can United States business absorb many more traditionally trained bottom-line disciples without losing still more of the innovation and enthusiasm that made possible its previous eras of success? And even in a well-rounded MBA program, do future managers develop those special and individual talents and energies that make for success?

Discounted cash flow analysis has been used as an example of a widespread management technique gone amiss. Robert Hayes and another Harvard colleague, David Garvin, note that American managers have turned to sophisticated analytic tools to evaluate proposed investments. The goal has been greater rationality in making investment decisions, yet the end results have been quite different: a serious underinvestment in the capital stock (the productive capacity, technology, and worker skills) necessary for viability. As techniques for using discounting calculations have gained acceptance in investment decisions, the growth of capital investment and R&D spending in this country has slowed. Hayes and Garvin believe this is more than simple coincidence. In an article entitled "Managing as If Tomorrow Mattered," in the May-June 1982 *Harvard Business Review*, they maintained that the discounting approach contributes to a decreased willingness to invest for two reasons: (1) It is often based on misperception of the past and present economic environment and (2) it is biased against investment because of critical errors in the way the theory is applied. The willingness of managers to view the future through the reversed telescope of discounted cash flow analysis is seriously shortchanging the future of their companies.

Breaking Away

Thomas Peters and Robert Waterman, in their best-selling book, *In Search of Excellence,* reported on their extensive analysis of sixty-two successful companies including IBM, DEC, 3M, and Hewlett-Packard. One avenue of their exploration was major new-product successes and failures. In every instance of success, the winning program was carried out by an "irreverent champion" who kept the idea out of the mainstream of the business. In all cases of failure, the program, idea, or champion had fallen into the tangle of the strategic planning process. The bureaucratic planning process, rather than enhance creative action, literally shut it down. (Readers wishing a fuller understanding of this highly important point should read Tracy Kidder's *The Soul of a New Machine.*)

Dartmouth's James Briant Quinn, a leading authority on innovation, concludes that fanaticism within an organization is crucial for rejuvenation and creativity. Economist Burton Klein, in examining fifty major innovations in the American economy over the last several decades, determined that none came from the company that was the industry leader at the time of the innovation. Even in the scientific community, professionals lament the diversion of technical talent into administrative matters and the massive detail demanded today in the application for and presentation of research grants. Assessment panels, committees, budget reviews, and the like are seen as overdirecting, overmanaging, and overadministering the course of basic research in this country to the detriment of creativity and innovation.

Teachers have been taking the brunt of the negative assessment of schools today. The real problem, however, is with administrations that overmanage the intellectual process; they require paperwork and structured plans that can drive even the most dedicated teachers out of the profession. The practice of management in the United States, in both public and private institutions, is based upon an implied view of human nature that owes more to military tradition than to anything else. People have to be directed, according to this perception; they have to be motivated—by fear, greed, praise, or whatever means—to perform their functions. But theorists and practitioners alike are beginning to understand that one does not motivate workers, one enables or encourages them to motivate themselves.

Learning to Forget

A great deal of the problem rests with an organization's inability to respond effectively to external change. When a response does occur, it tends to accommodate all the baggage acquired in all previous trips through the change process. Thus, new systems are heaped upon old, and little thought is given to how one might first clean out the existing structure. Sir Leuan Maddock of Oxford perhaps gives us the best language with which to discuss this point. He speaks of the difference between learning curves (which all organizations prize but which are fairly easy to institute) and forgetting curves (processes by which old or outdated skills are shed, old attitudes are discarded, old plants are scrapped, and old traditions are rejected). He contends that forgetting curves contribute more to success in engineering-based industries than do learning curves. Failures may be caused not so much by learning curves being too gentle as by forgetting curves being too gentle. To cling to outmoded methods of manufacture, old product lines, old markets, or old attitudes is to let newcomers race ahead. Completely new enterprises, on the other hand, have nothing to forget.

When John Welch, Jr., became CEO at General Electric in 1982, he began by focusing on forgetting. Welch blames the foreign threat to GE and other American companies, at least in part, on many of the management principles that GE itself espoused and pioneered in the preceding two decades—a time, Welch observes, when companies were "managed, not led." He says that managing assets as if they were investment portfolios, seeking short-term profits at the expense of long-term soundness, and emphasizing conservatism over innovation may have placed many American companies at a permanent disadvantage. He now wants GE executives to behave like entrepreneurs, not managerial bureaucrats. He is quoted in a recent *The Wall Street Journal* as "trying to reshape GE in the minds of its employees as a band of small businesses . . . to take the strength of a large company and act with the agility of a small company."

All this comes at a time when personal computers are proliferating and organizations speak of managing information more closely. Information housed in personal data systems can differ quite a bit from that traditionally centralized in an organization, because managers gather data that are never incorporated into central banks. It is estimated that over 200,000 personal computers are being used by white-collar employees in their daily work activities, a number expected to reach 400,000 by 1985. Although "experts" insist this must be better managed, others argue that it could be the very tear in the overmanagement blanket that could lead to revitalization of the overall system.

A Matter of Individual Style

It has become too easy to not think about the problem of overmanaging. One reason is the spate of books that neatly package motivational tricks and treat their readers as a uniformly styled population. Many of these books become best sellers, and everyone jumps on a new standardized theory bandwagon, with the implied outcome being across-the-board managerial improvement. Observation tells another story, one that cannot so easily be written about, taught, or otherwise sold to an eager audience. Prepackaged advice has compounded the overmanagement problem, largely because it implies or even explicitly states that one needs only to analyze success retrospectively and then copy it. You can know exactly what Herschel Walker does and how he does it, but that doesn't mean you can do it.

Management is an art, not a science. As such, it is an expression of individual style. Most importantly, managers are people. And people, whatever they may appear to be on the surface, are different inside. Thus, different managers hear music differently, see art differently, care differently. They have different wants and needs, failings and strengths, expectations and remembrances, home lives and community lives, joys and disappointments. Some are outspoken; some are reserved; most are somewhere in between. Some have material goals; some have psychic ones; most have some combination of both. Where, in all this diversity, is the common factor?

Actually, there are two common factors. The first is the responsibility for results. The second is the diversity itself. And so, regardless of the differences, it is these factors that must be understood and reckoned with in the culture of the organization. Responsibility is a form of harnessed energy; diversity is a manifestation of energy that is elusive, unchanneled, and intangible. When the two come together, another form of energy is released, and its product can be a splendid achievement or a dreadful fiasco. But when the two are suppressed or overdirected, particularly now that workers and managers are more independent, it is increasingly likely that the result will be mediocrity and frustration.

A key, then, is to allow the continual bursts of energy to happen and hope to head off the fiascos. But reality teaches us that if an enterprise is to achieve notable success, it will have to accept the fact that there could be equally significant setbacks. Such is the nature of risk, and everyone agrees that ours is a risky time. But this simple truth is what many managers seek to insulate themselves from.

We come, therefore, to the core of the problem: Many managers are intimidated by the prospect of giving up control because they fear negative results. What are some institutional myths that herd them toward overmanaging when, in their personal lives, they value the freedom to act, think, be challenged, and succeed on individual merits and unique contributions?

■ The belief that paperwork is an indication of work, of progress, of contribution. Observing the rituals of paperwork drains crucial energy from the achieving of real results in real operations.

■ The belief in the wisdom of the executives at the top or, even worse, their own belief in their wisdom.

■ The belief that one or a few external factors, such as changes in the price of the company's stock or the activities of just one competitor or the wishes of a politically or financially important constituent, are overwhelmingly important.

These are the barriers to the release of energy in any organization, public or private, large or small, and they prevent the organization from realizing its true potential for growth and success. These are the sorts of pressures, along with poorly designed compensation schemes, that frustrate the creative instinct and lead to overmanaging. They create an organizational environment in which the bright reds and vibrant greens of individual creativity and enterprise are so blended as to become the color of mud.

What Can You Do?

Effective managers will be those who understand the difference between a patronizing pat on the back and serious consideration of thoughtful ideas and solutions. (Serious consideration is more than ritual consideration. It entails a willingness to act on any idea, however unorthodox, that seems to be in the best interests of the organization.) Effective managers will be those who have somehow survived the debilitating illness of overmanaging (and that may take a good deal of introspection as well as organizational reshaping) or who have escaped it altogether. Here are some helpful guides:

■ Because GE tends to be a trendsetter generally, the Welch approach, including spin-off ventures undertaken by this major corporation, is worth studying. Perhaps what GE is doing is not totally applicable elsewhere, but parts of the new approach may be worth experimenting with in some form.

■ Intrapreneurialism, mentioned earlier in this book, is a concept introduced by management consultant Gifford Pinchot III. It is an organized process to encourage entrepreneurialism within large companies, and it should be looked into for what the process can teach you about ways to get around resistance to relinquishing overmanagement practices.

■ There are a number of recent books on the encouragement of entrepreneurial conduct within the organizational setting. You might carefully pick and choose from them some ideas that would seem to fit your personality and style and be feasible if introduced into the culture of your own organization. Be willing to work from small successes and to know yourself better than you may already; because if a good idea fails, you may have been the key saboteur without even knowing it. Your reluctance to take risks may dampen whatever efforts you make on the surface to ease up on overmanaging.

■ Paperwork should by fiat be cut across the board. Access to the copier should be limited, or quotas set, and all bureaucratic processes should be studied with an eye toward the elimination of, say, 25 percent of all written reporting procedures. These suggestions may sound frivolous. We are aware that many procedures are instituted as a matter of conforming to legal or regulatory requirements, but we are also aware that sometimes sweeping, across-the-board measures are necessary to weed out the unimportant, wasteful, and burdensome procedures that in every organization have long been carried out without thinking. Indeed, what we are proposing here is a sunset provision for bureaucratic managerial procedures. This may seem to run counter to the suggestion earlier that solutions need to fit the individual, but even within this sort of sweeping overhaul the possibilities for individualized adaptation and uniquely tailored solutions are plentiful.

■ Mavericks should not be isolated, nor should they be just tolerated. As in the old days, the court jesters may be a source of truth and wisdom. Their thinking and methods of behavior should be encouraged as a signal to others that there is no one best way to attack a problem or comport oneself. Unless in particular instances interpersonal problems become counterproductive to the goals of your operation, the acceptance of mavericks could be one of the most powerful clues you could offer to others about the nature of the environment in which they are working.

■ Examine your own life. Is it overmanaged outside the workplace? Are you too routinized, predictable, demanding of order and certainty? Change some of your own personal habits, and you may see the influence those personal changes can have on the way you manage your work environment.

PART 5

The Most Critical Factors Influencing Management Success in the Future

Evolutionary changes are not completely predictable . . . there is room in the world for what we call free will. Each individual decision to accept, resist, or change the current order alters the probability that a particular evolutionary outcome will occur.

Marvin Harris
Cannibals and Kings: The Origins of Culture[11]

CHAPTER 20

Vulnerability

If an institution is going to be responsive, it has to be insecure.

Ralph Nader

It has been said, with considerable justification, that the only constant today is change. Our civilization seems to be in a centrifuge that is accelerating wildly and spinning us around ever more rapidly. During most of human history, change percolated slowly through the layers of society, so that it was barely perceptible. Both people and institutions had time to adjust. As Daniel Bell wrote: "For millenia . . . children retraced the steps of their parents, were initiated into stable ways and ritualized routines, had a common book of knowledge and morality, and maintained a basic familiarity with place and family."

This tide of change, however, is being hurled against a seawall of institutional obduracy. By their nature, institutions resist change. Their strength has often been in their permanence, but today that very strength can be a major weakness. Institutions run the risk of becoming Maginot Lines, easily bypassed. The great vulnerability of all kinds of organizations comes from rigid and unchanging resistance to change.

One of the major manifestations of rigidity is continuing to view the world as it was previously defined, not acknowledging change, and not seeing that changes outside the specified boundaries can profoundly alter the organization's environment. The eruption of a Mexican volcano in the spring of 1982 produced enormous quantities of sulfur compounds in the atmosphere, which significantly affected the climate off the coast of Peru, which caused a drastic decline in the anchovy population, which in turn had a serious adverse impact on bird life there. The results included a great reduction in anchovy meal for feeding poultry and a substantial loss of revenue to the fertilizer industry, which uses bird droppings—all of which created problems for people and institutions ranging from buyers of chicken parts in supermarkets to economically troubled third world governments.

Environmental Concerns

Quite obviously, seemingly remote events can matter. But because the plan does not allow for them, they are ignored; and their consequences thus become unpleasant surprises. Currently, for American business, one of the major sources of unanticipated surprises is environmental concerns. Even though the 1960s and 1970s provided painful and costly lessons, there is still a reluctance to anticipate new developments. Businesses often find themselves, like generals, fighting the previous environmental battles while new areas of combat are opening up. There is growing concern among health and safety experts, for example, about the possibly harmful effects of high electrical and magnetic fields. A study of deaths among working men in the state of Washington from 1950 to 1979 showed that the incidence of leukemia among men working around such fields was twice the normal rate. If those results are confirmed by further studies, it is apparent that the cost to industry and government of protecting workers will be enormous. Even if not confirmed, the suspicion will remain; and there will have to be some kind of response. If the response is not voluntary, we can be sure, given recent history, that it will be mandated.

Environmental health and safety issues are perhaps *the* battlefield of the coming decade. Populist politicians, a rising force, are seizing upon the issue. Jim ("Whole Hog") Hightower, the Texas Commissioner of Agriculture, ran and was elected as a populist in 1982 with the help of what he called a "rainbow coalition" that included environmentalists. The little-noticed but potentially very significant decision in 1982 by the voters in Berkeley, California, to ban electroshock therapy indicates one wave of the future—local community control over, or punishment of, practices by professionals and industries that are labeled harmful or dangerous.

The New Consumer

Consumer groups are forming more cooperatives to provide direct competition with retail establishments. Economist Hazel Henderson describes a "counter economy" of nonmonetized economic activities, including barter, home gardening, and do it yourself, that displaces economic activities through normal channels. Like the underground economy, the counter economy is unmeasurable, but all observers agree that its size is substantial.

Internationally, too, vulnerability can strike like a hidden snake. Japan, which brought the American automobile industry to its knees and whose challenges in communications, computers, pharmaceuticals, and even fashion have spread fear and trembling throughout the western world, finds itself vulnerable to the rise of "new Japans." As Japan's labor costs rise and its industries become mature, Taiwan, South Korea, Hong Kong, and Singapore mount challenges that concern Japan's leaders. American appliance manufacturers are suddenly finding that changes in demographics, energy costs, lifestyles, and house buying have created a demand for smaller, European-style home appliances, and they are now facing a competitive challenge that was unanticipated and for which they were unprepared.

In the health field, hospitals and doctors are finding that growing numbers of people are going to clinics and independent emergency medical centers (sometimes called medical McDonalds) to save both money and time. More fundamentally, significant numbers of people are substituting self-care and preventive medicine for the traditional patterns of health care. Not many doctors, hospitals, or pharmaceutical companies are yet aware that their competitors include growers of health food and manufacturers of jogging shoes.

And as people become accustomed to finding alternatives, for whatever reasons, they find nothing incongruous in getting traditional products and services from nontraditional sources. In such an environment, brand names also lose their hold on the consumer. Private label brands are capturing large slices of the market. According to a 1981 survey by the Gallup organization, more than half of all consumers consistently bought private-label brands. And no-brand products—generics—also are making substantial gains at the expense of costlier name brands, even in cigarettes. Following a trend that became well established in Europe in recent years, L&M in 1983 introduced generic cigarettes in the United States at savings ranging from $1.20 to $1.70 per carton. (Generics, it should be noted, tend to appeal most to middle- and upper-class consumers.)

Political Intervention

And, of course, government is a great factor in vulnerability. It can insulate organizations against vulnerability, as in the cases of Chrysler and Lockheed. But more often, it creates vulnerability. Internationally, for example, Bangladesh and other third world countries issue decrees banning sales of pharmaceuticals they consider ineffective, hazardous, or unnecessary, and the result is serious inroads into the markets of pharmaceutical multinationals. Parker Brothers in effect loses its monopoly on the Monopoly game because the U.S. Supreme Court upholds a competitor's right to market a game called Anti-Monopoly, thus making the word "monopoly" a generic term. Another decision, also by the Supreme Court, creates new liability for organizations that issue product standards and codes.

The grass roots political movement targeting on utility companies (which, like all monopolies, tend to become too complacent), does not make the mistake of a head-on, direct assault. Its members take an indirect and far more dangerous approach: they work for having public utility commissioners elected by popular vote. That approach has succeeded in almost one-quarter of the states already. The record shows that in such states rate increases tend to be smaller.

Actions of the executive and legislative branches, both federal and state, are so important that many large companies more and more see that one primary job of the chief executive is government relations. In the financial services industry, for example, acts of Congress and regulatory decisions determine who can compete with whom and in what areas. Banks, particularly savings banks, suffered heavily from money market fund competition, primarily because Congress prevented them from competing effectively. Congress removed the bar to competition, and the brokers' money market funds suffered. Winners and losers are often determined by the effectiveness of pressure groups.

As the judicial branch assumes more of a de facto legislative role and as Americans continue to look to the courts for solutions, the problem that institutions face is the difficulty of exerting pressure on the courts. How do you lobby the court?

Public Attitudes

Public attitudes toward institutions play a major role in vulnerability. Survey after survey shows that the American public by and large dislikes and distrusts most of the major institutions of our society. That includes both big business and big government. These pervasive negative attitudes are generally misinterpreted as economic illiteracy by many business leaders who believe that if the people only understood fully, they would approve. So there are regular attempts, through advertising and public relations, to "educate" the people about the American economic system. Nonsense. Most members of the public understand as much about the basics of the American economic system as most business people do. They are not, for example, against the notion of profit. They are, however, angered by abusive practices, overextended perquisites, and excessive profits, especially when the latter are seen to benefit a few rather than be reinvested to benefit many. Knowledge and trust do not have to correlate.

There is a general fear of the power of big institutions. That does not mean that people feel such institutions are unnecessary, but it does mean that people want protection against them. And it does mean that the fear creates a real vulnerability.

In recent years the fear has been manifested in the extraordinarily rapid spread and wide acceptance of disinformation: patently false, damaging rumors about companies. McDonald's, for example, was accused of using worms in its hamburgers. That was obviously absurd—because, for one thing, worms are more expensive than beef—but it caused a substantial reduction in McDonald's business across the country. Procter & Gamble was the victim of a rumor that it was owned by Satanists. At one point, the company was receiving more than 12,000 calls a month about the rumor.

The fear is also manifested in scapegoatism. Big business makes a good target. Thus, when the women's rights movement was making its last desperate fight to secure passage of the ERA in 1982, there were full-page ads blaming the insurance business as a primary opposition force.

Crime

Big business makes a target for others whose motives are much less noble. Internal and external attempts and successes at sabotage, for personal gain or revenge, create significant vulnerabilities. As the Tylenol incident of 1982 suggests, they can become major media events and be precursors of a wave of similar attacks that are severely debilitating and costly. High on the list of activity here is computer-aided crime.

At a time when information is a critical resource, industrial espionage is no small consideration. We have been made well aware of cases of Russian and Japanese efforts to purchase corporate secrets, but there are hundreds of domestic leaks each day. They prompt massive security measures including antisnoop devices and lie detector tests.

The Ivory Tower Syndrome

A factor that exacerbates business vulnerability is an ivory tower syndrome that afflicts so much of the management of all our public and private institutions. In the late 1960s a Harvard Business School professor, George von Peterffy, attempted to construct a model of how public issues eventually wind up as legislation affecting business. The particular issue he chose to base his model on was automobile safety. As it turned out, he was not able to come up with a workable model, but he did unearth a most intriguing fact: The Washington representatives of the American automobile companies, throughout the years immediately prior to enactment of safety legislation by Congress, were substantially accurate in warning their managements of what was coming. But their managements didn't believe them.

People who comment on the ivory tower problem tend to do so in terms of physical isolation—that is, the heads of organizations are walled off from reality by human and other buffers. The fact is, more often than not, walls do not an ivory tower make. As the von Peterffy anecdote clearly illustrates, the ivory tower is commonly intellectual rather than physical and is almost always self-constructed.

And it's not just business. Educational institutions, willfully ignoring demographic and economic indicators of unmistakable significance, continue to spew out degree holders for shrinking or nonexisting job markets. Similarly, government agencies proceed inexorably along roads long since deserted by the public.

Napoleon, when asked after his stunning victory in Italy how he made his army cross the Alps, replied: "One does not *make* a French army cross the Alps; one *leads* it across." That kind of understanding, without which there can be no true leadership, has never been a common commodity, but today it seems rarer than ever. The Connecticut Mutual Life Insurance Company, in its comprehensive study on American values in the 1980s, showed among other things the divergence in values between the American public and the leadership segments. When asked to name the qualities they look for in leaders, the public most frequently mentioned honesty. None of the leader groups listed honesty as one of their three top choices. The study also showed that the public was considerably more concerned with religion and morality than were any of the leadership groups.

The bright young men and women who follow what many consider to be the ideal career path—prep school, Ivy League undergraduate school, elite graduate school (such as Harvard Business School), and ultimately the management ranks of a large public or private institution—are as removed from the everyday reality of most people as were medieval monks and nuns. By the time they get to top-management positions, they are further insulated by having associated primarily, if not entirely, with others like themselves, all of whom live in the same upper-middle-class communities, belong to the same clubs, and go to the same resorts. They don't know the multitudes who work for them, buy from them, and vote on their issues. More often than not, their only exposure to the masses is through TV sitcoms, and they tend to think of a population made up of Bunkers, Jeffersons, and Dukes—cute but dumb.

What You Can Do

How can managers deal effectively with vulnerability? There are three steps:

Step 1. Recognize that one's organization is vulnerable in the many ways described. That requires avoiding complacency, having a scanning system that allows you to be sensitive to changes in the external environment, and developing an institutional as well as an individual capacity to understand the meaning of such changes.

Step 2. Recognize that the environment is vastly more competitive now and that the nature of competition itself has changed. The traditional strategic planning tools for competitive analysis may now do more harm than good, because they do not allow for factoring in unanticipated competition from outside the industry.

Step 3. Understand that the key to success—even survival—in such a complex competitive environment is *marketing*. Nowadays, professionals such as doctors and dentists have to market; even museums are marketing.

These steps require that managers come out of their ivory towers and cultivate objectivity. They must be able to appraise, daily if necessary, what they assume to be true about themselves, their organizations, and their world and to discard whatever is no longer consistent with reality. That is not to say that managers should have no standards, no systems of enduring and strongly held values. Values and a description of reality are not the same thing. All of us must constantly determine, however, to what extent our value system influences or disturbs our ability to see the world as it really is.

One way to do that is to keep one's feet on the ground. Managers should regularly leave their comfortable quarters and get out into the field. Generals should visit the front lines; vice presidents of industrial firms should spend part of every week on the shop floor; supermarket executives should periodically work as cashiers.

Managers should expose themselves to contrary thought. If you read *U.S. News & World Report* because it gives you a perspective on the news that you approve of, try reading *Mother Jones* or *South,* because they will tell you things you don't want to read. Keep saying to yourself: "I know damn well this isn't so, but what if it is?" Every time you catch yourself saying "That's ridiculous!" or "That can never happen here!" ask yourself if you are really being objective.

The corporate sector is not alone in its vulnerability. Sectors that are dependent upon government funding, whether government agencies or nonprofit organizations supported in large measure by government grants, have found that their programs can come to a grinding halt in the aftermath of ill economic or political winds. And challenges from such sources as the Right-to-Lifers, James Watt, and Phyllis Schlafly defy those who believe that hard-fought wars can ever really be won, regardless of one's allies and regardless of existing laws and judicial rulings.

"When a thing is no longer useful," said Darwin, "it will cease to exist." The role of manager is to maintain the usefulness of the organization and not, as many seem to think, to preserve it as is. Economist Mancur Olson uses the term "economic sclerosis" to describe institutional and societal rigidities that prevent the flexibility needed for growth in difficult times. In turbulent times, such rigidities can simulate the appearance of strength, but it's the same kind of strength that the Titanic had.

CHAPTER 21

Legitimacy

There are basically two forms of contractual agreement between institutions and society. One is legal; the other is social. Neither is immune to the turbulence of modern times. Neither will remain unchanged in the course of the coming decade.

An institution exists as a formal entity because it addresses a perceived need. That need may be identified with a particular segment of the public, a particular product, or a particular market. The institution organizes around a charter which, when adopted, filed, and approved, legitimizes its existence. Principles of ownership, funding, and management are spelled out, and a body of law, ranging from taxation and accounting to liability and scope of activity, is applied. That, in a nutshell, is the legal contract.

However, there is not necessarily a complete correlation between what a lawyer might maintain is legal and the legitimacy granted by society as a whole. Most institutions have contented themselves with the legalistic interpretation and have generally assumed that, in doing so, they have covered all the bases of legitimacy. But ultimately it is society that confers legitimacy, and not necessarily or entirely through its laws.

The Challenge to Institutions and Professions

Government agencies ranging from the FTC to the CIA have in recent decades extended their activities beyond the limits of public approval and have caused outrage and heated debate. There are those who would have such agencies extend their scope of activities even further, whereas others believe that such power usurps basic constitutional rights and therefore operates outside an acceptable field of legitimacy.

Many public agencies, on the other hand, are viewed as not delivering the services to which the public believes it is entitled, at the very least as an adequate return for taxes paid. Municipal services have come under the same attack. Some programs have lived on past their original usefulness and exist only to perpetuate themselves. The legitimacy of the Social Security system is questioned as its implied promise to pay future generations who contribute now is substituted for its legal requirement to merely transfer payments from workers to retirees. The implied promise is inconsistent with the long-developing economic crisis facing the system.

Malpractice suits have hit just about every profession in existence. John McKnight, of the Center for Urban Affairs at Northwestern University, observed in an article for *Resurgence* in 1980 that the basic tool for control and oppression in modern industrialized societies is the power to label people as deficient and declare them in need. "Helping" professionals are the force behind this, and a revolt is developing against them. McKnight cites the reasons for the attack on professional legitimacy:

1.   The increasing inefficiency of the system as evidenced by the decline of student achievement scores, a stable life expectancy while medical costs escalate, and a sense of spreading injustice while the number of lawyers doubles.

2.   The arrogance of the professionals. Elitism is now being countered by consumers, including patient advocates, parent groups, and client councils.

3.   The cure is often worse than the disease (also known as iatrogenesis). The argument is that professionals are harmful, schools produce ignorance, hospitals and medicine produce sickness, and the justice system produces criminals.

Organized religion also has been challenged. Some people question whether a church has a legitimate mandate from society to engage in confrontational activities in the political arena. The role of a church as an adversary—not just in the political arena but also as an active participant in moves to effect change in the operation of private corporations as in investment policies—places it, in the minds of many, in a questionable position.

The media are being challenged on the ground that they often exceed their area of legitimacy. There are many who accuse today's journalists of creating rather than reporting the news. Another challenge is described by Stephen Barlas in a 1981 article for *Columbia Journalism Review*. Barlas asserts that journalists are making more money on the lecture circuit than ever before. Fees have risen dramatically; businesses and trade associations pay upward of $5000 for big names. Network news correspondents command top dollars. Of some concern among journalists, their publishers and networks, and the public at large is the possible conflict of interest raised by this practice.

The same concern is raised with regard to politicians and even expoliticians who still retain their connections and influence. Are high-paying speaking engagements a legitimate way for these people to supplement their incomes despite potential conflicts of interest? The two sides of this issue continue to be hotly debated.

Perhaps this concern will pale in comparison with two factors regarding legitimacy and political practice: the skyrocketing costs of campaigning and the use of the political action committees (PACs) that come close to dominating the finances of politics at the national level. Some politicians who have left Washington, D.C., have actually blamed the burgeoning growth of PACs for their feeling that they can no longer do an effective job. The legitimate roles of elected officials, they say, are to serve their constituents back home and to obey the dictates of their own consciences. But they feel the heavy pressure from moneyed interests now prevents them from doing either.

Corporate Legitimacy

And then, of course, we come to the issue of legitimacy as it relates to the corporate sector. In recent decades the nature of corporate ownership has undergone profound change. Many more individuals have been purchasing small blocks of shares, but an increasing percentage of shares has become concentrated in the hands of institutional investors. Major corporations have grown enormously in complexity. One consequence is an increasing gap between ownership and management; managers are much more likely to exercise autonomy in decision making. How can one reconcile the short-range interests that dominate the thinking of management and Wall Street speculators with the long-term interests of many other major and minor owners? Stockholder activism, one outgrowth of the legitimacy challenge facing publicly owned corporations today, seems likely to increase as the pulls and pushes continue.

An interesting twist in this is the growing concern about the dilemma of corporate counsel. Detley Vagts, writing in the *Harvard Business Review* in 1981, states that the relationship between chief executive officers and their lawyers is changing. Over the past few years, a series of cases has emphasized that corporate lawyers should "act for the corporation and not for management, and where the interests of management and the corporation conflict, counsel must follow the corporate interest." Furthermore, the lawyer's traditional role vis-à-vis his client and society also is being challenged. The corporate attorney was the client's own protector and advocate. This relationship is changing; it is becoming similar to that between a CEO and an auditor, and it makes lawyers "auditors of their client's compliance with the law." Some government agencies are increasing the strains by trying to enlist lawyers as "involuntary allies in enforcing agency rules." The SEC, for example, has been pushing for including lawyers on outside boards and on audit committees.

The IRS has suggested that lawyers may be held responsible for designing "abusive tax shelters," reported Linda Greenhouse of *The New York Times* in 1981. In her article she pointed out that, of the American Bar Association's twenty sections, the Section of Corporation, Banking and Business Law is the largest with a membership of more than 42,000. The current ABA Code of Professional Responsibility states that the corporate lawyer owes his allegiance to the corporate entity itself, not to any particular person connected with the corporation. The proposed new rules say that a lawyer may inform outside authorities if "the highest authority that can act on behalf of the organization insists upon action . . . that is clearly a violation of law and is likely to result in substantial injury to the organization." This rule runs counter to the legal profession's deeply held belief in loyalty to the client and confidentiality.

One accusation leveled at multinational and transnational corporations is that they are increasingly operating beyond the law by removing many of their operations from the United States and undertaking financial deals on foreign shores and in "safe harbors." One scenario places the transnational corporations of the future on remote islands with virtually unrestrained charters to do as they will as long as various legal requirements are met in areas where they undertake production or market their products. Theoretically, this is plausible. And there is currently no question that many corporate dollars flow through such safe channels. The Israeli economist Dan Bawly writes[12]

> One suspects, although it has not been proven, that financial institutions and banks sometimes knowingly aid and abet the subterranean economy. Behind the *Establissements* and *Anstalts* in Lichtenstein and Luxembourg, the funny-named companies in Panama, the Dutch Antilles, the Cayman Islands, and the Bahamas, trust accounts are kept and other forms of investments maintained with little likelihood of being traced to their real owners.

In a footnote to this, Bawly goes on to say:

> The notion that very many people are probably involved in these undertakings was reinforced in 1978, when a senior official at Citicorp of New York charged that funds were marked up and channeled through the bank from France to a tax haven in the Caribbees.

Another attack on the technical legitimacy of the corporation flows from the government bailout of Chrysler. If the legitimate role of the corporation is to provide a return or else suffer a loss for its stockholders, where do tax dollars, or the promise of them, play a role? Or is there another contract in existence alongside the legal one?

The Social Contract

The fact is that there is another, greater source of legitimacy. It is, to use John Locke's term, the *social contract*. It is housed not in a body of law, but in a body of public expectations. Those expectations, as they apply to the corporate sector, are currently seen to be as follows:

■ The corporation has a responsibility to its employees. That responsibility is related to providing jobs and job security, fair treatment and compensation, insuring safety on the job, and nondiscriminatory hiring and promotion practices.

■ The corporation has a responsibility to its customers for providing full and accurate information and a safe product at a reasonable cost.

■ The corporation has a responsibility to the community in which it does business to ensure that the environment is not damaged, that resources are not wasted, that the community fabric is not placed in jeopardy, and that a part of the profits is plowed back into community services.

■ The corporation has a responsibility to its investors to provide both a short- and a long-term profit.

Some parts of this social contract are now written into law, especially those involving safety, environmental impact, product information, and nondiscrimination in the workplace. But with expectations of some hard economic times ahead, one of the major parts of the social contract—the responsibility to employees—will create serious tension. Plant closings, displacement of workers by advanced automation technology and ultimately robots, and the diversion of tax incentive dollars into acquisitions and mergers that create no new jobs directly are examples of current conflicts that challenge the legitimacy of corporate behavior in management's, or even stockholders', best interests.

It is equally important to recognize that the social contract, being unwritten, is not fixed. It changes as public circumstances and expectations change and as values change. Furthermore, the changes are not determined by the corporation so much as they are by the public. In the future, corporations—and other institutions as well—will need to monitor changes in the social contract regularly and continuously. The only guarantee of existence for institutions is continued legitimacy.

The social contract and failure to recognize its importance could constitute the most serious threat to corporate America's autonomy of operation in the coming years. What must be fully realized is that the public, and not some legal entity, has extended the social contract and can withdraw it. Thus, accountability for actions will be a serious issue for managers, and effective management will require an enhanced sensitivity to shifts in public and societal expectations and demands. Who might be accountable for what and to whom is the subject of the next chapter.

CHAPTER 22

Accountability

The issue of legitimacy is ages old but is never permanently settled. The same holds true of its counterpart—accountability. It is generally believed that in free societies the highest arbiters of accountability are the marketplace, the polling booth, and the church. However, all three of these have been affected in recent years by the growth of bureaucracy, the thrust toward decentralization, an increasingly litigious society, changes in lifestyles, new technology, a heightened concern for resources and the environment, and the proliferation of special-interest groups. These, in turn, have come to raise anew the questions of who is accountable to whom and for what.

Liability

Legal accountability, known as liability, has been the first to undergo change. The issue of product liability is perhaps the most obvious case in point. Since the early 1970s, the number of product suits in which plaintiffs seek punitive damages has increased dramatically and the amount of damages awarded by juries has risen astronomically. According to Victor E. Schwartz, former chairman of the Commerce Department's Task Force on Product Liability, the increase in punitive damage claims and awards is due to a change in "the nature of evidence." Plaintiffs still have to convince a jury that a manufacturer acted recklessly, "but a company can be put in the dock for choosing between cost and safety in complex engineering matters." Thus we witnessed the famous and costly recall cases exemplified by Firestone's tire, Ford's Pinto, and articles of clothing not conforming to the Flammable Fabrics Act. Some landmark decisions, involving DES and asbestos, are worth citing here because together they have significantly affected the nature of legal accountability.

In 1976, Judith Sindell, suffering from cancer, sought damages from the makers of a drug her mother had taken 26 years earlier to prevent miscarriage. Since she had no idea which company made the drug, she took the approach that the generic, DES, was made by many companies, so she sued the top five manufacturers on the ground they should all be held liable. In May 1980, California's highest court agreed with her.

In 1981 the Appellate Division of State Supreme Court in Manhattan ruled that "a consumer harmed by a generic drug could sue a drug manufacturer for damages even though it could not be established that any particular company had made the drug that caused the injury." The defendant in this case was Eli Lilly & Company. The judge said that Lilly was liable because it had tried, along with other drug manufacturers, to obtain FDA approval for DES and to market it without testing it or heeding studies done in 1938 that warned of potential hazards.

The DES decisions have shaken the legal community. Lawrence Rout, a reporter for *The Wall Street Journal,* noted that the decisions promised to affect not only thousands of similar drug suits but legal wranglings concerning countless other products as well. Lawyers, who are not notoriously unopportunistic, are trying to "stretch the ruling to its limits," according to Rout. Assessments of impacts range from "an epic victory for consumers" to "a disaster for the legal system." Almost everyone agrees that the decisions represent a radical change in product liability law, because they relieve the plaintiffs of a great deal of burden in proving that a particular manufacturer is liable. The courts have, in effect, decided that technological advances and complex distribution systems result in many identical products that can't be traced to a specific producer. All producers, therefore, are to be held accountable.

A second major precedent grows out of lawsuits involving on-the-job exposure to disease-causing substances. Such cases are on the upswing in number and cost. In 1980 over 300 companies were facing close to 15,000 individual claims, many of which were related to events that occurred more than 20 years earlier. For example, a New York court certified a class action motion against seven defendants, including Dow Chemical, a manufacturer of the defoliant Agent Orange. Taken to its extreme, this suit could involve all 2.8 million Vietnam area veterans.

Asbestos producer Johns-Manville has become a landmark example. Several years ago J-M believed that it was amply insured against asbestos cases it might lose or choose to settle and that soon the number of new suits brought against it would level off. Instead, the number of plaintiffs kept increasing. Some of them were collecting over $1 million each, and the average claim was settled for about $25,000. In a move that left the business community profoundly shaken, Johns-Manville took the only way out that it could take: It declared bankruptcy.

The asbestos case serves as a precedent that could threaten the solvency of some insurance companies. A federal appeals court decision in 1981, which applied to more than 6000 lawsuits brought against the Keene Corporation in New York, stated that insurers are fully liable for damages awarded against a manufacturer for diseases that bore any connection to the policy period even if the diseases were not manifested until after the policies had expired. The ruling also required insurers to indemnify manufacturers for liabilities due to exposure *before* the policy period began; it stated that each insurer is fully liable for damages awarded if any phase of the disease overlapped with any part of the policy period.

Given those developments, it is easy to understand why managers see the liability aspect of accountability as a major threat to their organizations. One can identify in the current scene several time bombs that managers should note. They include video display terminals (VDTs), which are alleged to cause headaches, backaches, and even miscarriages; fluorescent lighting, which eliminates parts of the natural light spectrum and is now being implicated in dental cavities, migraines, and even skin cancer; radon poisoning, a potential by-product of energy-efficient architecture, which results from inadequate ventilation and internal-external air exchange; groundwater pollution caused by chemicals and industrial effluents and cited as the cause for health problems ranging from skin rashes to kidney malfunctions to birth defects in many communities; and nuclear radiation hazards for employees, communities where plants are located, and communities through which nuclear material and wastes are transported. Even low-level radiation from electrical lines, microwave ovens, and home video centers is increasingly suspect.

In addition there is the notion of cumulative trauma, which holds that all of an individual's employers, past and present, are liable for payment of workmen's compensation if a case can be made that death or disability is attributable to stressful conditions on all the jobs. (A heart attack victim's widow won such a case several years ago in California.)

The Changing Perception
of Institutional
Accountability

Such cases, and the changes they portend, are having important and growing effects on institutional accountability. The following examples indicate the nature of just some of those effects:

■ Richard Black, AM International Inc.'s chairman and chief executive officer, sued the company in 1982. He alleged financial cover-ups and misrepresentations that induced him to accept his position and buy stock in AM. A "big eight" accounting firm, Price Waterhouse, was dragged into the suit on the ground that it knew of and covered up the misrepresentation.

■ Michael Chow, owner of Mr. Chow's (a New York Chinese restaurant), filed suit following a scathing review of his restaurant in the

Guide Gault-Millau in 1981. He sought damages for "willful and malicious" statements.

■ Accounting firm executives are now legally accountable for mistakes, willful or not, reported or not, made by subordinates.

■ Malpractice suits have skyrocketed in number and kind. Even schools are being sued for failure to teach.

■ An increasing number of employees have brought suit against organizations that fired them for blowing the whistle on illegal or harmful practices. Led by Michigan, several states have enacted legislation to provide further legal protection for whistle blowers and force greater accountability on employers.

Societal Expectations

As with legitimacy, accountability has both its legal aspect (liability) and its social aspect. The latter is found not in a specific body of law, but in an amorphous body of public expectations. Sometimes the expectations go on to become law, as in the case of environmental pollution standards, equal-opportunity principles, restrictions against foreign dumping of products, and nutritional information requirements. But unlike liability, this aspect of accountability is not always clear, nor is it permanent. It is often enacted via regulatory standards, which change with economic or political conditions.

Indeed, we might say that these societal expectations are increasingly likely to become politicized and to transform and shape the agendas of special-interest groups. As we develop in the following sections, special-interest groups among the public have become a powerful force in altering the nature of accountability in the corporate world. Also, they have begun to exert much influence on how the government levers change.

The landmark study of corporate accountability, *The Modern Corporation and Private Property,* was written in 1932 by Adolf Berle, Jr., and Gardner Means. At that time, Berle and Means concluded that government was an effective deterrent to corporate power. Edward Herman contradicted that study at the close of the 1970s. In his report, *Corporate Control, Corporate Power: A Twentieth Century Fund Study,* Herman mapped the growth and changing structure of the corporation from 1900 to 1975. He concluded that the power of government to check corporate action was not as great as Berle and Means had believed. He cited improved communications and controls, geographic dispersion, and the enhanced adaptability and mobility of the large corporation as having contributed to the growth and maintenance of corporate power. He contended that although business essentially views government as an adversary, it practices a kind of "crybaby capitalism," using government as a crutch.

Herman further contended that, despite all efforts to curb its abuse, business is the most powerful sector of society and, overall, tends to be a destructive force. He wrote that, while helping to create enormous wealth, corporations have broken down community links and brought forth new problems whose solutions require mechanisms that do not now exist. Herman, a professor of finance at the University of Pennsylvania's Wharton School, believes that the way to alter corporate behavior is to increase public ownership, enlarge the role of government as producer, and reduce business leverage.

This argument, which has to a large extent been adopted by the so-called neoliberals, is now being heard more often. It is increasingly being looked upon as an acceptable alternative to traditional regulation. But critics say that its advocates do not fully recognize that fixing accountability in the public sector is no easier than in the private sector. Some would say it is a substitution of one evil for another.

Still, it is sobering to think that the age-old argument that the private sector will be held accountable for its action by the marketplace is now being so widely challenged. The fact is that although corporations may be ultimately held accountable for poor management through increased penalties or declining markets, many managers escape accountability. Workers, for example, are increasingly angered by the fact that layoffs, freezes, and cutbacks affect them more than the top managers whose decisions were responsible for creating the negative circumstances. Golden parachutes and other forms of what *Fortune* recently called "the madness of executive compensation" don't sit well with those who feel such practices effectively immunize managements against the dreaded plague of accountability.

The argument of Herman et al. misses another key point: The public is increasingly holding *all* institutions to a higher standard of accountability these days. This even applies to TV networks when the issue is violence on TV as it affects children and to nonprofit research laboratories when the issue is the dearth of results from the National Cancer Institute's $8 billion for cancer research.

Holding Government Accountable

The issue of government accountability is as significant these days as that of corporate accountability. If the perception is that the marketplace has been unable to exercise enough leverage on the private sector, there is a similar perception that the voting booth has been equally unsuccessful when it comes to the public sector. The rise in number of initiatives and referenda, if continued in the future, could promote more direct dialogue between the populace and the collectors and expenders of tax dollars. The question is whether the bureaucracy and myriad special interests can continue to maintain their leverage in light of taxpayer and voter discontent.

Even in the defense establishment, insiders say that accountability is virtually absent. Writing in *The New York Times Magazine* in 1982, retired General David C. Jones, chairman of the Joint Chiefs of Staff from 1978 to 1982, criticized the nation's armed forces for being rigid. He charged that conflicting bureaucracies were unresponsive to changing conditions and that authority and responsibility were greatly diffused. We won World War II, he said, not because we were smarter, but because we and our allies were bigger, we had time, we had geographic isolation to mobilize America's industry, and we had superb codebreaking capabilities. When President Truman tried to integrate the often competitive armed forces, Secretary of the Navy James Forrestal rejected the proposal on the grounds that a single armed forces chief of staff could become too powerful and threaten civilian control. Forrestal lived to regret that judgment when he became the first secretary of defense and found himself impotent in dealing with service autonomy.

Since Forrestal's time, the efforts of presidents, secretaries, and chairmen have proved futile in establishing a sufficient degree of accountability to bring under control the problems of cost overruns, duplication of effort, uncoordinated budgets, requirements outpacing capabilities, absence of priorities, unmet schedules, inefficiency, short-range perceptions, conflicts of interest on the part of service heads whose power is measured by dollars they win for their projects, and inadequate attention to the end product: combat effectiveness of the fighting force.

There are many who would like to be able to fire judges, regulators, bureaucrats, commissioners, and many others who appear to behave as if they were unaccountable to anyone for their decisions and whose decisions seem often to be counter to society's needs.

Holding Managers Accountable

The winds of change are blowing accountability away from its past mooring. Marketing and employment decisions are now being judged by their impact on the environment as well as on the bottom line. Retroactive accountability quite obviously has been institutionalized, but so have expectations about using foresight to avoid unintended consequences. The new federalism seeks to disperse accountability, whereas public-interest groups seek to centralize and intensify it. Seniors are held accountable for the action of juniors. Companies are held accountable for the actions of others in the industry of which they are a part.

It is no wonder that there is such confusion as to whether the various elements of our society fully understand and appreciate all aspects of accountability. If accountability is seen as ephemeral and insubstantial, because guiding ethical and theological principles have been supplanted by a patchwork of situational ethics, because bureaucratic procedures have come to dominate our largest commercial institutions, and because the oversight bodies themselves are only vaguely accountable, where does a manager look for guidance?

Managers, especially those in senior positions, should learn to be more comfortable with decision making in a fishbowl. Given the fact that employees, the press, stockholders, and special-interest groups will continue to clamor for increased disclosure, some types of closed-door decisions that are made without involving the affected parties could be disastrous.

Strange as it may sound, some organizations are using philosophers to help establish and implement policy decisions. More should do it, and at the highest levels of management. Moral and ethical principles sometimes need to be highlighted and objectively factored into decision making, and managers today are not equipped to do that without help. Too often these days, managers who make what they think are marketing, personnel, or production decisions are seeing those decisions evaluated—and criticized—as moral ones.

Managers should study the major and minor publics and interest groups—their *stakeholders*—and determine what their relationships to the organization are now and may soon be. The study should include not only shareowners, customers, and employees but such groups as retirees, whose stake is in the continuation of their pensions, and the local press, whose stake is in the organization as a source of news. Unfortunately, most organizations today pay lip service to monitoring emerging stakeholder group interests but do little to counteract emerging pressures until they become full-blown and costly. Many of the stakeholder groups are gaining in power and expertise. Their tactics now range from selective buying (boycotts) to sabotage, from stockholder activism to the spreading of rumors, from intimidating sponsors to pushing for control over investments, mergers, and acquisitions. These are not mere nuisances. They are matters of organizational life and death—of power, control, and survival. Monitoring stakeholder expectations of accountability and responding appropriately should be taken seriously by managers, particularly because some of the issues may have 10- to 20-year life spans.

Reserves or coinsurance systems should be explored and, when feasible, set up for unexpected future liability challenges. The threatened solvency today of some companies that have been hit by retroactive accountability cases should serve as a lesson to many others that the possibility of such judgments in the future ought to be factored into long-range financial projections and contingency plans. The backup systems might be cooperative across an industry because of the court judgments citing overlapping liability.

Actions and decisions of subordinates should be monitored for effects upon stakeholder groups, especially customers and employees. These are the two groups most likely to resort to litigation over grievances. Heading off potential liabilities becomes a must at a time when managers are increasingly liable personally for negligent, wrongful, or damaging actions by subordinates.

A strengthened network of bottom-up internal communications, matched with the promise of active attention to complaints, could bring to the surface not only employee concerns but also issues that might eventually be championed by external-interest groups.

Whither Corporate Social Accountability?

The expectation that the corporation has a responsibility to the greater society mushroomed in the 1970s. Beyond the issues of affirmative action, employment quotas, consumerism, and environmentalism, there were continuous knocks on corporate doors for donations to the arts, universities, various charities, and myriad social aid programs. With the new federalism's cutbacks in social and maintenance services come new knocks at corporate doors for stepped-up giving. Not all of the requests are charitable in nature. Increasingly the inquiries relate to partnerships in potentially profitable endeavors that also meet societal needs or the merging of public affairs activities with the interests of segments of the public suffering from program or service cutbacks.

At a time when most companies are preoccupied with survival and the bottom line, the tendency is to continue a hodgepodge of contributions programs and complain of the confusion, complexity, and cost of the new demands. Yet some companies have begun to look at giving, charitable and otherwise, in a new light. Some managers are looking at their long-term survival considerations and are attempting to link them to some strategic assessments of which failing societal services will leave their companies in a weakened future position. Several, for example, are exploring ways to counter the epidemic of unemployment and the increasing mismatch of skills and literacy to long-term corporate employment and consumer needs.

Today's supermanager is one who will recognize the need to superimpose a long-term strategy on corporate giving. One model for doing so is presented in Table 22-1. For a pharmaceutical company,

Table 22-1
Strategic Profile

Business Base	Societal Situation
(1) Industries in which company operates	Unmet societal needs
(2) Need to hire skilled employees	Skills not in adequate supply
(3) Facing displacement of workers	Retraining not readily available
(4) Locales in which company operates	Infrastructure problems:
	■ Affects survival (profit, business)
	■ Affects employees (transportation, schools, security, etc.)
	■ Affects health and well-being of community
(5) Concerns and interests of managers and employees	Expertise and volunteers in short supply
(6) Appreciation for role of culture	Demand for "software" funding and development (includes arts)

line 1 might mean health care for the poor and aged; for a bank, it might mean loans to small businesses. Each line could be weighed by its relevance to the long-term needs of the company. A trucking company might find line 4 of more urgency overall than line 1, 2, or 3. The important thing is to impose a strategic discipline—one that is linked to corporate survivability and growth—on the corporate dispensation of charitable contributions, public affairs efforts, public policy positions, and product and service strategy.

Moving On and Up

We have not, in this chapter, covered the roles of the board of directors and the chief executive officer in the major movement toward heightened accountability. At that level of the organization, accountability becomes entangled with governance. And governance is the subject of the next chapter.

CHAPTER 23

Governance

In the nineteenth century, the life insurance business was rent by a fierce ideological dispute: Should the companies be operated for the benefit primarily of shareholders or of policyholders? It was never settled; indeed, the argument still rages. So we have mutual companies, owned by their policyholders, and stock companies, owned by stockholders.

Today all American institutions are being forced to examine the same question: for whose benefit does the organization operate? As business in particular struggles to deal with the question, the issue increasingly becomes governance—how a corporation is controlled. A recent report from SRI International's Business Intelligence program (entitled *Shared Control: Sea Change for a Fourth Wave of Regulation*) examines some of the ways in which corporate governance is being challenged now—and will be challenged even more in the future.

The report forecasts "increased limitations on management rights," including "greater participation by employees in decision making," more "involvement of government, community and interest groups in decisions," and "more explicit definition and protection of employee and other stakeholder rights."

As in every other area of our economy and society today, there is no longer passive acceptance of established procedures and rules in institutions. Consent, the primary basis for control, is not given in perpetuity. In essence, those who control institutions today are being subjected to a kind of zero-base assessment: they have to demonstrate that they are entitled to hold power. And it is becoming increasingly difficult to base the response on tradition.

■ The political left, ranging from the radical left (for example, *Mother Jones* magazine) to the moderate left (for example, neoliberal ideologue Robert B. Reich of Harvard), demands public control over, or shared control with, corporate management. The neoliberal platform includes planks calling for government planning for private-sector investment, increased worker participation in management, and allocation of capital to chosen industries. *Mother Jones* advocates an economic plan that would give workers control over pension funds, increase workers' ownership of business, mandate guaranteed employment, and diminish the ability of corporations to relocate.

■ Two eminent Episcopal bishops, Paul Moore, Jr., of New York and John H. Burt of Ohio, in an op-ed page article in a 1982 *The New York Times*, joined in the call for modification of corporate governance. "We ask," they wrote, "whether it is not time to explore alternatives to corporate and conglomerate ownership that removes decision-making and control from local communities." Episcopalians have not heretofore been particularly distinguished by antiestablishment ideology.

■ The American Law Institute created a furor in corporate management ranks in 1982 when it proposed a new set of rules on corporate governance. So vehement was the opposition, in fact, that the institute postponed voting on the proposals for 2 years. What the business leaders particularly objected to were rules calling for a majority of outside (noncompany) directors on boards and for outside directors to be in the majority on key board committees such as audit, nominating, and compensation.

■ Unions, too, are getting into the act. The United Auto Workers, for example, asks in return for the concessions it has made to the struggling U.S. automotive industry that it have a say in decisions on pricing, plant closing, and subcontracting—all prerogatives of senior management. Anthony Mazzocchi, of the Oil, Chemical, and Atomic Workers Union, writing in *The New York Times,* says that unions can avoid economic catastrophe only by challenging management's right to manage. Workers, he writes, must begin to assume direct responsibility for the decisions that determine the economic direction of the country. He also calls for legislation to control "wasteful and unnecessary" mergers. Even Lane Kirkland, president of the AFL–CIO, would like to see workers participating in investment decisions. Some observers feel that business has already invited the camel into the tent by opening their books to unions in an effort to justify give-backs or slowdowns in wage increases. General Motors, for example, in order to prove that it was using union concessions to reduce car prices, agreed to let a union-appointed auditor study confidential accounting data.

■ Publications ranging from *The New Republic* to *Fortune* have been sharply critical of top executive compensation. The articles have carried such titles as "The Gargantuan Salaries of Business Executives" and "The Madness of Executive Compensation." Claiming that senior executive compensation must be more closely related to performance, the critics also call for board compensation committees made up of outside directors in the hope that would result in a more objective determination of management pay and perquisites.

■ Conservative writer Kevin Phillips sees a growing "radicalization" of the middle class as economic conditions worsen, and he believes one result will be a decline in the autonomy of senior management.

■ Internationally, there is a continuing erosion of the autonomy of senior business executives. Sweden's Social Democrats, restored to power in 1982, campaigned on a platform that would by the end of the decade give unions effective control over major corporations. Under the plan, new taxes would be channeled to wage earner funds that would use the money to buy up the stock of Swedish companies. The funds would be managed by union appointees. The European Parliament has for some years been debating, amending, and otherwise trying to avoid coming to a decision on the notorious Vredeling proposal, which would require all companies operating in any member country to consult with unions on major decisions in every country in which the company does business.

■ The courts, too, have complicated the issue with decisions that limit the ability of senior executives to hire, fire, and promote. Most recently, there have been rulings which have, in effect, said that there are implied, if not explicit, contractual relationships when workers are hired, and these restrict management's traditional right to fire at will.

These external pressures, along with internal pressures such as those discussed in Part 3, are resulting in shifts in the nature and practice of corporate governance. The appointment of women and blacks to the boards of major corporations has both reflected and contributed substantially to the fight for equality, even if some observers claim that not nearly enough has been done in that direction. Board members are themselves reasserting their theoretical preeminence. More and more, board audit committees are consisting of a majority of outside directors, for example, and these committees are increasingly keeping a cold, sharp eye on managements. Paul Kolton, chairman of the Financial Accounting Standards Advisory Council, former head of the American Stock Exchange, and a director of several major corporations, says that this is the most significant change in boards in recent years. The audit committee, he says, is a "new beast." Audit committees can—and do—retain outside counsel as well as auditors and conduct investigations of management. Kolton also suggests that major corporations have nominating committees made up entirely of outside, or "disinterested," directors, as is already required of investment companies. There is increasing pressure for alternatives to the traditional "old boy" approach to selecting directors.

The prominent economist Norma Pace, a director of a number of important corporations including Sears, says that the line between directing and managing is increasingly fuzzy. This has in large part been due to the new liability exposure of directors, but the same exposure has caused many board members to want to retreat from taking on too much responsibility for knowledge of intricate operating details.

What Should the Board Do?

Thus, there exists a critical dilemma at the board level of most enterprises. It is compounded by public expectations of boards of directors, indeed, even by management myths regarding the role of the board. Members of the public and many middle-management personnel actually envision a more "managerial" role for the board than, in fact, is the case. There has been little research on the perceived role and nature of the board. However, several anecdotal observations are worth mentioning because, taken together, they shed some light on the debate about governance we are likely to see heightened in the coming years.

It is universally understood that boards of public companies represent the interests of the stockholders; in fact, all the members of such boards must be stockholders. But there are two widely held and conflicting perceptions concerning the role of board members. The first is that the board is merely a rubber stamp for management, that it does little on its own initiative, that meetings, held in plush quarters, are cursory, and that the main purpose of a board is to meet legal requirements. The other perception is that the board runs the company, that its members vote on the major and minor strategies to be undertaken by the company, that market, product, government affairs, personnel, and planning decisions are all within the scope of the board to initiate, review, ratify, execute, monitor, and change.

Unfortunately, in some companies the first of these perceptions is an accurate reflection of board activity. Surprising to many, and fortunately for our corporate institutions, the second is absolutely wrong. There are many boards that are not merely rubber stamps or puppets of management, but even they try to remember the line, however vague, between governing and managing. No board should be expected to manage the business it governs. It should, however, take seriously its responsibility to see that the company is managed capably. Therefore, the greatest responsibility of the board is to select the chief executive and ensure an adequate pool for management succession. It can do so in any number of ways. One is to tie the chief executive's compensation not only to financial results but also to the development of excellence in senior people throughout the organization. Another is to press constantly for information about the kind and availability of back-up management at the top levels of the organization.

A second major responsibility of the board is to see that the enterprise does not violate its charter. A growing concern, however, is that what is legally required (the letter of the law) is not always in keeping with what society expects (the spirit of the law). Now that more directors are being held legally accountable for actions (decisions) that deal with shades of legal interpretation and the number of stockholder suits is growing, some responsible and respectable directors are taking some unfortunate actions. They include withdrawal from board service, limiting board service, and retreating from making some hard decisions or asking some hard questions. Once again we have the paradox: The increased liabilities promote more astute governance and limit it at the same time.

A great unfulfilled information need is to educate the public, public-interest groups, management, and even directors themselves about the roles, purpose, and pressures residing at the board level. In the absence of a good body of research on the perceptions that exist, on the emerging thinking of board members, on the general practices and procedures that have worked well or have failed dismally, the board's role in corporate governance will remain in the shadows of general ignorance and misinformation. That can create long-term damage to the workings of a free-market system. Shadows distort, and they play tricks on our ability to make enlightened judgments.

Corporate Social Responsibility

Closely connected with questions about the role of the board is the issue of corporate social responsibility. How and by whom is it determined? By the managers or by the owners?

President Reagan connected the concept of private-sector initiatives to budget cuts for social programs. Among the reactions was one by Milton Friedman and his adherents, that senior executives have no right to use stockholder money for social or charitable purposes. Others, however, feel that a corporation, like an individual, has a responsibility to its community and must contribute to the well-being of that community.

The crux of the issue, of course, is executive autonomy. If senior managers have the authority to decide the corporation's social responsibility, they determine what that responsibility is and how best to meet it. Today, however, there is increasing doubt—even within management ranks—that executives can act with that degree of autonomy. More companies are turning to their boards. Board committees on social responsibility, theoretically at least, acknowledge the ultimate authority of the stockholders. Some companies, such as those in the life insurance business, have an industrywide cooperative approach to help determine how to deal with corporate social responsibility. And some companies are waiting for government to tell them what to do.

The Role of Government

Government does abhor a vacuum. Both the executive and legislative branches of the federal government have in recent years devoted considerable time and thought to the various elements of corporate governance. In 1980 the Securities and Exchange Commission issued a massive staff report on corporate accountability that exemplified the commission's preoccupation with corporate governance. One of the major recommendations was that there be a distinct separation between the roles of chief executive officer and chairman of the board. Another was that the CEO be the only member of management on the board. It is interesting to note that a number of business leaders, including Paul Kolton, see considerable merit in these recommendations.

In a thoughtful paper on this subject delivered at Oxford University in 1981 James C. Armstrong, director of corporate policy analysis for AT&T, pointed out quite correctly that SEC activities in recent years "have focused on improving shareholder access to the proxy machinery and increasing the amount of information made available to shareholders. Both activities promote the furtherance of what has come to be called 'shareholder democracy.'" And Congress, as Armstrong also pointed out, has been sniffing around the edges of the subject with growing interest. Although there seems little chance at present for enactment of federal chartering legislation, as proposed by Ralph Nader, some kind of federal minimum standards legislation—specifically focused on fiduciary standards for directors—is not out of the question. Furthermore, we are likely to see more legislation setting standards of accountability for both directors and internal executives, including provisions for criminal liability.

Responding to Challenges to Governance

More and more senior executives are becoming aware of the need to deal with the significant challenges to their authority. Some are digging in their heels or circling the wagons; others are looking for ways to accommodate to the pressures. Rafael D. Pagan, Jr., a top executive of Nestlé, a giant multinational, has written that multinationals must make positive responses. They should acknowledge property rights in jobs and give adequate notice before closing factories, and they "must open their files" to consumers and other publics.

As part of the bicentennial celebration in 1976, the life insurance business brought together a group of industry, government, and academic leaders to discuss "Freedom and Control in a Democratic Society." Many questioned whether the title should have been freedom versus control, but that oversimplified the issues. The fact is that freedom and control are interrelated and interdependent. Control of some can ensure freedom for others. Freedom without control can become anarchy, which can be the heaviest weight on freedom.

Challenges to existing modes of governance need not end in diminished freedom for executives. Prudential, which became the largest insurance company in the world because of its aggressive, forceful leadership, did so under a board which includes six public directors appointed by the governor of New Jersey. Chief executives can continue to have both authority and autonomy and can continue to be leaders even if present systems of governance undergo radical change.

If you are now, or if you expect to become, a senior executive, you can anticipate newly emerging challenges. You will be challenged by external forces, such as government intervention, and by internal forces, such as worker demands for autonomy and participation in decision making. Consequently,

■ You will need to find ways to share authority without fully relinquishing control. Leadership can be even more important when it operates within limits. All signs point to a move away from rigidly structured, hierarchical organizations in which titles and positions carry their own authority.

■ You will have to work constantly at gaining and maintaining the consent of those who work for you. In years to come, authority to govern will increasingly flow from below as the work force continues to become more educated, more highly skilled, and more concerned with individual feelings of control.

■ You will need to find ways for your organization to get more early warning on shifts in public expectations of institutional governance. Some organizations, for example, are adding social scientists to their government relations staffs in an effort to move away from the customary fire-fighting mode toward one that includes foresight and sophisticated analysis of long-term trends.

Real power is as much an attribute of the individual as it is of the position. Studies done for the U.S. army, for instance, have shown that in battle, more often than not, leaders emerge from among the ranks independently of the existing hierarchy. The challenges to governance do not have to mean an end to executive authority; indeed, the result can be an enhancement of authority if it can be justified.

CHAPTER 24

Interdependence

Everything is connected to everything else, reads the first law of ecology. One of the curses of our western ways of thought is that we see the world as if we were looking at an illustration through a magnifying glass; we see, separately, the component dots and consequently tend to lose sight of the fact that they exist only to make up an entire picture. Alfred Kinsey, who was a great entomologist before he achieved fame as a sexologist, once wrote: "It is a fundamental of taxonomy that nature rarely deals with discrete categories. Only the human mind invents categories and tries to force facts into separate pigeon-holes. The living world is a continuum in each and every one of its aspects."

Perhaps some of us are able to see this fact clearly enough in nature but are unable to see it in other spheres of life. A University of Wisconsin professor of ecology, Stanley A. Temple, hypothesized some years ago that the Calvaria trees are dying out on the Indian Ocean island of Mauritius because of the extinction of the dodo bird some 300 years ago. According to Dr. Temple, the coat of the Calvaria seed is so tough that the only bird that could crush it was the dodo. So since the demise of the dodo, the Calvaria seeds have been unable to germinate.

We are beginning to be aware of the linkages among all of the elements of nature. Almost half of all prescriptions dispensed in the United States contain natural substances, most of which are derived from plants. A growing concern among scientists about the escalating destruction of the South American rain forest is that valuable sources of necessary medicines and foodstuffs may be irretrievably lost. Researchers at the Harvard Botanical Museum have so far identified more than 1000 plants from the rain forest that have value as foods, drugs, or industrial substances, and fewer than half of all the plants there have as yet been identified and described. A related concern has to do with the threat to genetic diversity. The spread of high-yield varieties of many crops is resulting in homogeneity; and where wild varieties do grow, they are being destroyed by forest clearing. If, as has happened before, a new blight strikes, the absence of diversity could mean that an entire crop would be wiped out.

Damage to the environment has both obvious and subtle impacts on human life. We know the consequences of air and water pollution as far as birth defects, lung diseases, and cancer are concerned. But there is as yet limited awareness that such pollution may be a factor in male sterility. Researchers at Florida State University have discovered an apparent link between a decline in male sperm count and the presence in the environment of toxic chemicals such as PCBs.

We have already discussed international interdependence in Chapter 8. But as we witness the increasing intractability of the international economy and the inability of economists or economic theorists to make things right, it is necessary to emphasize again that what happens in the remote jungles of Nigeria and the out-of-the-way villages of Indonesia and the cities of Europe happens to us as well. No nation is totally self-contained; all nations are affected by what happens in each. C. Fred Bergsten, director of the Institute for International Economics, pointed out in 1982 that stagnation in the U.S. economy cannot be dealt with effectively without taking into account how closely linked our economy is to the world economy:

■ Over 20 percent of U.S. industrial output is now exported.

■ Export accounts for approximately one out of every six jobs in manufacturing.

■ Two out of every five farm acres produce for export.

■ Almost one-third of all U.S. corporate profits come from international activities.

Obviously, said Bergsten, it is inconceivable under these circumstances that the United States can achieve a healthy economy unless the world economy gets healthy.

Making the Links

There is heated controversy in scientific circles about the relation between national security and the flow of scientific and technological information. Government military and security agencies are attempting to exert tighter control over such information that may have significance in military and economic competition, particularly, of course, information that the Soviet Union wants and needs. Even though many scientists agree that leakage of technology is serious, they are concerned that the attempts to control it are overkill. A recent report from the National Academy of Sciences contends that open scientific communication has not heavily damaged U.S. security and that attempts to "restrict access to basic research would require casting a net of controls over wide areas of science that could be extremely damaging to overall scientific and economic advancement as well as to military progress."

The leaders of all segments of American society have always proclaimed their commitment to education. But we are now seeing how flaws, failures, and inadequacies in education are having important and largely undesirable consequences in our economy. Consider, for example, the decline in foreign language study. More than one-fifth of all high schools in the United States teach *no* foreign languages. Less than 10 percent of our colleges require foreign languages for entry. As a consequence, American managers, largely ignorant of other languages and cultures, are at a disadvantage in a time when business is increasingly international. And that disadvantage affects our ability to compete with foreign companies.

We are now realizing that cultural patterns that have lasted for millennia can have unforeseen and possibly harmful consequences if left unchallenged in a time of major change. For example, cultural patterns have discouraged women from entering such professions as engineering in large numbers. Now we need more engineers, and most people, regardless of their view of difference between the sexes, would welcome more women into the profession.

There are many other ways in which unrecognized linkages and unanticipated second-, third- and fourth-order consequences show how like a web the world really is.

■ Philosopher Christina Hoff, writing in *The Hastings Center Report,* shows how the replacement of individual good deeds by large-scale public and private charitable institutions resulted in a loss of community. That can lead to self-indulgence and a serious decline in private benevolence.

■ Psychologists are mounting a serious challenge to Cartesian dualism. More and more studies and experiences show that the mind and body are not separate, as Descartes propounded. That is undermining the dominant medical approach, which treats disease only by treating the body. In the new medical field of psychoneuroimmunology it has already been shown that the immunological system of the body can be so affected by stress that its capacity to combat cancer is reduced.

■ In his book *Minds, Markets and Money: Psychological Foundations of Economic Behavior,* Shlomo Maital lays the blame for the failure of economic theory on the fact that economics has divorced itself from the other social sciences. Since so much of actual economics in the world is the result of seemingly irrational behavior by individuals and institutions, Maital feels that economics must entail the study of politics, sociology, and psychology if it is to mirror and predict accurately.

Investment banker Felix Rohatyn, who was forced to become aware of interconnectedness by his involvement in the fiscal problems of New York City, once wrote: "The components of major problems are being studied narrowly, with little thought about their relationship with other aspects of the same problem."

The Effect on the Workplace

It is important for managers to understand that awareness of the inter-connectedness of all things, of the fragility of the structure of nature, and of the fact that we live in an environment that does have real limits has a substantial and growing effect on the values and behavior of consumers, employees, voters, and regulators. People are changing the way they live; they are focusing more, as we pointed out earlier, on doing rather than having. Both voters and regulators are acknowledging that there may be problems we cannot solve by overwhelming them with money or other resources. Workers and even managers are deciding that it is not as important as they once thought to work harder for advancement that merely results in more material acquisition.

The Challenge to Managers

It is important for managers to understand that the complex underpinnings of human behavior resist categorization. Theories of organizational and human behavior are Procrustean beds that are inadequate—and dangerous—substitutes for thought and analysis. "For want of a nail," as the poem goes, "a kingdom was lost." The stakes are high today; in a time of turmoil and transition, organizational existence as well as individual well-being can depend an ability to see the connections and yet not be overwhelmed by them.

These are the days of flowcharts, models, feedback loops, complicated matrices, cross-impact analyses, and systems design. Many of these tools are helpful in the analysis of the interdependence of events and issues and decisions. They do not, however, constitute the true science that many of their users would have others believe they do; neither are they the frivolous, faddish, or fringe elements of the management process that their detractors would have them be. Sometimes these devices can point up unanticipated and even counterintuitive results of seemingly benign decisions. Sometimes they can show how several problems can be addressed by one course of action. Most often, they serve as a conceptual aid; they point out interactions to those who tend to think linearly. "If A, then B, then C" is an outdated mode of operating in a climate of interdependence. More often, the case is: "If A, then D, F, and G and ultimately Y and Z, which diminishes the profitability or feasibility of A."

Interdependence, more than just an academic concept, is a way of thinking about the world: the larger context in which countries and people exist, and the smaller contexts in which institutions are managed and people live and work. To make the most of one's resources, whether capital, people, money, or materials, and to maximize the returns on one's decisions is to accept, in general, the idea that nothing happens in a vacuum. Public opinion studies are not predictive because of the impact of the unfolding of events from day to day. There are people who believe there is a loss somewhere in the system for every gain. And every decisive action changes the context in which all future decisions will be made.

The supermanager sees this, uses appropriate and available tools to help anticipate consequences, and is serious about establishing decision systems that reach beyond the simplistic, limited, and pitfall-fraught linear thinking of the past.

CHAPTER 25

Morality

Suddenly, morality is a management issue—one that is now much larger than anyone had anticipated and one that seems likely to become ever larger over the next decade. The 1960s and 1970s were a time of what Daniel Callahan, director of the Hastings Center, calls "minimalist ethics"—an ethical focus on gratification of the individual almost to the exclusion of the community. Callahan, along with many other philosophers and moralists, believes that our society can no longer afford that value system, that we now need a stronger sense of community that can come only from a more universal, shared standard of morality. No longer, according to these thinkers, can we say, "If it feels good, do it"; no longer can we afford to be tolerant of all moral viewpoints if we want to restore cohesion to our society.

Philosopher Alan Goldman, in his book *The Moral Foundations of Professional Ethics,* says that ethics should not be classified according to one's profession or work, that there should be no differentiation from a universal standard of ethics unless it leads to greater rights for all people. From that perspective, the concept of professional ethics is being attacked. Within the legal profession, for example, scholars and practitioners are engaged in heated debate over whether a lawyer's duty to his client must be subordinate to his duty to his community. Both medical doctors and philosophers are struggling with questions of the right to live and the right to die, and answers are neither quick nor clear.

The New Religion; the New Coalition

Behind this turmoil is a pervasive feeling that the narcissism and self-centeredness of the recent past, although productive of much individual satisfaction and growth, have frayed the social fabric. A new emphasis on religion is interpreted by some as signifying, at least in part, a desire for a firm, clear core of morality. Even liberal writers and publications are calling for restraint in self-expression and self-gratification. A profamily coalition, so called because of its opposition to abortion, pornography, the ERA, homosexual teachers and preachers, and the banning of prayer in public schools, has pulled together a lot of resources to change laws and public policy—and particularly to promulgate an Old Testament–based standard of morality for individual behavior.

Most observers characterize this coalition as being reactionary, as trying not so much to stop the tide of social change as to turn it back. It is true that many if not most of the members of the so-called Moral

Majority yearn for an earlier, simpler, sterner time, but there is an underlying revolutionary element in this new old theology that has enormous potential for forward rather than backward change in our value systems. That element is the concept of *stewardship*. Fundamentalist Christian theologians are in effect reinterpreting Genesis; they are saying that it was God's intention to give human beings not dominion over the world and all its creatures but stewardship for it. Dominion, quite obviously, means that the world is ours to do with as we choose. Stewardship, on the contrary, means that we may be held accountable for returning the world undamaged.

Around this emerging theology an interesting coalition is forming. Striking some observers as incongruous, the coalition includes environmentalists and civil rights groups as well as fundamentalist clergy. The theology is manifested in opposition to exploitation—not just exploitation of resources but exploitation of people. It is anti-materialist and, most significantly, antiindustrial. It goes beyond Marxism in criticizing all forms of industrial society, whether capitalist or socialist. It holds that industry is not merely an economic activity but a moral one as well and must therefore be judged in the context of a new morality. Humanity has no right of eminent domain; humanity is not the highest point in a hierarchy of nature. Thus, the animal rights movement mounts ever stronger opposition to the use of animals in scientific and commercial laboratories on the grounds that mankind has no inherent right of superiority than can justify hurting or otherwise exploiting nonhuman creatures.

The Dilemmas Facing Management

And so managers will be facing more moral dilemmas in the years to come. And dilemmas they are, because dilemmas, unlike problems, have no easy answers. In the case of moral issues, they may not even have a readily discernible right or wrong. As an example, genetic screening has triggered a great deal of controversy. Some large industrial companies use genetic screening tests to determine whether workers have inherent susceptibility to the illnesses caused by certain chemicals used in industrial processes. From the management perspective, the screening is a humane response to concern over possibility of damage to human beings. Workers who have genetic susceptibility would not be required to have contact with chemicals dangerous to them. But others are highly critical of the screening on the ground that a company must assume responsibility for making the workplace safe and should not be permitted to shift that responsibility to individuals who can control neither the workplace nor their own susceptibility. A dilemma.

Managers will increasingly face conundrums of that kind. The difficulty in arriving at satisfactory solutions is perhaps one reason why there appears to be such a hunger for an unchanging, universal moral base. The pragmatism that has characterized morality in our society in recent times no longer seems adequate.

The companies that decided to market infant formula products in third world countries believed they were making a marketing decision. Therefore, the information used in making the decision was marketing information—potential size of market, costs of distribution and transportation, profit potential, etc. To their surprise, they were told after the fact that they had made a moral decision, and a wrong one at that.

Most managers are unprepared, by either training or experience, to deal with such dilemmas. As a result, managers too often attempt to evade that kind of responsibility. The consequences are more dehumanizing of the organization—more bureaucracy as a refuge from accountability—and ultimately even greater problems for management. Just as a succession of mayors of New York City deferred making difficult financial decisions until one mayor finally was forced to make them, so managers are hoping to leave to their successors the necessity for dealing with today's moral dilemmas.

Relations between Individuals and Organizations

When viewed in the new moral context, the relations between individuals and organizations also becomes far more complex. Consider loyalty as an example. There was a time when the loyalty of an employee was taken for granted, but different times and different people have made it an issue far removed from yesterday's simplicity. As a result of shifts in attitudes toward work, the focus on self, the increasing mobility of the work force (and of business itself), unionization, more emphasis on professionalism, greater questioning of authority, and the increasing depersonalization associated with size and the tendency toward bureaucracy, managers will quite obviously have to put more effort into earning and maintaining loyalty. It can no longer be taken for granted.

Whistle blowing (the act of snitching on one's employer) is a relatively new phenomenon that can be directly traced to both the decline in loyalty and the new focus on morality. Morality may dictate that service to the community takes precedence over loyalty to the employer. Indeed, it may demand that an individual who is accountable to society and to God *must* blow the whistle on wrongful or harmful acts of his or her employer. Whistle blowing, of course, does entail some risk. Chances are that most employers have not yet arrived at the state of grace that enables them to turn the other cheek. But the risk has diminished, somewhat at least, since states, starting with Michigan in 1981, have started enacting laws protecting whistle blowers.

Crime

The issue of crime against corporations also represents a kind of dilemma.

■ In recent years, employee thefts have risen at an appalling rate. Herchell Britton, executive vice president of the Burns International Security Service, estimated in 1981 that white-collar crime added up to more than $70 billion a year. The FBI has a backlog of almost 20,000 cases of white-collar crime. Retailers in the United States lose goods worth more than $20 million a day, and far more of the loss is due to employee theft than to shoplifting.

■ According to a poignant and disturbing article in *The Wall Street Journal* in 1981, the American Seed Company, which for 60 years had used children to sell packets of garden seeds, went out of business. Why? Because, increasingly, the kids were keeping all the money instead of sending the company its share.

■ A 1981 survey by *The New York Times* revealed an increasing incidence of deception by job applicants, including false information about educational background and job experience.

People who commit crimes against corporations invariably defend their actions (to themselves if not to society) on the ground that the victims are constant and flagrant criminals. By that reasoning, the rip-off mentality is transformed into a Robin Hood one.

What Managers Must Do

One of the key difficulties managers face in dealing with the developing emphasis on morality is the inadequacy of their preparation.

Graduate schools of business may have one course in business ethics (should you or should you not pay bribes in foreign countries?), but in few, if any, can there be found awareness that management will increasingly operate in a moral context. Quite obviously, a first step is to provide better training so that future managers will at least be better equipped to come to grips with the complexities of their decisions. Already some large companies—Bristol-Myers and Prudential are examples—have met with philosophers or hired them as consultants in an effort to help managers ask the right questions in trying to determine the moral implications of management decisions. Hospitals also are exploring the use of philosophers in an attempt to resolve the moral dilemmas posed by the limited time, talent, and economic resources available for health delivery.

To understand what society will expect from those in charge of its institutions, managers must become familiar with the theology of stewardship. At its most basic level, stewardship means that alternatives to experiments on live animals and the depletion of the rain forests must be found. On a more complex level, it means that thoughtful managers must consider whether the eventual result will be a very different, perhaps less hierarchical, structure and what that might mean to human resource management and organizational efficiency.

Some observers deride the term "business ethics" as being an oxymoron in the same category as "Postal Service" and "military intelligence." Peter Drucker, perhaps the most respected of all business writers, says there can be no separate ethical code for business. That reflects growing societal pressure for standards to which all must adhere. Managers can anticipate that behavior viewed as immoral by society at large will not be justifiable on pragmatic grounds.

Consultant Joseph Coates suggests, perhaps with tongue in cheek, that the mounting problem of computer crime can be dealt with to some extent by setting an IQ ceiling for computer operators. Others feel that the rip-off mentality, which appears so often in young people in computer work, reflects such value shifts as are embodied in the misnamed erosion of the work ethic and can be dealt with only by new forms of organizational responsiveness to individual needs. Certainly managers must now see the issue of loyalty as one that must be increasingly two-way. Can a manager demand loyalty from employees who know that he or she may later lay them off?

Corporate social responsibility, discussed in Chapter 23, has too often been treated by managers as a public relations matter. In reality, however, it is a moral one. When the Moral Majority threatens to boycott corporations that sponsor what its members consider to be objectionable shows on TV, we see that even the most conservative elements in society have de facto accepted a far-reaching concept of social responsibility for business. But yesterday's social responsibility is not necessarily tomorrow's and managers will need to be constantly sensitive to changes in the social contract. Whether that will be via the hiring of consulting philosophers, the installation of public issues–tracking systems, a personal immersion in readings and grass roots organizations, or some combination of those approaches will depend on the nature of the individual manager and the organization for which he or she works.

CHAPTER 26

Disintermediation

Throughout the country, people in ever-larger numbers hurry from their homes on weekends to sit behind booths in, or browse through the aisles of, thousands of flea markets. In some places red tag sales, garage sales, and street fairs are once-a-year events. But in almost every town, every district, every city, and every county of the United States there are standing flea markets that occupy parking lots, theaters, old warehouses, malls, meadows, mountainsides, and Main Street. There is hardly anything you can't buy at a flea market instead of at a retail outlet, whether it is to decorate your home or your body. The total amount of money that changes hands at flea markets on a typical weekend afternoon is beyond estimate. And, indeed, it is meant to be. No statistics can accurately reflect the economic impact of flea market transactions, because most of this business is off the books— unreported and untaxed.

The flea market is a major element in the underground economy, which may be approaching one-third the size of the GNP. Even if we deduct from that amount the transactions attributable to organized crime, we still have an enormous amount left—a vast network of informal, uninstitutionalized economic activity. This bypassing of established institutions and officially recorded transactions is only one form of what is increasingly being referred to as *disintermediation*.

In a narrow sense, disintermediation is described as the displacement of funds from traditional banking and savings institutions when depositors seek higher yields by investing on their own. Application of the principle beyond the savings function leads us into an assessment of a bypassing phenomenon that is sweeping the country in many ways. It is related to what social scientists call the assertion of individual autonomy. As people feel increasingly remote from the outcome of what they do, as the institutions they are part of appear increasingly complex and overwhelmingly large, they try to win back control, to go back to simpler and more direct transactions. They seek to eliminate or reduce intermediaries. In a sophisticated and complex economy like ours today, that may seem quixotic, but it should not be underestimated as a force.

The Costs of Intermediation

Figure 26-1 is a very much simplified model of the ideal of basic economic relations. Such a simple flow might be true, for example, of a transaction in which a farmer sells eggs to buyers who come to his door. In the price of the egg, the farmer has considered (but not exactly calculated) his cost of feeding and housing the chickens. "I want an egg," says the customer. "I've got one, and it'll cost you two cents," says the farmer. "Sold," says the customer. End of transaction.

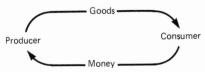

Figure 26-1   Basic economic relations.

What happens when the economy gets more mature, more developed?

■ A trucker can deliver the eggs to a market farther away and expand the farmer's volume, but that will cost the ultimate customer another cent an egg for the transportation.

■ A box maker sells the farmer the boxes and crates needed to send the eggs to market. That costs another ½ cent per egg.

■ Retaining a lawyer and an accountant adds another ¼ cent to the cost of the egg.

■ For the cost of expanding the farm to service the new market, figure another cent per egg.

■ An insurance company insures the farmer's newly expanded chicken farm and egg transportation. Add another ¼ cent per egg.

■ A worker to help with the increased workload adds another cent to the cost.

■ And the retailer, who sells the egg in the remote market, marks the egg up another cent.

So now the customer can get an egg from the farmer for 7 cents instead of 2. Intermediation has added 250 percent to the cost of the original transaction. Chances are that the producer and retailer have never met. The entire transaction is one of middlemen and all their associated costs.

Figure 26-2 is a flowchart that can only approximately describe the cumbersome and convoluted new system of transactions. In reality, the economy is much more complex than that. And therein lies the point. The very complexity of it all has set some people to thinking seriously whether it's *all* worth it *all* the time.

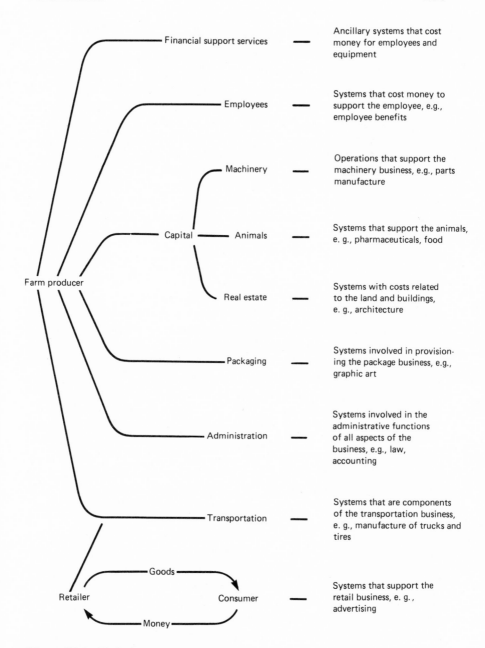

Financial support services — Ancillary systems that cost money for employees and equipment

Employees — Systems that cost money to support the employee, e.g., employee benefits

Machinery — Operations that support the machinery business, e.g., parts manufacture

Capital — Animals — Systems that support the animals, e. g., pharmaceuticals, food

Real estate — Systems with costs related to the land and buildings, e. g., architecture

Packaging — Systems involved in provisioning the package business, e.g., graphic art

Administration — Systems involved in the administrative functions of all aspects of the business, e.g., law, accounting

Transportation — Systems that are components of the transportation business, e. g., manufacture of trucks and tires

Farm producer

Retailer

Goods

Consumer — Systems that support the retail business, e. g., advertising

Money

Figure 26-2 Today's economic relations.

Defrocking the
Professional Priesthoods

Another manifestation of the phenomenon is what we call the defrocking of the professional priesthoods. The desire to take back control of one's life is reflected in a growing unwillingness to continue one's traditional submission to professional expertise. Does the doctor, lawyer, architect, teacher, engineer, legislator, parent, boss really know better? The questioning has been intensified by a rising level of education of the public, changing technology, inflation, and a declining faith in traditional institutions and the people who run or influence them. Malpractice and liability problems haunt not only doctors but also accountants, lawyers, architects, and even morticians, beauticians, and members of the clergy. Second-guessing and bypassing the professionals are definitely new national pastimes.

The do-it-yourself phenomenon is generally seen as a combined economic and recreational movement: people make or repair things themselves; they use their hands as therapy and save money. But it is more than that. People who have developed confidence in their ability to be masons or cabinetmakers—or even gardeners, for that matter—find it not so difficult a step to replace providers of services, and not just providers of manual skills. Thus we see people making their own wills and handling their own divorces. There are neighborhoods that have formed their own parapolice patrols. Because it affects everyone intimately, the health field is very directly impacted. Alternative and do-it-yourself health systems and approaches abound; diet, nutrition, and exercise are more than mere obsessions—they reflect individual efforts to take charge of one's own health. Schools also are now increasingly subjected to critical assessment; many parents and taxpayers are dissatisfied with the results of leaving education to the bureaucrats. There have been court cases in which parents have demanded the right to educate their own children.

Professionals who have been confronted with this time of turbulent change, such as economists, engineers, and physicians, find that either their theories are no longer believed or their skills and knowledge are quickly outdated. Machines can teach, monitor our health, tend to our financial transactions, help us reduce our stress, forecast the economy (as poorly as any economist), and diagnose the problems in our cars and computers. Alternatives to traditional forms of schooling, health care, legal processes (for example, moves to increase arbitration or bypass standard litigation), religion, psychotherapy, and legislation (via initiative) are increasingly adopted. New markets for new products are being created as people seek low-cost ways of getting around the high cost of traditional, institutional, professional intermediary services.

Getting Around the Costs

Other costs of playing by the system also are fueling disintermediation. One pattern of reasoning heard when a middle-class wife is considering returning to the work force is: "Let's see. I can make X a week if I go to work for the Ajax Corporation. Transportation will cost me A. Child care will cost B. Taxes will come to C for me, and D for the two of us because our income bracket will be higher. New clothes and cleaning bills will cost E. Lunches out will cost F. Now, $X - (\$A + \$B + \$C + \$D + \$E + \$F) = \$Y$. Only Y! I'm not going to work a whole week for Y. It's not worth it. I'd rather do babysitting, or work off the books at the corner shop for two days, or just do the flea market on weekends."

The high *cost* of living today just to support the *earning* of a living is very much on the minds of working people, even those in high-ranking management positions. Increasingly, large corporations are finding senior or promising people who one day decide the whole business is just not worth it and leave to make stained glass or raise the children or write a book. A significant minority of talented and creative people are no longer just fantasizing about running off to the South Seas; they are beginning to ask themselves whether the costs of entering the system, remaining in it, earning through it, purchasing through it, and saving through it are still as acceptable as they once were.

New media are helping people find direct access to the information they need and liberating them from reliance on those who have traditionally controlled that access. Some of these media are publications such as *The Whole Earth Catalogue* and *The People's Yellow Pages*. But the revolutionary factor is electronics. Computerization and the networking of individuals and interests via electronic bulletin boards promise to be major forces for acquisition of knowledge and skills over the next decade.

Paul Hawken has stated that we are seeing "a *dissolution* of power away from the polity and the corporation into what only could be called the ebb and flow of information within the culture, a frustratingly diffuse locus."[13] Hawken goes on to conclude that, as the relations between resources, capital, and labor shift, some economists believe they can reverse the process by massive infusion of capital investment into production. Other economists see innovative relations between people and "mass" as the solution. Thus an apparently contradictory world is going in two directions at once: Corporations adjust to poor rates of return on their investments in existing plants, equipment, and research by concentrating resources, capital, and secular power. Individuals respond to the poor rate of return they receive from their life's work by *disintermediating* the same institutions, adapting, and decentralizing. Hawken, for one, is betting on the individual to get the upper hand.

Getting Satisfaction

Let's look at this from the perspective of one important human need—satisfaction. Without attempting to define it, we can have a feel for what satisfaction might mean in any number of circumstances, as well as the ways in which intermediate institutions provide us with or deprive us of satisfaction. Joseph Coates, formerly with the U.S. Congressional Office for Technology Assessment, uses the following illustration. In Italy if a man saw someone smash into the back of his brand-new car, he would open the other car's door, drag the driver out, punch him in the face, and threaten worse if the fellow didn't agree to pay full damages. The new-car owner would therefore get direct and immediate satisfaction. In the United States, if a man saw someone smash into his new car, he would place calls to three intermediaries: the police, the insurance company, and his lawyer. Then he would go home and dream for weeks about how he would have liked to punch the other fellow in the face. He has little if any satisfaction. What he does have, however, is a new set of hassles.

Psychologists who have studied the effects of minor but frequent irritations of daily life conclude that hassles are more closely linked to, and may have greater effect on, our health than major misfortunes. Most previous research in this field operated under the premise that major changes—both positive and negative—produce the kind of stress that, on a cumulative basis, increases the potential for physical and mental illness. It appears that hassles are more directly correlated to mental and physical health. The more frequent and intense the hassles, people reported, the poorer their overall mental and physical health, particularly in the short term. Indeed, major life changes may have the most direct impact on people through the daily hassles they provoke.

Corporate managers are in many important ways indistinguishable from those around them in the desire to avoid hassles and also in their feeling for many of the other factors that fuel disintermediation: getting a good bargain, taking control of their own health, deciding on alternative ways to invest their money, learning new skills, getting information from informal networks, intervening in the local educational bureaucracy, and withholding even a token something from the scrutiny of the IRS. So can Hawken be far wrong? How long can the corporate manager continue to wear two hats as the personal disintermediator and the corporate centralizer? Perhaps for a long time. But the former role will ultimately affect the latter, as some recent evidence shows.

In the early 1970s, when the new youth-centered values were making themselves felt in the United States, a Yankelovich, Skelly and

White study showed that the corporate managers most likely to hold more of the new values were those who had college-age children. Quite obviously, personal exposure in one's own home and life is a significant factor in value formation.

The Impacts of Disintermediation on Corporate America

What, then, might you expect to see as disintermediation increasingly extends beyond financial institutions? Will it transform the character and structure of business organizations in the next 5 to 10 years? And if so, how?

The most obvious area of impact will be in products. Certainly, the financial industry, first to feel the force of disintermediation, has been changed significantly by the almost torrential flows of cutomer dollars seeking higher ground. That has taken its toll on the savings and loans associations and has forced the life insurance business into a state of unprecedented turmoil. Banking will never again look the same as it did in the mid-1970s.

Corporations, even while being disintermediated themselves in their traditional lines of business, can serve as receptacles for disinter-mediated funds from elsewhere. For example, the health industry, as mentioned earlier, has begun to shift the focus of both product development and marketing from the health practitioner to the health consumer. Do-it-yourself diagnostic equipment and dietary supplements, for instance, can be aimed at sizable new markets. Publishing houses are already aware of the profit potential in do-it-yourself books. Retail chains are capitalizing on the appeal of storefront dentistry, optometry, and tax counseling.

Disintermediation also means that loyalty to brand names is not what it used to be. One study, done by William D. Wells, director of research at the Needham, Harper & Steers advertising agency, has supplied evidence of a sharp decline in brand loyalty in recent years. The study showed that agreement among men with the statement "I try to stick with well-known brand names" fell from 80 percent in 1975 to 64 percent in 1980. Among women, who had expressed less brand loyalty to begin with, agreement also declined steadily through those years, from 72 percent in 1975 to 56 percent in 1980.

For the most part, marketers are finding the following qualities heading the list of consumer preferences: easy to use, quick, convenient, uncomplicated, long-lasting, good quality, cheap, clearly understood, multipurpose, clean, healthful, and a host of similar attributes that one would expect to be appropriate in a time of growing disintermediation. People want to be able to understand instructions without consulting someone else, to get good use out of a product so they won't have to replace it too soon, to know that the product is not harmful to their own or anyone else's health, and to face no hassles in its use or repair. That is true whether we are talking about cars or floor polish or cosmetics or underwear or lighting fixtures.

Perhaps most significant will be the massive changes that retailing will undergo into the 1990s with the proliferation of wholesale outlets, farmer's markets, cooperatives, flea markets, street vendors, barter exchanges, and computerized shopping by mail or telephone.

Even trade and professional associations are challenged by disintermediation. They can no longer count on the willingness of their members to compromise or accommodate themselves to some common denominator. Much to their shock, many large Washington-based trade associations, whose primary purpose is to lobby for the common goals of their constituencies, find their member companies opening their own Washington offices and dealing directly with regulators and legislators. The Business Roundtable, comprised of chief executives of the largest corporations, serves to bypass not only trade association lobbyists but each company's lobbyists as well, even if that was not a part of the initial intent. In addition, the proliferation of computer data banks offered by software developers can provide individual companies or professionals with the kind of shared-cost information formerly available only from an association.

Disintermediation is the culmination of a competitive economy. Business is reaping the fruits of intense efforts in which the consumer, asked to choose, ultimately becomes the decision maker. Adam Smith would approve; for it means that no provider of goods or services, no matter how successful today, can thrive or even survive without accommodation to such major shifts in marketplace values and evaluations.

And no manager can be successful without considering how to respond, whether by developing new products, new services, and new delivery systems, by finding ways to reduce reliance on intermediaries between the company and the consumer, or by arranging internal processes that provide more direct access to workers. The sum of all this can mean a more productive organization.

CHAPTER 27

Gatekeeping

During the Iranian hostage crisis it was reported that the real power in Iran was wielded not by the parliament or the president or even the Ayatollah Khomeini, but by those who decided who would be granted an audience with Khomeini. And it is widely understood in Washington that if you want to communicate effectively to a representative or senator, you had best do it through some key staff person. Traditionally, of course, it has been a senior executive's secretary or administrative assistant who served as both a buffer and a filter between the executive and the demands for his or her attention. These are the gatekeepers. And their important role in serving as the means of access between information and decision making is becoming even more important as we rush pell-mell into the information age.

Information Overload

It is widely believed that one of the hallmarks of the information age is that we have too much information or, to use the popular phrase, we have information overload. Estimates are that the volume of information has been increasing at a rate that is greater than 10 percent a year. The number of scientific journals worldwide increased from 18,800 in 1978 to 62,000 in 1981. Many people in government and business in recent years have complained about the burden imposed on them by the explosion of information. Indeed, one of the reasons for the eagerness with which some forms of electronic communications have been embraced is the belief that they will reduce the flow of paper. But a recent study by the International Resource Development Corporation forecasts that, on the contrary, electronic mail will actually accelerate the use of paper and will result in more than 20 billion messages, on paper, by the early 1990s.

Author Ted Mooney, in his highly acclaimed 1981 science fiction novel *Easy Travel to Other Planets,* saw humanity afflicted by what he called "information sickness"—a response of epidemic proportions to information overload that was characterized by disconnected speech, apparent disorientation, and a desire to touch everything. Other writers and intellectuals have warned against societal disorientation caused by the massive move to a scientific age based upon information and communication.

But the concept of information overload is a wrong one. The human brain can take in more information than even the biggest of computers. It is not the quantity but the quality of information that is the central problem of the information age. Quality, at a time when information is both abundant and cheap, is a function of utility. What really distinguishes bits of information is how specifically useful they are to the recipient. People who complain about information overload are really saying that they are getting too much nonuseful information or too much information whose usefulness is not clear to them. Managers who receive multitudes of voluminous studies on market dimensions, buyer behavior, demographic and income trends, political preferences, and a myriad of other elements of the environment know too well that it is all unrefined ore.

The problem calls for gatekeepers. In this case, the role of the gatekeeper is to be the bridge between information and action, that is, to provide the utility value that transforms data into actionable information and to refine the raw ore into usable material.

Decentralization of Gatekeeping

There is much potential for centralized information management, and therefore centralized gatekeeping, in the new computer and communications technologies. Even as far back as George Orwell's *1984* it was predicted that the new technologies would produce a society controlled by a handful of infocrats at the center of a web of communications and information channels. In reality, the decentralizing effects of the new technologies have been at least as strong as, if not stronger than, the centralizing ones.

Political analyst William Schneider, writing in the journal *Public Opinion,* shrewdly points out how coverage of foreign policy news has made the American public more aware of foreign developments and more involved in questions about foreign affairs. Before TV became the primary news source for at least two-thirds of the public, most Americans skipped over foreign news in their newspapers or magazines. You can't do that with TV. The intrusiveness of the medium has made foreign policy increasingly subject to public judgment and, consequently, less exclusively reserved for a small foreign policy elite.

The same is true of business news, which now is no longer confined to the back page of a daily newspaper. Quite often, the lead stories on the evening news, and on the front pages of the newspapers, focus on economics and business: the fluctuations of the Dow Jones average, corporate mergers and takeovers, the results of meetings of OPEC ministers or Common Market officials, automobile company sales results, and so on.

The possibilities for centralization of the gatekeeping functions have not gone away, however. It has been proposed, for example, that we can bring together all of today's reference books and research materials into one giant electronic encyclopedia, which would contain everything known to all people, would be accessible to everyone, and could be updated constantly. It sounds like a wonderful idea. But who would decide what would be included and what left out? Is convenience or even efficiency the most important criterion when judging information resources? In spite of the enthusiasm some scholars have for this proposal, others believe it smacks too much of Big Brother.

The Gatekeeper's Power

Denial of access to information may be as significant as denial of access to decision makers. The gatekeeping function ideally works both ways. Selection is involved; selection entails judgment; and judgment hinges upon bias. The hidden agenda of a gatekeeper—Khomeini's appointments secretary, for example—can shake the world. It can be argued that revolutions in communications and information technology have made authority more rather than less dependent upon gatekeeping. Thus, there is mounting concern about the potential for unelected and even unknown persons to achieve virtual control over organizations and even societies by determining what information makes its way to the top, ultimately to affect decisions and actions. Indeed, technology can make gatekeepers, as controllers of mysteries beyond the understanding of their superiors, more powerful than those they purportedly serve.

The Struggle for Control

Very few people in our economy make things anymore. Most workers in the United States today—by some estimates, 70 percent or more—handle information. Sit in any office building in a large city and look out your window at the buildings around you. All you see is people like yourself, in offices like yours, speaking on the telephone, talking to others, moving paper from one place to another, or doing the daily crossword puzzle. Information workers. No wonder that so much of the struggle within organizations, within countries, and between countries and organizations is based on the control, manipulation, valuation, and symbolism of information.

One of the many complaints third world countries have against the developed countries is that the latter have remote-sensing satellites that can pinpoint undiscovered natural resources in the developing world. In that way developed countries can know more about developing countries' resources than those countries themselves. If the resources are coveted ones, as is so often the case, who will benefit most from this critical gatekeeping function of having access to and passing on the information? This is at the core of the growing disparity between information-rich and information-poor countries, and some observers are concerned about what they see as a form of colonialism: information imperialism. Canada has publicly expressed fears that the United States may own all its secrets. France has tried to control the outward flow of information through tariffs. The U.N. General Assembly has for some time been engaged in one of its seemingly endless and futile debates over whether countries have the right to demand and receive data gathered about their territories by remote-sensing satellites. Countries all over the world are sensing that their own gatekeeping functions are being usurped by others through technological expertise and economic motivation.

Third world countries are enacting legislation to control data banks within their borders, particularly with respect to data flows across borders. India has even gone so far as to attempt to tax *Time* for stories about India that appear in the magazine.

Information has often been viewed as the basis for power. If it is the basis for power, then control of information is power itself. Unlike previous sources of power, such as land and money, information has to be made into something else, something usable, to pay off in power. That fact is not yet widely recognized. Indeed, most efforts to capitalize on the power potential of information seem to come from a miserly perspective. The new world is full of Scrooges who seem to think that by hoarding information, keeping it secret, they will gain or maintain power. But the true gatekeeper knows that power really resides in the use, and not the storage, of information.

Frank Press, president of the National Academy of Sciences, is worried that in the United States this miserly approach may end up harming rather than protecting the national interest. He and others feel that closing the gate on sensitive research could damage the nation's basic research capability and ultimately weaken the competitiveness of United States industry, perhaps even to the point of forcing some companies to locate elsewhere. The future may see some "information havens" perhaps performing the equivalent of Switzerland's and the Cayman Islands' roles in international finance. These gatekeeping safe harbors may be the high-tech backyards for many multinationals that find movement of data across national boundaries increasingly difficult.

The All-Pervasive Dependency

Today's librarians are being renamed; information management is their new job. Today's managers are information managers. Today's consumers are information managers. Today's investors are information managers. But today's leaders are managers of people who manage the information. Being once, or many times, removed from the sources of information makes them more dependent upon media and staff to digest, reform, package, present, and draw conclusions from the world of numbers, events, ideas, and communications. That is no minor consideration. It has escaped few who master their personal and organizational environments that communications skills are critical.

The passing on of knowledge or intelligence has become an art. Computer designers have opened up a whole new industry to compete with overheads and slides: computer graphics. "Intelligent" typewriters with memories have been enlisted as noncoms in the information communications onslaught. Data banks that provide gatekeepers with massive research findings or published materials or networking of ideas are proliferating. Newspapers have been accused of distorting the news by the very same politicians who wake up in the morning to digest a cup of coffee and the local daily. Ironically, the president of the United States gets his news from a news digest prepared overnight by his staff from TV and publication news reports. So the president gets his news filtered through the hidden agendas of his staff, who in turn get their raw material from sources reflecting the hidden agendas of reporters and editors. If the president doesn't get firsthand information, who does?

The Key: Linking Information to Action

Information, like air, cannot be contained by a gate. It leaks out. It can go from place to place in the minds of people. And people, unlike natural resources, are never totally owned. The new technologies make exclusiveness even more difficult to achieve. The spread of personal computer terminals in organizations, for example, is undermining attempts to manage information more closely. It is estimated that close to half a million such terminals will be in use in business by 1985. People manipulating their own data bases for their own purposes present what many observers see as a critical problem for management. To the extent that workers on all levels can operate autonomously in the collection and manipulation of data, vital or not, management can feel with some justification that its own authority is diminished.

Perhaps the central conflict of the information age will be—indeed, already is—in the Khyber passes and Dardanelles through which information flows. While multitudes focus on gathering and storing and classifying information, and others seek to gain strength from information, the ones likely to benefit are those who fully master the art and promise of gatekeeping, who know how to find and select relevant information, how to translate information into motivation, and therefore how to link information to action. Mastering the art will help ensure a greater degree of prosperity for your organization and, even more, enhance your own value to that enterprise. Such mastery requires:

■ Recognizing how perceptions can be greatly affected by the biases, filters, and values of those who supply information.

■ Understanding that information, unlike other forms of wealth, can be shared and still wholly retained. Indeed, astute sharing can increase the value of information.

■ Developing a program for mining the lodes of information in your organization. One large company recently discovered it was spending $2 million a year on publication subscriptions and had nothing to show for it but loaded library shelves. The need is to adopt one of the now existing mechanisms that can help take the information beyond its entry point—the individual reader—and integrate it into the planning and decision processes in the organization.

■ Learning to read material for what it means, not just what it says. This entails asking questions such as: What is in this that our competitors might have missed? Does this signal a change from conventional wisdom? Is there anything in this that will motivate others to act, and if so, how can it be tapped?

■ Knowing enough about the new information technologies to retain and maximize your gatekeeping power.

Apart from your role in your organization, recognize the critical part gatekeeping plays in your personal life. What information influenced your last decision in the voting booth, and why? In retrospect, was it accurate? What information led you to make whatever disappointing investments you may have made? From whom did it come? What sources of information are you relying upon to appraise your children's career choices?

What kinds of hype tend to work most effectively on you, to render you most vulnerable to making an unwise decision as a consumer, citizen, or investor? Semiotics, a discipline that studies communication through images, tells us that the use of pictures, symbols, tone, and context can manipulate people more powerfully than language alone can. Examining the knowledge, motives, and objectivity of the keepers and purveyors of information that affects you financially, interpersonally, and in your role as citizen can be a wise course of action before you set your jaw firmly and believe you are in full control of the facts of the matter.

CHAPTER 28

Transition

1960s social scientists and other observers noted that some tal changes were occurring in western society and in the tates in particular. There were some who hailed these developᴏᵖ. s as the dawning of the age of Aquarius, as proclaimed in the popular musical *Hair*. A new age of peace and love and harmony, the triumph of brotherhood, the sharing of the evergrowing pie, the spread of the beneficial social movements of environmentalism, consumerism, and equal opportunity. *The Greening of America,* as it was called by Yale professor Charles Reich.

Then, in the mid-1970s, it was the age of Narcissus, the me generation, illuminated by such diverse figures as historian Christopher Lasch and writer Tom Wolfe. Supposedly it was a time of selfishness, self-love, and self-indulgence.

And now the 1980s, which perhaps might be called the age of Osiris. Osiris was a principal deity of the ancient Egyptian religion who was drowned and then reborn each year, symbolizing the rhythm of life along the banks of the Nile. Like Osiris, we, too, may be going through a cyclical transformation—the latest of a number, such as the Reformation, the Industrial Revolution, and the Renaissance, that have marked human history. As history shows us, during such transformations the institutions that comprise the framework of the dying society crumble and fall apart, a necessary precondition to the construction of the new institutions of the new society.

Many scholars agree that such a transformation is taking place now. Harvard sociologist Daniel Bell, for example, has written extensively about the transformation to what he calls postindustrial society. Historian Barbara Tuchman entitled her study of fourteenth-century Europe *A Distant Mirror,* reflecting her belief that the transformation from medieval to renaissance society mirrors our own age of transformation. In that context what has been called narcissism may merely represent what happens to people when they are between old institutions and new institutions, in a holding pattern while they wait for new places to land. The fact is, we tend to define ourselves, at least to others, in terms of institutional affiliations. If you ask people, at a party or on an airplaine, who they are, note that in almost all cases they respond by telling you their affiliations.

> I'm an accountant. I work for General Foods. I live in Scarsdale. I'm an Episcopalian. I'm married. I have two children. I graduated from Yale.

> I'm a housewife and mother with three kids. My husband teaches. I'm originally from Dayton. I belong to the Junior League.

Such people haven't told you much about who they are; they have told you what their institutions are.

The Stress on Institutions

Institutions, of course, resist dissolution. There is what we call the March of Dimes phenomenon, in which the achievement of a stated institutional goal becomes secondary to the perpetuation of the institution itself. Thus we see threatened institutions fighting back: the outbreak of Islamic reaction, the rise of the so-called neoconservative movement in the United States, the back-to-basics crusade in education, the rapid development of the evangelical Christian movement.

What results from this institutional turmoil is a kind of societal split personality. Apparent paradoxes and dichotomies abound, in society and even within individuals, to a far greater degree than in less turbulent times. (Epidemic schizophrenia appears to be a factor in all periods of transformation, by the way. It may be that we can forecast social change by tracking the incidence of schizophrenia.)

An example of our schizoid age is to be found in our attitudes toward science and technology. Public interest in science and technology has never been higher. New scientifically oriented publications are emerging almost weekly; *Connections,* a science series on PBS, had one of the largest audiences for any program ever on that network. Yet, at the same time, technology as villainous, as threatening to our lives and well-being, is a theme that has characterized much of our literature since World War II. Significantly, nowhere is that more evident than in science fiction. The back-to-nature movement has a strong antitechnology bias. Neo-Luddites brought suit some years ago against the University of California to enjoin it from developing agricultural machinery that might put people out of work. E. F. Schumacher's "appropriate technology" in effect demands that we restrain technology so as to keep it under human control.

Other signs of stress on our institutions are everywhere. Our government institutions, embedded in solidified traditions, seem on the surface to be incapable of action as they try to handle new situations with antiquated structures. The two-party system no longer provides coherence and control in Congress. The executive department gets ever larger and ever more bureaucratic and unmanageable. Yet beneath this surface green shoots are emerging to bypass obstacles and continue the business of government.

Green Shoots

Within Congress new structures such as caucuses have arisen to fill the organizational vacuum left by the declining parties. The first caucus was established in 1970; there are now more than thirty. Ad hoc groups also have been springing up in large numbers in recent years to provide focal points for member interests.

As the conflict between Congress and the president intensifies, the third branch of government—the judiciary—assumes a greater role, even to the point of becoming a de facto legislature. This development, together with Congress's efforts, tends in the long run to limit the powers of regulatory bodies that have heretofore been relatively unaccountable. The sum of all this confusion is, remarkably, a governmental system that is considerably more responsive to the needs of the day than is generally perceived. In the process, substantial and significant changes are taking place within that system.

Institutional turmoil and change are perhaps most evident in our religious institutions. One of the most remarkable examples of what has been happening is the evangelical Christian movement in the United States. A recent book about that movement by Jeremy Rifkin and Ted Howard, *The Emerging Order: God in the Age of Scarcity,* presents a brilliantly realized picture of an institution both resisting and being transformed by change.

The evangelical movement now encompasses about 45 million people in the United States, many if not most of whom feel that they are returning to a "mystical bygone era," a rigidly defined time of certainty and faith. They are building their own Christian community as an alternative to the secular society around them. This entails "total church living complexes" of homes, stores, banks, restaurants, motels, beauty shops, nightclubs, and discos—all certified Christian. The movement has its own TV network (now the fourth largest and still growing), 1300 radio stations, 2300 bookstores, record companies, a billion dollar publishing empire, its own nationwide directory of Christian businesses, and more. And it has its own educational system, with more than one million children attending over 5000 evangelical elementary and high schools, in which the fundamentalist interpretation of the Bible serves as the basis for knowledge.

It is significant that these people are striving to develop an alternative to what has traditionally been considered a Christian society. They believe, obviously, that society has become too secular and not sufficiently Christian and that they must therefore find their own way back. Yet, as Rifkin and Howard point out, they may in reality be building a new institution instead of recreating an old one.

Education, too, reflects the confusion and turmoil of this age of transition. There are many who decry our current public education system as failing us. "Johnny can't read and write or add and subtract." About 40 percent of the population of Philadelphia has been deemed functionally illiterate, that is, incapable of reading beyond a fourth-grade level. SAT scores had been on a long-term skid downward, and they have only recently leveled off. It is estimated that the number of functionally illiterate adults in the United States exceeds 30 million. The high school dropout rate across the country is viewed as alarming.

Yet many young people today are mastering at mind-boggling speed the computer technology that will guide communication, computation, recreation, and engineering in the future. Is it possible that abstract, nonlinear, and motor skills will come to dominate over linear, rational, and written skills in the future? After all, our forebears needed skills to survive that only a handful of us need to have today. Each age needs its own skills, and it may be that the educational system, run by people from a previous day, lags behind the new needs.

The Crisis of Followership

A consequence of all these push-pull struggles is what the media call the decline of leadership. Supposedly the people are clamoring for leadership, and many observers feel that the calls are not being answered. What is more likely is that people these days are increasingly less amenable to being led. And while they may appear to be calling for a strong leader on a white horse, chances are that if such a leader does show up they'll steal the horse. Thus what is called a crisis of leadership may more appropriately be termed a crisis of followership.

What Lies Ahead

For many people, those whose sense of security is dependent upon their affiliations with strong institutions, the tidal wave of change that characterizes our time is horrifying. They see themselves as perched at the edge of the western sea, about to be swept over into the abyss, with nothing ahead but darkness swarming with unknown and terrifying monsters. Others see ahead a brave new world, Utopia, with the destruction of today's institutions freeing humanity to become like the angels.

Pay your money and take your choice. We don't really know what the future holds. There may be another Dark Ages coming, or we may be bathed in the light of a new Renaissance, or both. If anything is sure, it is that humanity has a survival instinct that is even stronger than that of its institutions. The death of institutions does not have to mean the death of people. Like neophyte swimmers, we have to believe that we will not drown if we let go.

The real message of the legend of Osiris is not that he died, but that he was reborn.

Demographic shifts, economic shifts, geopolitical shifts, ideological shifts, lifestyle shifts, institutional shifts, market shifts, governance shifts—everything that we have discussed throughout the book reflects the fact that we are in the midst of transition.

Is this a "third wave," as Toffler calls it, or a twenty-third wave? For intellectuals, the debate could be significant. But for those who must get on with the process of managing their institutions and their lives, the question is probably irrelevant. The most important point is that the transition is systemic, is real, and is disconcerting as well as refreshing. In many ways it can be like a spirited new horse ridden successfully by those with initiative, foresight, understanding, creativity, tenacity, and will. That is an impressive list of attributes. Part 6 will help show you how to acquire them.

PART 6

Supermanaging for Organizational and Personal Success

In practical matters the end is not mere speculative knowledge of what is to be done but rather the doing of it.

Aristotle
Nichomachean Ethics

CHAPTER 29

Supermanaging
Your Work

You can have any number of positions of authority and function within your work environment. To be a supermanager, you must first acknowledge the variety and complexity of responsibilities you have to your peers, your professions, and your employees, as well as those you have to yourself. Your assessment of those responsibilities will differ with your own nature, your position, and the culture of your organization.

The Senior Executive: The Strategist

As head of your organization, or as an executive in the top levels of a large one, you have the responsibility to create and communicate a vision of the institution and its destiny. That requires a fresh look at the nature of change, the uneasiness it creates in the workplace, and the interpersonal skills needed to weld your people and your possible courses of action into an instrument that will foster and implement your vision.

Vision is neither daydreaming nor wishful thinking. It is the creation of a desirable and achievable future. *Institutional vision must grow out of a disciplined and participatory process set up within the organization for the purpose of continuously scanning the external and internal environments and identifying reasons for change, opportunities to master change, and people best suited to understand and implement new processes and procedures.*

A beginning step toward institutional vision is an assessment of what your organization's culture is and whether in its current state it can contribute to success in the turbulent times ahead. Five of the most important factors to pursue in making such an assessment (which might even be in survey form) are:

1. **Acceptance of risk.** Do people throughout the organization believe that risk taking is not welcomed by the organization? Or do they truly feel that the path to personal success within the organization is a willingness to take risks?

2. **Perceptions of employee autonomy.** Do employees generally feel they are treated as individuals with intelligence and motivation? Or do they feel that there is an internal environment of strict controls and limitations on their participation in decision making, job design, workplace structuring, and upward communication? Is long-term loyalty encouraged, or is turnover prevalent?

3. Attitudes toward innovation. Has the organization relayed a constant stream of communications that promote the status quo in the nature of its products, markets, and human resources? Or are there always one or more processes available to allow for *and accept* innovative ideas, solutions, and approaches?

4. Openness of communication and information sharing. Do the various line and staff functionaries tend to protect their hierarchical and segmented flows of information in the belief that information is power or that one department's gain is another's loss? Or is there a corporate approach, up and down, that encourages sharing of data and analyses for the greater good of the organization?

5. Clarity of objectives. Is there internal confusion about what the organization's major goals are? Is there a general perception, for example, of whether profit or growth is the primary moving force or whether overall market share or targeted market dominance is the desired approach? Is the firm driven by customer and market needs, or does the impetus come from such internal factors as commitment to existing products?

When you have the answers, or at the very least a clarification of the issues raised by these questions, you can get on with the business of either reshaping the internal environment or bolstering it. Communication of a strategic vision is critical at this stage, if it has not already been clearly accomplished. As an executive you can not be a supermanager if your employees are not committed, do not understand their relations to your objectives, do not find their rewards (compensation, promotion, interpersonal) commensurate with their personal perceptions of your vision, and do not feel your vision is adequate to the nature of the times, the expectations of the public, and the actions of the competition.

Another factor to be considered is the enhancement of your own visibility with the key segments of your external publics. Training in communications and continual exposure to a variety of groups, both friendly and hostile, are necessary steps in your becoming a vital force for your organization's success. Relations with the various levels and segments of government will increasingly occupy your time, so you will need to acquire and/or sharpen your political skills to accomplish your goals and protect your organization. Remember too that the increasing accountability of executives requires you to weigh your decisions in terms of both their political and societal liability and their impacts on profit and other bottom-line goals. To that end, you need more than strengthened legal protection flanks; you must have intellectual protection as well. To get it, you should have more people around you who see the world differently from you, and you should seek the opinions of others who are not normally included in your decision-making staff. Examples are philosophers, sociologists, consumer activists, and political analysts.

The Middle Manager: Executing the Strategies

If you are a middle manager, you are caught in a difficult place at a difficult time. Told that organizational trimming is a necessary cost-saving activity, you suspect that it is within your ranks that this has been, is, or will be felt most. As workers at lower levels demand more say in their own job design and reward systems, you recognize that some of your *raison d'être* is undermined. Because of demographic realities (older people holding onto their jobs and the baby-boomers fiercely competing for available positions), you are concerned about your prospects for advancement. As you witness the growing capabilities of technology to take over some of your functions, you suspect that computerization and automation might ultimately threaten your role within the organization or, at the very least, transform it. How do you become a supermanager in the face of such change?

The easiest way for you to become redundant or obsolete is to refuse to either change or accept change. You must now reconceptualize your value to your organization. Just as you would promote any product or service to the marketplace, you must be able to demonstrate your own value-added contributions. You might do so through five avenues of personal growth or redevelopment.

1. **Stop searching for ways to motivate your people and begin to construct an environment in which they motivate themselves.** This would put your personal stamp, not that of some general theory or formula, on your own organization. If you deal with your employees as individuals and establish a climate in which maximum productivity can take place, it will be far more difficult for someone or something to fill your shoes than if you had merely left behind an administrative system that did not maximize performance and indeed minimized the need for managerial excellence.

2. **Learn to network.** The hierarchy gradually has begun to give way to the network in the advancement of successful people and successful programs. Networking, both informal (purposefully socializing with peers from other parts of the organization) and formal (participating in task forces, forming committees, and recommending and en-

couraging employee involvement across line and staff functions or areas of specialty or expertise), is increasingly important as a means of access to power. It can promote your visibility, increase your facility in a variety of organizational activities, broaden your base of personal and professional affiliation throughout the organization, open up to you new avenues of communication and career advancement, and link you to the best thinking available as you undertake projects. It also reduces impediments you may have been confronting where your work overlaps with that of another department or area.

3. Don't attempt to justify that which you can't personally justify. Merge your personal integrity with the prestige of your position and be willing to revise or even do away with systems you have designed or inherited that are no longer consistent with the needs and interests of the organization. To cling to outmoded ways out of fear of loss of turf or purpose would be to intensify your inner *personal* conflict about your worth to the organization, increase your level of stress, and probably decrease your vitality and ingenuity. And in the event the changing times claim your programs as victims, your close association with them will increase your vulnerability. *However,* that does not mean you shouldn't fight to protect and promote activities that may seem unpopular but, to your mind, are worthwhile and necessary in these complex and challenging times. The real point here is to be true to yourself and to your perceptions of what you should be doing to move your enterprise along the appropriate path for the future. Selective enthusiasm, rather than broad-gauged protectionism or despair, will increase your value to the organization.

4. Anticipate. Install systems that help you anticipate emerging issues and challenges. Value those working with or for you who have demonstrated an ability to anticipate. The more events you can truly manage, the more you are viewed as *managerial.* And managing is a much more valued skill than administering. In turbulent times you can expect that your human resource needs, your technological needs, and your information needs will constantly shift, whether rapidly or gradually. Develop the radar that tells you the sort of people you should be hiring. (Aside from the skills you anticipate needing, search out the job seekers who are comfortable with change, upheaval, and uncertainty. You will find you have to spend less of your time and energies reassuring them, so you will have more of your time left for harnessing their contributions.) Satisfy yourself that you have the firmest possible grasp on the emerging social, economic, political, and technological factors that could affect your areas of responsibility. The fewer surprises you let senior management get hit with each year, the more you will be viewed as having things under control. That is no insignificant mantle to wear in times such as these.

5. **Translate effectively.** Basically, as a middle manager, you are a gatekeeper. It is through you that information is channeled to the top of the organization. Too often the greatest mistake made by managers is thinking that information is independent of the manner in which it is communicated. It is not; nor should it be. The voluminous report may speak well of effort but speak not at all of insight, implication, or value added. The management summary may be cleverly composed but may lose all the richness and depth of understanding embodied in preliminary material.

In times of complexity, information is a rather cheap and readily available commodity. There are many providers, from internal to government to private data houses. Insight, implication, application, and skill in communication are *not* readily available. *When someone asks for information, more often than not what he or she really wants is an insight or solution.*

Review the nature of the information that leaves your desk. Is it just information? Or are you genuinely and personally excited by the intriguing nature of what is contained in your document or presentation? Have you truly considered your audience and what would motivate it to act on your information? Is there enough in what you have to say that is new? Have you made pronouncements of change in a threatening manner, or have you skillfully assured the recipient that opportunity is to be had from seemingly threatening new circumstances? Have you thought through the internal political consequences of the information you are transmitting, even to the extent of having done some preliminary work in building a broad-based constituency in support of your information or suggested actions? And, most important, do you undermine yourself by appearing to believe that you are smarter than those to whom you are delivering the information and therefore oversimplify or excessively repeat the contents of your presentation? Finally, have you taken advantage of opportunities made available to you to bring others along in the acquisition and acceptance of information about change?

Markets, Products, Industries

Throughout this book we have made dozens of observations and suggestions regarding the changing nature of consumer wants, needs, and circumstances, of competition among and within industries, of the kinds of products and services most likely to be sought after in the coming years, and of the environment in which the multitude of changes is taking place. Yet we have barely scratched the surface.

Many people have despaired of a system that replaces a comprehensive knowledge of mathematics with hand-held calculators, believing young people will become lazy in their thinking. Many believe that arcade games are addictive and even destructive of young people's health, mental energy, inclination to pursue traditional recreational activities, and interpersonal skills. Yet these young technophiles are the people who will inherit the marketplace and the work force in the future. Can we adequately judge, from our timeworn perspective, the skills and interest they will need to survive in, cope with, and succeed in that future?

If you are a man and you could ask your great, great grandfather what skills you would need to survive in life, you would most likely be told that you need to be able to build a house. And, indeed, the Main Street of his time would sport, alongside the saloon, a general store stocked with carpentry and construction tools. Yet today, you may live in an apartment where all of your tools fit in a shoebox in your utility cabinet, or if you own a garage, you may have a larger supply of tools hanging on pegboards. There are no lumberyards on Madison Avenue, or Pennsylvania Avenue, or Ghiradelli Square. Your housing is built for you, and you wouldn't, in all likelihood, know how to even begin to properly clear ground for your shelter.

If you are a woman and you could ask your great, great grandmother what skills you would need to survive in life, you would be told that you need to be able to make clothes for your family. Today enterprising, thrifty people do make their own clothes, but very few if any of them start by weaving the fabrics. And so today our Main Streets boast department stores, boutiques, and fabric shops.

Would our predecessors click their tongues and say that we are unprepared for life? Times have changed very quickly in recent decades. What would once have taken one or two generations to recede from our mainstream system of commerce now takes only a few years. And to anticipate the new markets, the new products, and the shape of our new industries requires a mental telescope of sorts that can enable you to see well beyond today's horizons, forward to the new world whose shape, size, and color will not for a long time be discernible with the naked eye.

CHAPTER 30

Supermanaging
Your Life

As a child you accepted direction from those in positions of authority even when you couldn't believe your self-esteem was well served. When you were bold enough to ask why, your search for explanation was often ended by "Because I said so!"

If you managed to ask that question on a day when someone was willing to be patient and tell you the reason behind a directive, you were probably bored by the sensible, rational, and painstaking explanation of why you couldn't swim farther out, or eat another portion of ice cream, or punch Marvin on the nose for insulting your dog. At such times you may have wished that someone would just say, "Because I said so!," and leave it at that. As adults, we still have that same child within us. We still ask why, but we ask it of books, we ask it of professors, we ask it of bosses, we ask it of guidance counselors, we ask it of journalists, we ask it of our data banks, our lawyers, our stockbrokers, our ministers, our own consciences.

And what we often get are sensible, rational, belabored, and supportable facts of the case that lead us up to the point where, after hearing all that is to be said on the one hand and all that is to be said on the other, we must, in the end, make our own decisions. There are still days and times when we yearn for some person of authority to say, "Do it this way because I tell you to." Unless we have a dictatorial spouse or boss, we hear that answer less and less as we get older, and we are left to our own wits to make sense of the sea of information in which we swim.

Good News, Bad News

The bad news is that the quantity of information is increasing and the numbers and kinds of choices we all have to make also are increasing. And, eventually, whatever choice you do make must come from your own internal interests and motivation. There are those who turn to religion or charismatic leaders because they help to limit choice and therefore confusion. There are also those who take comfort in working in a rigidly structured work environment because there too both options and the responsibility for decision making are limited. But many find that these are not satisfying ways of maximizing their creative forces, meeting their need for self-fulfillment, or recognizing their desire to experiment with the options open to them.

The good news is that today experimentation is a more acceptable way of learning about what we want and who we are. It is also a more acceptable way of *living*.

Back in the early 1970s it was becoming apparent, not only to social scientists but also to business and government agencies, that the tradi-

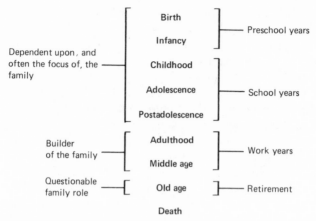

Figure 30-1 The traditional life cycle.

tional life cycle of substantial segments of the American population was being altered. The then Institute of Life Insurance (now the American Council of Life Insurance), the major trade association of the life insurance industry, issued a study in 1974 describing some of the changes taking place. The traditional life cycle was as shown in Figure 30-1. For increasing numbers of people, each of the elements in the continuum was and still is in a state of flux.

Education

We have begun to perceive that structured learning can begin much earlier than we had thought and can last over the course of one's lifetime. Preschool programs and educational television bring academia into the child's world much earlier, and home computer technology helps teach advanced functions to the very young.

The clean break that once existed between school years and work years has, for a large number of people, virtually disappeared. Continuing education is a fact of life for a great many adults today; it is estimated that persons over 30 account for more than one-quarter of the total number of students enrolled in undergraduate programs.

Adult and continuing education has become the fastest growing kind of instruction in the United States for reasons that include:

■ The desire of women to return to the work force in a professional capacity after taking time off to have and raise children.

■ The increases in leisure time, whether managed (for example, people who have moved closer to work to cut down on commuting) or involuntary (for example, people who have been laid off).

■ The do-it-yourself movement, which ranges in form from sewing and plumbing to computer programming and personal finance management.

■ The constant desire for job upgrading in fields that require additional education or new or higher credentials.

■ The increased incidence of primary careers that have been made obsolete by technological advances or rendered precarious by the tight job market, a cutback of jobs in a particular field, or budget cuts.

■ The growing dissatisfaction that many people feel with their primary career choices and which makes them look to different fields that might be more to their liking.

■ The rapid outdating of technical information that requires professionals to keep up with state-of-the-art processes, discoveries, data systems, and so on.

■ The simple fact that more people are more educated and have acquired both a taste for education and the resources to indulge it.

Thus education at any stage of life has become an option that is both acceptable and viable for the achievement of personal and career goals. With the world around you changing as it is, there is little time to regret a wrong career decision or an ignored talent or inclination. Indeed, there is no need to. You have both time and opportunity to pursue your interests for your future gain.

Careers

Henry Ford once told American car buyers they could have any color car they wanted so long as it was black. Look at the choices car buyers have now. And look at the choices people have when it comes to careers, not just at the beginning of their work life but at any point along the way. No career choice, whether made at the age of 15 or 50, need be permanent.

The development is not new. Early in the 1970s, an American Management Association survey found that nearly 50 percent of the 2821 management-level respondents had either changed or considered changing their occupation during the 5 years prior to the survey. At the same time—from scientists to managers—professionals were becoming less inclined to see themselves as employees of a particular company and were increasingly looking at themselves primarily as members of their professions. Radical career changes were becoming more common then. One survey in that period (the Institute of Life Insurance's *Monitoring the Attitudes of the Public*) indicated that 71 percent of the adult public approved of changing occupations in the middle of one's career and 56 percent approved of someone dropping out of the work force temporarily to pursue personal interests.

If you should decide that you would like to take advantage of the changing times and values and move yourself in one or more new career directions, there are available many counseling services that can help determine your personal strengths, weaknesses, and inclinations. Career guidance service is proving so popular, in fact, that you might even consider it for your own second or third career. Other fields that hold promise for the future include the following:

1. **Computer systems that augment traditional professions and services.** In the future, security, health and medicine, architecture, graphic design, education, financial management, and a myriad of other services will be delivered and performed with the aid of computers. There are immense entrepreneurial and corporate opportunities here, and as the machines get "smarter," the scope of opportunities will expand greatly.

2. **Fields that disintermediate traditional paths for delivery of goods and services.** Bringing goods or services to people in any one or more of the following ways in any one or more of the following fields could offer opportunities to alert individuals and managers:

Ways	Fields
Less expensive	Education
Less time-consuming	Legal services
Simpler	Health (includes medicine, diagnostics, nutrition, fitness)
More personalized, targeted	Home improvement
More self-involving	Personal financial management
Ecologically oriented	Games, crafts, hobbies
More convenient	Guidance counseling (career, stress, family, drugs, etc.)

Some of the ways may seem contradictory. For example, "less time-consuming" may appear to be the exact opposite of more "self-involving." But there are many people who are seeking one of the two as an alternative to their present choices. Knowing which people seek what (in other words, doing some market research and segmentation), or which directions your interests or talents would dictate will help you decide which market you wish to serve and how.

3. **Filling societal needs where publicly provided services have begun to deteriorate.** Privately financed services, including neigh-

borhood security forces, ambulances, day care, escorts for the elderly, afterschool cultural and athletic programs, and mail delivery, are only a few of the many possibilities open to the enterprising individual or institution.

4. Merging two or more disciplines to address a highly particularized need. If you are an unfulfilled lawyer and you know an unfulfilled social worker in the criminal justice system, the two of you could combine your expertise to open up a private and discreet service for families whose children tend to get into trouble with the law. Or if you are a frustrated artist and you know a frustrated teacher, you might combine talents to offer an afterschool art and cultural history program for working parents who are concerned about seeing their children occupied and cared for from 3 to 6 p.m. These examples serve to show how you can redirect your career without necessarily revising it altogether, always keeping in mind the way the world is changing and how you can utilize your knowledge, skills, and interests to capitalize on the newly forming markets and areas of need.

What's in an Age?

Chronologically, the traditional life cycle model also has been altered for large numbers of people. Adulthood is being delayed by the better educated, who remain in a postadolescent mode of experimentation with life choices such as mates, living arrangements, careers, education, and geographic location until perhaps their late twenties or even early thirties. The postponement of family life by this segment has meant that the need to make hard and seemingly permanent decisions comes later in the life cycle. But adulthood, once settled into, is often subsequently interrupted by another bout with adolescence that is now widely known as the mid-life crisis.

This raises an interesting question, however. When is mid-life? Perhaps more than any other challenge to the life cycle, the very fact of a difference in the aging process renders the traditional model questionable. Today a lot of people are remarrying in their fifties. This can often mean beginning a new family with a younger mate. Conversely, there are those who, satisfied in their mid-forties that they have accomplished all they wish to for the time being, elect early retirement, even if only temporarily. There are those who begin new careers at 65, because after jogging miles each week and paying close attention to diet and health, they feel their physical condition is too good to accept being put out to pasture.

What do we mean today when we use terms like "middle-aged," "elderly," and "young adults"? That is not an insignificant question for sociologists or market researchers or human resource specialists. But it is also of great importance to you, because you may have been considering your own life in a perspective that is outmoded for you. The choices you have as a person living in a time when 80 (and not 65) is seen as old, when you can be equally productive at 18 or 78, when your options with respect to family, location, career, and education are multiplied can be exhilarating. To supermanage your life in these times will not necessarily be easy; indeed, you may well make some wrong choices. But you will be able to choose again, move on, and grow more.

Investments

As you consider your financial choices in this time of personal flux and economic transition, you may want to consider much of what has already been said in this book about industries and opportunities presented by the changing times. *Housing,* because the population will continue to grow and because people will always need a place to live, will remain a wise investment choice for many years to come, despite transitional fluctuations based on interest rates, tax decisions, and inflation. But you should also be alert to the following four areas of opportunity:

1.   Medium-sized companies will continue to be good investment bets, particularly those based on or related to the locomotive technologies. As targets for acquisition, they offer opportunities for substantial stock appreciation. In the event the acquisition tide is stemmed, they are likely to continue growing at a more healthy and rapid rate than many of the larger companies, particularly those unresponsive to the changing world.

2.   As James Robinson, chairman and chief executive officer of American Express, has pointed out, we frequently act as though **the service sector** is not as real to our economy as the industrial. We tend to look at our economy with only one eye—the industrial eye—when we should be using two. Robinson advocates a total review not only of such measurements as inventories and money supply but of all the economic indicators that we rely upon to ensure that they reflect the reality of today's economy. An awareness that there can be other ways to measure the economy and performance of a given company can help you see investment opportunities that might be missed by those who rely on conventional analytic tools to assess future corporate growth and potential.

3. **Adult recreation and leisure,** already a $300 billion industry, will be one of the fastest growing fields in the future. The baby boom generation, which was weaned on a recreation ethic, and life cycle change, computer technology in the home, the revolution in health and fitness, the rising incomes of two-wage-earner households, and adult education are leading the industry ahead rapidly. Investment opportunities will multiply.

4. **Companies that are developing the beginnings of their own competition** will be in a stronger position in the future than those that leave the competition to their competitors. To the extent that a company demonstrates it (*a*) is aware of the many new directions from which competition may come as a result of innovative technology, financial shifts, marketplace changes, and so on and (*b*) is exploring goods and services that can meet the new challenges (even, possibly, ultimately replacing its own existing business), that company has a degree of flexibility and vision that can help ensure its future success. A company should be no more loyal to its own products and services than the market is.

There are obviously hundreds of other opportunities and hazards that you can consider. But our intention here is to acquaint you with the new kinds of assessments you need to make if you are to truly master your investment choices as you would your other life choices. These analyses are of a kind that are not included in the services offered by most traditional investment advisers.

Take the forces for change described in this book and play them back to your most trusted adviser(s) to see what changes, if any, your advisers would recommend in your current or contemplated investments. Are you convinced that your advisers are aware of all they should be?

No Limit to Options

To paraphrase President Franklin D. Roosevelt, the only thing you have to fear is fear of change, because it can paralyze you and keep you from achieving all that you might achieve. The real victims of change are those who resist it blindly, unthinkingly. "He who fights the future," said Kierkegaard, "has a dangerous enemy." Instead of dragging your heels and vowing to fight to the death, examine your options. It's crucial to recognize that you *do* have options. Resisting change is only one of them. Resistance may even prove to be the best option for you in any given situation, but you should come to that conclusion only after objective appraisal takes you there.

Every force for change combines hazard and opportunity. The fact is that the kinds of forces for change discussed in this book are generally neutral; they are neither good nor bad in and of themselves. Their consequences, however, can be good or bad, and it is the consequences that you can affect by your actions.

Technological change, which fills so many people with dread, can be a powerful force for good if directed to the welfare of humanity. Social change, which threatens so many people's perceptions of who and what they are, can result in freedom and accomplishment if used to liberate and nurture. Economic and political change, too, can be like blank canvases awaiting the hand of a skilled master.

In *A Woman of the Future* Australian novelist David Freland described a character whose "past was before him like a beacon; he would keep going in that direction and call it the future." To be in control, to master change, to be a supermanager in a time of rapid, turbulent, and confusing change, you must fall away from a past that prevents you from seeing the potential ahead.

References

1. Landon Jones, *Great Expectations: America and the Baby Boom Generation,* Coward-McCann & Geoghegan, Inc., New York 1980. Used by permission.
2. Address delivered at Dakota Wesleyan University, May 16, 1982. *Vital Speeches of the Day,* vol. 48, no. 21, August 15, 1982.
3. Neil Pierce, "Smokestack Chasers Who Miss the Point," *Washington Post,* May 1977. © 1977, The Washington Post Company, reprinted with permission.
4. Lawrence Minard, "A Chat with Fernand Braudel," *Forbes,* June 21, 1982.
5. *Nature,* July 8, 1982, p. 113.
6. *New Scientist,* October 14, 1982, p. 90.
7. From *The Breakdown of Nations* by Leopold Kohr. Copyright © 1957, 1978 by Leopold Kohr. Reprinted by permission of the publisher, E. P. Dutton, Inc.
8. Catherine Houck, "Triumphing Over the Fear of Success," *Cosmopolitan,* November 1982.
9. Richard M. Huber, *The American Idea of Success,* McGraw Hill Book Company, New York, 1971. Reprinted by permission.
10. Richard Cornuelle, *De-Managing America.* Alfred A. Knopf, Inc., New York, 1975.
11. Marvin Harris, *Cannibals and Kings: The Origins of Culture,* Alfred A. Knopf, Inc., New York, 1977.
12. Dan Bawly, *The Subterranean Economy,* McGraw-Hill Book Company, New York, 1982. Reprinted by permission.
13. Paul Hawken, "Disintermediation," *CoEvolution Quarterly,* Spring 1981.

INDEX

273

ABOUT THE AUTHORS

Arnold Brown and Edith Weiner are the principals of the prestigious New York-based consulting firm Weiner Edrich Brown, Inc. Their clients include many of the Fortune 500 companies, agencies of the federal government, and other consulting firms. Both are widely known speakers at business and educational meetings. They serve on a number of boards and advisory committees in the public and private sectors; they have coauthored many articles and columns on the future; and they have appeared on radio and television shows across the country. Weiner and Brown are recognized internationally as pioneers and innovators in the management of change.